Recent
Homiletical
Thought

Recent
Homiletical
Thought A BIBLIOGRAPHY, 1935-1965

EDITED BY *William Toohey, c.s.c.*
HOLY CROSS COLLEGE
WASHINGTON, D.C.

and *William D. Thompson*
EASTERN BAPTIST THEOLOGICAL SEMINARY
PHILADELPHIA, PENNSYLVANIA

ABINGDON PRESS
NASHVILLE
NEW YORK

RECENT HOMILETICAL THOUGHT

Copyright © 1967 by Abingdon Press

Library of Congress Catalog Card Number: 67-15948

SET UP, PRINTED, AND BOUND BY THE
PARTHENON PRESS, AT NASHVILLE,
TENNESSEE, UNITED STATES OF AMERICA

Preface

Almost everyone has an opinion about preaching. In the past thirty years, increasing numbers of people have put into print their reflections, theories, and accounts of preaching. This book is an attempt to list and comment upon most of the books and articles written in English during this period, and to list the scholarly theses produced.

The project was conceived in 1960 by the officers of the Catholic Homiletic Society, then a rather small group of priests and other persons interested in the renewal of preaching in the Roman Catholic Church. The scope of the project soon grew to include materials and editorial cooperation by Protestants, and the project became a fully ecumenical venture. It is hoped that teachers of preachers, preachers themselves, and students of preaching will find help here in their pursuit of knowledge about preaching.

The year 1935 was chosen as a starting point since it signalled a significant change in both Protestant and Catholic homiletical theory. C. H. Dodd, the distinguished British scholar, gave in that year his now famous lectures to King's College, University of London, published as *The Apostolic Preaching and Its Developments*. At the same time, Fr. Josef A. Jungmann, S.J., was at work on his *Die Frohbotschaft und unsere Glaubensverkündigung*, published at Regensburg in 1936 and released in English in 1962 as *The Good News Yesterday and Today*.

Until this time, no single, comprehensive listing has been available except Cleary and Haberman's *Rhetoric and Public Address: A Bibliography, 1947-1961*, published in 1964, and Caplan and King's *Pulpit Eloquence: A List of Doctrinal and Historical Studies in English*. As helpful as these are, neither one covers the wide variety of religious periodicals that have been searched for this bibliography. The Cleary-Haberman study covers less than half the time span of this one, and the Caplan-King bibliography stops more than twelve years ago. Appre-

5

ciation is acknowledged to both these sources, from which a number of citations have been drawn for this compilation.

Books. Nearly all the 446 books have been annotated, most often descriptively. In some instances, critical comments have been included. Following the standard bibliographical data, a "C" or "P" has been added to indicate a Catholic or Protestant author, if known. No sermon anthologies or books of preaching helps have been included since they are too numerous and do not reflect homiletical thought, the concern of this book.

Articles. The 1081 articles were chosen from a master list of twelve Protestant-edited periodicals, sixteen Catholic-edited periodicals, and eight scholarly journals in the field of speech. As articles from periodicals not in this list came to the attention of the editors, they were also included. The thirty-six journals which were thoroughly searched for the thirty-year period are listed in the appendix in categories of sponsorship.

Theses and Dissertations. The listing of 610 master's theses and doctoral dissertations was taken from Franklin H. Knower's "Graduate Theses: An Index of Graduate Work in Speech," an annual feature of *Speech Monographs,* and his "Bibliography of Communications Dissertations in American Schools of Theology," also printed in *Speech Monographs* (June, 1963). The listings were supplemented by materials supplied by William K. Clark, editor of the *Digest of Research in Religious Speaking,* no longer being published. Since Knower's listing began in 1934 and included a few studies done during the preceding decades, it was decided to include all appropriate listings for the sake of completeness.

The method of listing is topical, supplemented by an author index. Each item is listed only once, under the topic which seems to be its primary concern. The following explanation may help the user to discover most readily the materials he is seeking.

I. *General Works:* This is the broadest category, including textbooks, surveys, principles of preaching, lectures on a variety of preaching's aspects, and items with cryptic titles.

II. *Preaching and Theology:* The biblical and theological dimensions of preaching will be found in items listed here.

III. *Topics of Preaching:* Such works are included here as suggest topics to which the preacher can address himself.

IV. *The Preacher:* When the author's concern is with the preacher as a person, the material is listed in this category.

V. *The Congregation:* Listed here are materials concerning the persons to whom preaching is addressed: writings on the psychology of preaching, preaching's relationship to pastoral counseling, and the analysis of contemporary culture.

VI. *The Setting—Liturgical:* An item is listed here when it involves that type of preaching occurring as a part of a liturgical service.

VII. *The Setting—Special Occasions:* Missionary and catechetical preaching, conferences, retreats, and various other preaching situations are covered in this category.

VIII. *The Sermon:* Included in this category are materials which are concerned with the task of composing the sermon: choice of topic, outlining, illustrating, wording the sermon, planning the preaching program.

IX. *Delivery:* Use of the voice and body, oral interpretation in preaching, and matters of articulation and pronunciation are included in this category.

X. *History—Individual Preachers:* Material is listed in this category when the focus is on the preacher, either contemporary or historical.

XI. *History—Groups:* If two or more preachers are discussed, the item is listed here.

XII. *History—Periods:* When the item's concern is with a period of time, including the present, it is included in this category.

XIII. *History—Theory:* Here are included such materials as describe the theories of preaching held by practitioners and theorists of the past.

XIV. *Teaching:* This category lists materials concerning homiletical teaching methods, curricula, etc.

XV. *Bibliography:* Lists of published material in the field of preaching are included in this category.

Manifestly, this bibliography is not "complete" or "comprehensive." To list everything that has been written about preaching in this period would require searching materials in liturgical studies, church history, evangelism, priesthood and ministry, missions, and other fields. Neither is it infallible. No bibliographical work of this size and complexity can be free from error, however carefully checked are the materials. Users are invited to call attention to errors or omissions by writing the Catholic Homiletic Society, 4453 McPherson Avenue, St. Louis, Missouri 63108.

The compilation of this bibliography has been a labor of love by a great many persons to whom acknowledgment is given elsewhere. The editors commend the contributors heartily. They also commend this book to the world of scholarship with the prayer that the living God may use it to facilitate the preaching of his Word.

WILLIAM TOOHEY, C.S.C.
WILLIAM D. THOMPSON

Contributors

MILTON ADAMSON, C.S.C.
Holy Cross College, Washington, D.C.

ANATOLE BAILLARGEON, O.M.I.
Oblate College and Seminary, Natick, Massachusetts

DANIEL A. BARRETT
Wheaton College, Wheaton, Illinois

PATRICK BAYER, C.M.F. and the
Claretian House of Studies, Washington, D.C.

HAROLD A. BRACK
The Theological School, Drew University, Madison, New Jersey

FREDERICK M. BRUNER
St. Paul's Methodist Church, Warrington, Pennsylvania

DONALD BUGGERT, O.CARM.
and the Carmelite Fathers of Whitefriars Hall, Washington, D.C.

HERBERT J. DORAN
The Theological Seminary, University of Dubuque, Dubuque, Iowa

ROBERT W. DUKE
Lancaster Theological Seminary, Lancaster, Pennsylvania

FRANCISCAN FATHERS OF HOLY NAME COLLEGE
Washington, D.C.

9

EARL H. FURGESON
Wesley Theological Seminary, Washington, D.C.

RUDOLPH GAWLIK, C.S.C.
Holy Cross College, Washington, D.C.

FRANCIS E. HILL, O.M.I.
Oblate College, Washington, D.C.

LYNN BOYD HINDS
Pittsburgh Theological Seminary, Pittsburgh, Pennsylvania

DEWITTE HOLLAND
Temple University, Philadelphia, Pennsylvania

GORDON G. JOHNSON
Bethel Theological Seminary, St. Paul, Minnesota

PAUL KNIERIM
Eastern Baptist Theological Seminary, Philadelphia, Pennsylvania

J. EDWARD LANTZ
Interdenominational Theological Center, Atlanta, Georgia

ROBERT E. LUCCOCK
School of Theology, Boston University, Boston, Massachusetts

LOWELL G. MCCOY
Hebrew Union College—Jewish Institute of Religion
Cincinnati, Ohio

CHARLES MCELHINNEY, M.S.
LaSalette Seminary, Cheshire, Connecticut

DONALD MACLEOD
Princeton Theological Seminary, Princeton, New Jersey

HOWARD MELZER, S.C.J.
Sacred Heart Monastery, Hales Corners, Wisconsin

GEORGE H. MUEDEKING
Pacific Lutheran Theological Seminary, Berkeley, California

THOMAS OLBRICHT
Pennsylvania State University, University Park, Pennsylvania

Contributors

FORREST RHOADS
David Lipscomb College, Nashville, Tennessee

T. D. ROVER, O.P.
Dominican House of Studies, Washington, D.C.

LEO SANDS, C.S.B.
St. Basil's Seminary, Toronto, Ontario, Canada

EDWARD THEISEN
St. Francis Seminary, Milwaukee, Wisconsin

MARY JEAN THOMAS
University of Massachusetts, Amherst, Massachusetts

RICHARD C. WHITE
Lexington Theological Seminary, Lexington, Kentucky

FARIS D. WHITESELL
Northern Baptist Theological Seminary, Oak Brook, Illinois

DON R. WISMAR
Christian Theological Seminary, Indianapolis, Indiana

R. CLYDE YARBROUGH
The Theological Seminary, University of Dubuque, Dubuque, Iowa

11

Contents

BOOKS

Allen, Arthur
The Art of Preaching. New York: Philosophical Library, 1943.
93 pp. (P) A manual which first appeared in Great Britain dealing with the art of preaching, the setting and subject of the
sermon, and the preacher and his preparation.   1

Allgeier, Joseph L.
Canonical Obligation of Preaching in Parish Churches. Washington, D.C.: The Catholic University of America Press, 1949. 115
pp. (C) As the title of this doctoral dissertation indicates, it has
considerable usefulness for introductory appreciation of the duties
to preach as set down by the Catholic Church.   2

Aristotle
Rhetoric. Ed. by Lane Cooper. New York: Appleton-Century-
Crofts, 1937. 259 pp. Herein is found the classical framework so
helpful for homiletic theory—the sound principles of the art of
persuasion.   3

Atkinson, O'Brien
How to Make Us Want Your Sermon. New York: Joseph F.
Wagner, 1942. 179 pp. (C) An excellent work of self-analysis by a
member of the average Sunday congregation and also one of the
most readable works in preaching literature. The writer is an
advertising man, and his candid view of preaching will be of
service to an understanding of the reactions of the audience the
preacher faces.   4

Babin, Pierre

Crisis of Faith: The Religious Psychology of Adolescence. New York: Herder and Herder, 1963. 251 pp. (C) An important study by a catechetical scholar on the general question of the relevance of Christianity in the world of modern youth, relating the psychological understanding of young people to a dynamic faith. Indispensable for all preachers working with youth. 5

Faith and the Adolescent. New York: Herder and Herder, 1965. 128 pp. (C) Valuable book for all concerned with the communication of the Christian message to teen-agers, containing scholarly delineation of the authentic attitudes and dispositions they have, especially with regard to the meaning of God in their lives. 6

Bailey, Ambrose

Stand Up and Preach. New York: Round Table Press, 1937. 147 pp. (P) "This book is a testimony of joy . . . a testimony of confident faith in the Christian Church and in the power of the ministry." A popularized, impressionistic general survey of the work of preaching in the 1930's as one New England preacher saw it. Homiletical advices need to be read critically. 7

Barrett, C. K.

Biblical Problems and Biblical Preaching. Philadelphia: Fortress Press, 1964. 49 pp. (P) Two addresses by a noted British Methodist biblical scholar on the biblical background of preaching. 8

Barth, Karl

Community, State, and Church. New York: Doubleday & Company, 1960. (P) The third essay, "The Christian Community and the Civil Community," offers some definitions of the relationships which should exist between the Christian community and the state. Sections xxxi through xxxiii of this chapter suggest the need for political sermons within the church and the communication of church viewpoint in political matters. 9

Bartlett, Gene E.

The Audacity of Preaching. New York: Harper & Row, 1962. 159 pp. (P) The Lyman Beecher Lectures for 1961, dealing mostly with the philosophy of preaching in our times. The accent falls on the pastoral and prophetic note. 10

Baxter, Batsell Barrett

The Heart of the Yale Lectures. New York: The Macmillan Company, 1947. 332 pp. (P) An analysis of the Lyman Beecher Lectures on Preaching delivered at Yale between the years 1871 and 1944. The author selects and organizes what the lecturers have said about the preacher, the sermon, and the congregation. 11

Speaking for the Master. New York: The Macmillan Company, 1954. 128 pp. (P) Help for laymen who are called to give devotional talks or full sermons. 12

Berry, Sidney M.

Vital Preaching. London: Independent Press, 1936. 156 pp. (P) The Warrack Lectures for 1936. A survey of the preacher, the sermon, the study, the congregation, and the sanctuary. 13

Bishop, John

Study Notes on Preaching and Worship. London: The Epworth Press, 1952. 44 pp. (P) A supplement to Fred A. Farley's textbook, *Preparing to Preach,* prepared for correspondence students in England. The supplement follows the chapters of the textbook, covering the usual content of homiletical theory and contains test questions on which the student writes his examination. 14

Blackwood, Andrew W.

Biographical Preaching for Today. Nashville: Abingdon Press, 1954. 224 pp. (P) Stresses the condition of the hearer in contrast to his previous volumes which stressed more the content of the message. Part I deals with preaching strategy with adults and young people. Part II deals with sermon tactics and is an adaptation of homiletical principles to practical situations. One wonders why the volume was not entitled "Pastoral Preaching"; it does not deal with biography. 15

The Fine Art of Preaching. New York: The Macmillan Company, 1943. 168 pp. (P) Deals with sermon construction, use of biblical materials, and style. Views preaching as a fine art. 16

Preaching from the Bible. Nashville: Abingdon Press, 1941. 239 pp. (P) A textbook on how to prepare a sermon based on the Bible, with concrete examples of sermons based on biblical characters, expository lectures, sermons on books of the Bible and chapters of the Bible. 17

17

Blocker, Simon
The Secret of Pulpit Power. Grand Rapids: Wm. B. Eerdmans Publishing Co., 1951. 209 pp. (P) The secret of pulpit power is thematic preaching or the proclamation of God's self-revelation as contained in the Bible. Substance and form of the sermon are discussed, and six sermons are offered as examples.   18

Boaz, H. A.
The Essentials of an Effective Ministry. Nashville: Cokesbury Press, 1937. 137 pp. (P) Six lectures to southern Methodist ministers, touching lightly and inspirationally on all phases of the preaching task.   19

Bohren, Rudolph
Preaching and Community. Richmond: John Knox Press, 1965. 215 pp. (P) An excellent translation of lectures by a stimulating German pastor-theologian. While lacking unity, the book is filled with helpful insights based on sound biblical scholarship.   20

Booth, John N.
The Quest for Preaching Power. New York: The Macmillan Company, 1943. 229 pp. (P) An approach to sermon construction based on a study of the techniques of outstanding contemporary preachers.   21

Bowie, Walter Russell
Preaching. Nashville: Abingdon Press, 1954. 224 pp. (P) The purpose of preaching, use of the Bible relating theology to life, the construction and delivery of the sermon.   22

The Renewing Gospel. New York: Charles Scribner's Sons, 1935. 296 pp. (P) Lyman Beecher Lectures for 1935. An interpretation of the gospel which the Christian preacher needs "in this present time." A restatement of the content of the Christian message. Some chapters on the preacher and his people, and new challenges to the church.   23

Broadus, John A.; Jesse Burton Weatherspoon
On the Preparation and Delivery of Sermons. New York: Harper & Bros., 1944. 377 pp. (P) A revision of the textbook first published in 1870. A comprehensive survey of the structural and functional elements of the sermon with a consideration of the biblical foundations, style, and delivery of the sermon. Both authors were teachers in the Southern Baptist Seminary.   24

Brooks, Phillips
Eight Lectures on Preaching. London: SPCK, 1959. 281 pp.
(P) A reprinted selection of Brooks's famous lectures.   25

Lectures on Preaching. Grand Rapids: Zondervan Publishing
House, 1950. 281 pp. (P) A reprinted edition.   26

Phillips Brooks on Preaching. With a new introduction by
Theodore Parker Ferris. New York: The Seabury Press, 1964.
281 pp. (P) A reprint of Brooks's Beecher lectures of 1877.   27

Brown, H. C., Jr.; H. Gordon Clinard; Jesse Northcutt
Steps to the Sermon. Nashville: Broadman Press, 1963. 202 pp.
(P) An analysis of the *process* of sermon construction which
offers a chronology or steps to be taken in sermon preparation.
Parts of the sermon are identified, and the logical order in which
these are to be constructed is set forth. An operational approach
to homiletical theory.   28

Buchanan, Henry D.
The Art of Persuasion in Pastoral Theology. Philadelphia:
Dolphin Press, 1940. 96 pp. (C) A short treatise on the technique
of persuasion, as it has been employed in pastoral experience
with the sick, converts, marriage cases, hardened sinners. Only
minimally relevant to preaching.   29

Buege, William A.
Preaching With Power. St. Louis: Concordia Publishing House,
1956. 47 pp. (P) A short, insightful series of lectures by a
Lutheran.   30

Burnet, Adam
Pleading With Men. Westwood, N. J.: Fleming H. Revell
Company, 1935. 189 pp. (P) Warrack Lectures, Edinburgh, 1935.
Deals with liturgics, sermon construction, and sermon writing.   31

Buttrick, George A. *et al.*
Preaching in These Times. New York: Charles Scribner's Sons,
1940. 179 pp. (P) The Lyman Beecher Lectures for 1940, one of
two occasions when these have been presented by a group of
lecturers. Other contributors are E. M. Poteat, A. H. Bradford,
E. M. McKee, W. A. Smart, and E. F. Tittle.   32

Caemmerer, Richard R.
Preaching for the Church. St. Louis: Concordia Publishing
House, 1959. 327 pp. (P) An outstanding textbook especially
helpful on preaching the Christian year.   33

Cairns, Frank
Prophet of the Heart. New York: Harper & Bros., 1935. 149 pp. (P) The Warrack Lectures for 1934. A warmhearted call, written in first person, for the human touch in preaching, balanced by theology and craftsmanship.   34

Carney, Thomas A.
A Primer of Homiletics. Houston: Standard Publishing Co., 1942. 143 pp. (C) An aid to competence in the pulpit, this work contains sections on the human character of Christ; sermon preparation based on the little method of St. Vincent de Paul; mechanics of public speaking; and an analysis of the sermon on the mount. Presented in a light, popular style, needing, admittedly, fuller development and examples.   35

Chappell, Clovis G.
Anointed to Preach. Nashville: Abingdon Press, 1951. 124 pp. (P) The essence of what one Methodist preacher learned from a long ministry spent in the pastorate. He considers the preacher's call, his major emphasis, the preparation and delivery of the sermon.   36

Chilcothe, Thomas F., Jr.
The Excellence of Our Calling. New York: E. P. Dutton & Co., 1954. 192 pp. (P) An abridgement of Phillips Brooks's lectures on preaching.   37

Cleland, James T.
Preaching to Be Understood. Nashville: Abingdon Press, 1965. 126 pp. (P) The Warrack Lectures for 1964. A readable discussion of the knotty problems of contemporary preaching—the source of the preacher's authority, the gospel as "proclamation," the principles of sound biblical interpretation, the place of homiletic technique, and the significance of the nature of the church for preaching.   38

The True and Lively Word. New York: Charles Scribner's Sons, 1954. 120 pp. (P) A survey of the preaching task in five lucid lectures.   39

Cowan, Arthur
The Primacy of Preaching Today. New York: Charles Scribner's Sons, 1955. 128 pp. (P) The Warrack Lectures for 1954. Upon his principal thesis that "the fundamental purpose of corporate worship is the proclamation of God as revealed in Christ," Cowan offers commentary in chapters which expound

the importance of preaching today: expository preaching of the Old Testament and the New Testament, doctrinal preaching through the Christian year, and the manner and matter of preaching. The lectures are amply illustrated from literary resources by means of which the author demonstrates the effective use of expository material.   **40**

Craig, Archibald C.
Preaching in a Scientific Age. New York: Charles Scribner's Sons, 1954. 119 pp. (P) The Warrack Lectures of 1953 by the lecturer in biblical studies at Glasgow University. After consideration of the peculiar dilemmas confronting the contemporary preacher and the problem of biblical criticism, the author moves on to particular discussion of preaching in a scientific age on miracle, resurrection, and the last things.   **41**

Davis, H. Grady
Design for Preaching. Philadelphia: Muhlenberg Press, 1958. 294 pp. (P) Currently the most widely read general text in preaching among Protestants. A lively style illuminates a concept of preaching which is biblical, relevant, and contemporary. Outstanding.   **42**

DeWelt, Don
If You Want to Preach. Grand Rapids: Baker Book House, 1957. 168 pp. (P) A survey of the preaching task by a conservative, evangelistic-oriented preacher.   **43**

Dolan, Albert H., O.Carm.
Homiletic Hints. Chicago: Carmelite Press, 1952. 80 pp. (C) Pamphlet containing a program for the preparation, construction, and delivery of a sermon. It is addressed to seminarians and young priests, and combines speech theory with the fruit of personal experience.   **44**

Douglass, Truman
Preaching and the New Reformation. New York: Harper & Bros., 1956. 142 pp. (P) The Lyman Beecher Lectures at Yale for 1955 addressing the emerging pattern of ecumenical thought and action as it affects preaching today. The main thesis is that a new and vigorous content can come to preaching from the movements toward Protestant unity. The Word can no longer be preached in fullness from separated pulpits. A final chapter summarizes the characteristics of preaching the new reformation.   **45**

Doxsee, Herald M.
The Layman Speaks. Anderson, Ind.: Warner Press, 1965. 144
pp. (P) A public-speaking text addressed to laymen who are beginning to learn how to speak to church groups.   46

Drury, Ronan, ed.
Preaching. New York: Sheed & Ward, 1962. 149 pp. (C) A collection of recent articles by several writers (all Irish but one);
two outstanding contributions are Charles Davis' on the theology
of preaching and Joseph Dowdall's on the function of the homily.
Most of the other essays are concerned with kinds of preaching:
dogmatic, moral, etc.   47

Ellison, John M.
They Who Preach. Nashville: Broadman Press, 1956. 180 pp.
(P) A broad survey of the minister's preaching task by the first
Negro president of Virginia Union University.   48

Evans, William
How to Prepare Sermons. Chicago: Moody Press, 1964. 158 pp.
(P) Reprinted lectures by a Bible institute teacher who used
traditional categories and orthodox theology. The theory is
illustrated by copious sermon outlines.   49

Farley, Frederic A.
Preparing to Preach. London: The Epworth Press, 1939. 88 pp.
(P)   50

Farmer, Herbert H.
God and Men. Nashville: Abingdon Press, 1947. 203 pp. (P)
The 1946 Lyman Beecher Lectures: helping the preacher lead
his people in the actual business of being a Christian.   51

Feehan, John M., ed.
Preaching: A Symposium. Cork: Mercier Press, 1953. 70 pp.
(C) A collection of very candid and valuable comments on the
present status of preaching by members of the laity, as they see it. 52

Fénelon
Dialogues on Eloquence. Ed. by Wilbur S. Howell. Princeton:
Princeton University Press, 1951. 160 pp. (C) Important treatise
on sermon preparation, extemporaneous delivery, style, and
sermon content—one of the great classics of homiletic theory.   53

Ferris, Theodore Parker
Go Tell the People. New York: Charles Scribner's Sons, 1951.
116 pp. (P) The George Craig Stewart Lectures, Seabury-West-

ern Theological Seminary. The purpose, content, and form of
a sermon plus the personal problems of the preacher.   54

Flood, Dom Peter
*The Priest in Practice: Preaching and Some Other Priestly
Duties.* London: Burns and Oates, 1962. 164 pp. (C) The first
eight chapters of this work consider various aspects of preaching:
preparation and kinds of sermons suited for special occasions
(days of recollection, tridua, retreats) ; the place of erudition in
sermons; and the delivery, gestures, position, and personal ap-
pearance of the preacher himself. A very personal sharing; some
worthwhile information.   55

Francis de Sales, St.
On the Preacher and Preaching. Trans. with introduction and
notes by John K. Ryan. New York: Henry Regnery Co., 1964.
110 pp. (C) The famous letter of 1604, with illuminating introduction and helpful notes; still very worthy of attention.   56

Fritz, John H. C.
Essentials of Preaching. St. Louis: Concordia Publishing House,
1948. 73 pp. (P) A refresher course in homiletics for preachers.   57

Preacher's Manual. St. Louis: Concordia Publishing House,
1941. 390 pp. (P) A study in homiletics, with the addition of a
brief history of preaching, sermon material, texts for various
occasions, and pericopic systems.   58

Garvie, A. E.
The Christian Preacher. New York: Charles Scribner's Sons,
1937. 477 pp. (P) A reissue of a standard text of 1921 featuring a
generous history of preaching, a discussion of the preacher himself, and preaching methodology.   59

Gibbs, Alfred P.
A Primer on Preaching. Fort Dodge, Iowa: Walterick Print
Company, 1946. 207 pp. (P) A textbook, compactly written by a
member of the Plymouth Brethren, along traditional lines. (Rev.
in 1951, name changed to *The Preacher and His Preaching*) .   60

The Preacher and His Preaching. 3rd ed. Fort Dodge, Iowa:
Walterick Print Company, 1951. 441 pp. (P) A thorough text on
homiletics, with clear illustrations for many points.   61

Gilkey, Langdon
*How the Church Can Minister to the World Without Losing
Itself.* New York: Harper & Row, 1964. 146 pp. (P) Keen insight
into the problems of preaching relevantly to a secular age.   62

Gregory the Great, St.
Pastoral Care. Westminster, Md.: The Newman Press, 1950.
281 pp. (C) An important preaching manual from the middle
ages, with significant contributions on audience analysis with
particular occasions in mind.   63

Hance, Kenneth G.; Harold A. Brack
Public Speaking and Discussion for Religious Leaders. Englewood Cliffs, N. J.: Prentice-Hall, 1961. 254 pp. (P) A clear and
comprehensive guide, written for clergy and laymen who speak in
church groups.   64

Haselden, Kyle
The Urgency of Preaching. New York: Harper & Row, 1963.
121 pp. (P) The place and importance of preaching today and
the urgency with which it should be done.   65

Haynes, Carlyle Boyaton
Divine Art of Preaching. Washington, D. C.: Review & Herald
Publishing Association, 1939. 256 pp. (P) General material
prepared as a reading course for Seventh-Day Adventist
preachers.   66

Hill, J. R.
Preaching the Word. London: Pickering and Inglis, 1958. 105
pp. (P) A homiletical guide for lay preachers.   67

Ireson, Gordon W.
How Shall They Hear? London: SPCK, 1958. 222 pp. (P)
Principles and practices of present-day preaching, plus twelve
sermons illustrating the principles. Clear, lucid writing by an
Anglican clergyman.   68

John Eudes, St.
The Priest: His Dignity and Obligations. New York: P. J.
Kenedy & Sons, 1947. 306 pp. (C) Part II of this volume contains
the Saint's treatise on "The Apostolic Preacher." Noteworthy for
its many inspiring and practical bits of advice to preachers.   69

Jones, Bob, Jr.
How to Improve Your Preaching. Grand Rapids: Kregel Publications, 1960. 126 pp. (P) (Rev. and enl. from the Revell ed. of
1945) A brief, helpful book by a fundamentalist preacher-
dramatist.   70

Jones, Ilion T.
Principles and Practice of Preaching. Nashville: Abingdon Press, 1956. 272 pp. (P) A practical book along somewhat traditional lines. For the man "at whatever stage of his ministry who wants to learn to preach more effectively and is willing to pay the price of the learning." Extensive bibliographies. 71

Jordan, G. Ray
Preaching During a Revolution. Anderson, Ind.: Warner Press, 1962. 192 pp. (P) A general reading book for inspiration and individual study by ministers and those who are interested in communicating more effectively with others as a part of their church work. Suggests adaptations of the traditional approaches for the pulpit of the 1960's with its contemporary crises, the new techniques, and methods produced by the skills of mass communication. 72

Kennedy, Gerald H.
God's Good News. New York: Harper & Bros., 1955. 182 pp. (P) The Lyman Beecher Lectures of 1954 presented with the characteristic Kennedy sagacity and resources of wide reading. Indicates helpful directions for preaching and offers many personal hints. 73

His Word Through Preaching. New York: Harper & Bros., 1947. 234 pp. (P) Treatment of how to bring the message and method of preaching together, combining the presuppositions of Christianity with preaching's dramatic character, its imaginative vitality, and its existence as deed. 74

Krieger, W. Harry
Angels Having the Gospel to Preach. St. Louis: Concordia Publishing House, 1957. 45 pp. (P) Consists of two principal addresses on effective preaching, based on the premise that God supplies help to eager learners through the efforts of human instruments. The man, the message, and the method are simply and effectively treated by a pulpit pastor out of his own experiences. 75

Lantz, John Edward
Speaking in the Church. New York: The Macmillan Company, 1954. 192 pp. (P) A general, brief text written on an elementary level and using insights from the speech disciplines. 76

Leabel, Pius A., C.P., ed.
St. Vincent Strambi's Guide to Sacred Eloquence. St. Meinrad, Ind.: Abbey Press Publishing Division, 1963. 138 pp. (C) A good

guide for today's preacher, containing a review of the basic rules of rhetoric. It emphasizes the "soft sell" in the pulpit, stresses simplicity in style and the manifestation of genuine emotion. The chapters on "familiar discourse" and the use of the Bible to reconstruct for the people the full context of life situation are of particular interest. 77

Liske, Thomas
Effective Preaching. Rev. ed. New York: The Macmillan Company, 1962. 293 pp. (C) One of the most popular recent texts for Catholic preaching courses; heavy dependence upon principles of public speaking. 78

Lockyer, Herbert
The Art of Praying and Speaking in Public. Grand Rapids: Zondervan Publishing House, 1952. 59 pp. (P) A brief, practical book written by a British fundamentalist preacher. 79

Louttit, H. I.
Commanded to Preach. New York: The Seabury Press, 1965. 111 pp. (P) The George Craig Stewart Memorial Lectures in preaching at Seabury-Western Seminary. A general approach. 80

Luccock, Halford E.
Communicating the Gospel. New York: Harper & Bros., 1954. 183 pp. (P) The Lyman Beecher Lectures for 1953. Perceptive and sound, with many literary references and allusions. How to interpret the gospel for the world of insecurity, futility, and fear and, in the face of all the obstacles that stand in the way, not to obscure nor strip it. 81

McCallum, James R.
A Short Method for Pulpit and Sermons. London: James Clarke & Company, 1942. 96 pp. (P) 82

McIntyre, R. E.
The Ministry of the Word. London: Thomas Nelson & Sons, 1950. 117 pp. (P) The Warrack Lectures of 1949 on the importance of preaching, the use of the Bible and dogma, and originality in preaching. 83

Mackenzie, Hamish C.
Preaching the Eternities. Edinburgh: Saint Andrew Press, 1963. 130 pp. (P) The Warrack lecturer for 1963 touches lightly the traditional topics for a survey: the importance of preaching, the preacher himself, techniques, dangers, etc. 84

MacLennan, David A.
Pastoral Preaching. Philadelphia: The Westminster Press, 1955. 156 pp. (P) Provides helpful definitions of pastoral and Christian preaching, a good statement of the objectives of preaching, and some cogent advice about the delivery of the sermon.   85

Entrusted with the Gospel. Philadelphia: The Westminster Press, 1956. 128 pp. (P) The Warrack Lectures for 1955. A sprightly discussion of the preacher's responsibilities, the nature of his commission, the congregation, and the possibilities of preaching.   86

Macleod, George
Speaking the Truth—in Love. London: SCM Press, 1936. 127 pp. (P) The Warrack Lectures of 1936 on "the modern preacher's task." A helpful survey.   87

MacNutt, Sylvester F., O.P.
Gauging Sermon Effectiveness. Dubuque: The Priory Press, 1960. 139 pp. (C) A handy collection of criteria for the evaluation of a sermon: its subject matter, arrangement, style, and also the ethos of the preacher; a guide for students making sermon evaluations from the vantage point of speech theory.   88

Macpherson, Ian
The Burden of the Lord. Nashville: Abingdon Press, 1957. 157 pp. (P) Discusses the preaching of Christ as Savior and Lord, contemporary Power, Judge, and Ruler of the world. Considers desirable characteristics for a man who preaches. The craft of sermon construction is clearly and succinctly discussed. The delivery of the sermon aptly but briefly treated.   89

McVann, James, C.S.P.
The Canon Law on Sermon Preaching. New York: Paulist Press, 1940. 190 pp. (C) A doctoral dissertation tracing the development of ecclesiastical legislation on preaching from the earliest times to the modern code of canon law; valuable for understanding the pronouncements of councils and popes.   90

Marcel, Pierre C.
The Relevance of Preaching. Grand Rapids: Baker Book House, 1963. 110 pp. (P) Translation of a scholarly work by a French Reformed pastor who calls for a balance between the eternal Word and the needs of the world.   91

Michonneau, Georges; François Varillon, S.J.
From Pulpit to People. Trans. by Edmond Bonin. Westminster, Md.: The Newman Press, 1965. 224 pp. (C) Translation of a 1963 French publication of short essays on various aspects of the preaching apostolate; especially strong in areas of language and the question of adaptation, weak in sphere of theology of preaching and the renewed sense of liturgical preaching.   **92**

Missett, Luke, C.P.
The Pews Talk Back. Westminster, Md.: The Newman Press, 1946. 83 pp. (C) A nontechnical collection of essays on various aspects of sermon composition and delivery; practical approach, including numerous illustrative anecdotes.   **93**

Montgomery, Richard Ames
Preparing Preachers to Preach. Grand Rapids: Zondervan Publishing House, 1939. 249 pp. (P) A basic textbook written in a light style.   **94**

Morlan, George K.
Layman Speaking. New York: R. R. Smith, 1938. 242 pp. (P) An evaluation of preaching by a layman who reports research on laymen's likes and dislikes, the kinds of sermons they remember, and his own suggestions for improvement in preaching.   **95**

Morrow, Thomas M.
Worship and Preaching. London: The Epworth Press, 1956. 103 pp. (P) The first half of the book is concerned with the conduct of worship and attitude toward ministry. The second half deals with the making and delivery of the sermon. Prepared as a prescribed text for candidates who are preparing themselves for the lay ministry.   **96**

Murphy, Thomas R.
A Priest Must Preach. Milwaukee: Bruce Publishing Co., 1945. 287 pp. (C) An engaging book of Sunday sermons prepared on Saturday night, with a post-Sunday analysis and matter-delivery criticism. It presents a novel method of gauging the effectiveness of one's Sunday sermon on the following Monday.   **97**

Nes, William H.
The Excellency of the Word. New York: Morehouse-Gorham Co., 1956. 158 pp. (P) Presents the topics "The Preacher and the Bible," "The Use of Images," "Preaching Is a Time of Anxiety," and "Priesthood and the Word." A Survey of Homi-

letics Education by Noah E. Fehl is appended. More theological
than rhetorical in content.   **98**

Noyes, Morgan Phelps
Preaching the Word of God. New York: Charles Scribner's
Sons, 1943. 219 pp. (P) Lyman Beecher Lectures of 1942. Gen-
eral reflections from a pastor.   **99**

Oman, John B.
Concerning the Ministry. Richmond: John Knox Press, 1963.
180 pp. (P) A rather wordy but helpful series of reflections on
preaching by a British preacher and teacher upon his retire-
ment. (A reprint of the 1937 Harper Bros. ed.)   **100**

Oxnam, G. Bromley
Preaching in a Revolutionary Age. New York: Abingdon-
Cokesbury Press, 1944. 207 pp. (P) The Beecher Lectures of
1944. Considers the nature of a revolutionary era, urges that
preaching be relevant to the era and that the preacher "speak of
sin where sin is."   **101**

Park, John Edgar
The Miracle of Preaching. New York: The Macmillan Company, 1936. 184 pp. (P) Lyman Beecher Lectures for 1936. The
author traces the miracle of the inspiration of the sermon
idea, feeling that there are some preachers who make sermons
and others "in whom sermons are born." He believes that preaching must be a by-product of life and that usually the best sermon
ideas evolve after the mind and heart have been induced to
operate. He sees preaching also as an aid to the growth of the
congregation.   **102**

Patton, Carl S.
The Preparation and Delivery of Sermons. New York: Willett,
Clark & Co., 1938. 191 pp. (P) This book combines insights concerning the nature of preaching and its primary importance in
the minister's work with the practical mechanics of sermon structure, style, preparation, and delivery. The author believes that
preaching is an art that must be learned by doing and that the
first requisite for a good delivery is to have something to say. **103**

Pearson, Roy M.
The Ministry of Preaching. New York: Harper & Bros., 1954.
127 pp. (P) The author discusses the purpose and content of
preaching, the nature of the congregation, the credentials and

roles of the preacher, and the preparation and delivery of the sermon. He sees preaching as proclamation, demonstration, and implantation.   104

Phelps, Austin
The Theory of Preaching. Abridg. and rev. by Faris D. White-sell. Grand Rapids: Wm. B. Eerdmans Publishing Co., 1947. 167 pp. (P) A comprehensive but seriously dated homiletical theory.   105

Pike, James A.
A New Look in Preaching. New York: Charles Scribner's Sons, 1961. 107 pp. (P) Bishop Pike discusses things which make communication difficult in our changing times. By the use of the common idiom and ideology he seeks to bring preaching back to the people and to give freshness to old truths. The book is organized around concepts of modern salesmanship, such as market survey, the product and its packaging, the salesman, the store.   106

Pittenger, W. Norman
Proclaiming Christ Today. New York: The Seabury Press, 1962. 148 pp. (P) The author feels that much of the lack of power in contemporary preaching arises from the confusion of the preaching office of the minister with the minister's work as teacher and other pastoral functions. He develops the thesis that as preachers we are engaged only in confronting our listeners with the very Word of God under the headings: the gospel we proclaim, the setting of the gospel, the people to whom we preach, problems in proclaiming the gospel today, etc.   107

Read, David H. C.
The Communication of the Gospel. Chicago: Alec R. Allenson, 1952. 96 pp. (P) The Warrack Lectures for 1951. The author seeks to help the preacher bridge the "expanding gulf between the thought and language of the inner church and those of the contemporary world."   108

Riley, William Bell
The Preacher and His Preaching. Wheaton, Ill.: Sword of the Lord Press, 1948. 146 pp. (P)   109

Rogers, Clement F.
The Parson Preaching. New York: The Macmillan Company, 1947. 130 pp. (P) A practical text for Anglican seminarians, written in a delightful style.   110

Rust, Eric C.
Preaching in a Scientific Age. Birmingham, England: Berean Press, 1951. 24 pp. (P) A thoughtful reflection in a single lecture by one trained both as scientist and theologian.　　111

Sanford, Jack D.
Make Your Preaching Relevant. Nashville: Broadman Press, 1963. 93 pp. (P) A pastor makes a vigorous plea for preaching which is in simple language, but which is also soundly biblical. A strong emphasis on the preacher's need for personally experiencing the truths about which he preaches.　　112

Sangster, W. E.
The Approach to Preaching. Philadelphia: The Westminster Press, 1952. 112 pp. (P) Six lectures delivered at the six Methodist theological colleges in England in 1950. A very general but useful little book.　　113

Power in Preaching. Nashville: Abingdon Press, 1958. 110 pp. (P) The thirty-ninth series of Fondren Lectures delivered at Perkins School of Theology, containing practical advice about preaching.　　114

Sayres, Alfred Nevin
That One Good Sermon. Philadelphia: United Church Press, 1963. 95 pp. (P) A unique survey of the preaching task, put into the words of a hypothetical parishioner who talks to an inquisitive homiletics professor about his pastor's preaching.　　115

Scherer, Paul
For We Have This Treasure. New York: Harper & Row, 1944. 212 pp. (P) The Lyman Beecher Lectures for 1943, providing one of the most helpful and stimulating recent surveys of the task of preaching.　　116

The Word God Sent. New York: Harper & Row, 1965. 261 pp. (P) One of America's foremost preachers shares a rich lifetime of reflection about the task of preaching. In masterly style, his essays on the theology and craftsmanship of preaching blend with a group of his sermons. The extensive cross references are designed to help readers follow Dr. Scherer's theory into his practice. One of the best books on preaching in many years.　　117

Schloerb, Rolland W.
The Preaching Ministry Today. New York: Harper & Bros., 1946. 113 pp. (P) Lectures delivered to the summer conference of ministers and religious leaders at Union Theological Seminary

in 1945. A brief appraisal of the preaching function and an elementary treatment of the nature and purpose of preaching.   **118**

Schulze, Frederick
A Manual of Pastoral Theology. St. Louis: B. Herder Book Co., 1944. 380 pp. (C) In a section on the teaching of divine truth, there is a rather standard, manual-type consideration of various aspects of preaching.   **119**

Sharp, John K.
Next Sunday's Sermon. Philadelphia: Dolphin Press, 1940. 324 pp. (C) Basic text for preaching courses; in its era, one of the most useful treatises available.   **120**

Sittler, Joseph
The Ecology of Faith: The New Situation in Preaching. Philadelphia: Muhlenberg Press, 1961. 104 pp. (P) The Beecher Lectures for 1959. A reassessment of the minister's role as preacher in contemporary society, analyzing the demands of the new situation and the resources to meet them within the heritage of the church. A responsible attempt to achieve relevance in the communication of the gospel.   **121**

Sleeth, Ronald E.
Persuasive Preaching. New York: Harper & Row, 1956. 96 pp. (P) A brief treatment of recent findings in the study of persuasion as they apply to preaching. A good introduction by one who is trained in speech and involved in teaching homiletics.   **122**

Snyder, Russell D.; Otto A. Piper; Oscar F. Blackwelder; Fred C. Wiegman
Reality in Preaching. Philadelphia: Muhlenberg Press, 1942. 168 pp. (P) Seven lectures on various aspects of preaching by four well-known preacher-theologians.   **123**

Sockman, Ralph W.
The Highway of God. New York: The Macmillan Company, 1942. 228 pp. (P) The Lyman Beecher Lectures for 1941 dealing with the minister and his message. The author seeks to shed light on the task by a study of Jesus' appraisal of John the Baptist's preaching. Somewhat dated now, the book pulsates nonetheless with realism and hope which are timeless.   **124**

Soper, Donald O.
The Advocacy of the Gospel. Nashville: Abingdon Press, 1961. 120 pp. (P) The Lyman Beecher Lectures for 1960 which at-

tempt to think through the particular needs of the present age and to find an answer to the pulpit's seeming irrelevancy. Somewhat lacking in theological depth.   125

Sperry, Willard L.
We Prophesy in Part. New York: Harper & Bros., 1938. 201 pp. (P) The Lyman Beecher Lectures for 1938 dealing with the "liberty of prophesying" by means of historical survey and analysis of the prophetic function. Seriously dated now, the book seems to plead for a Christian humanism in which religion is defined as "a struggle for perspective" and the *sine qua non* of preaching is freedom of expression.   126

Spurgeon, Charles H.
Lectures to My Students. Grand Rapids: Zondervan Publishing House, 1955. 443 pp. (P) Reprinted from an earlier work of 1894, these lectures cover everything from the minister's call to his delivery of sermons. Although wordy and seriously dated, these lectures are valuable not only for historical reasons but also because of much practical advice from a leading figure in the late nineteenth-century pulpit.   127

Stamm, Frederick Keller
So You Want to Preach. Nashville: Abingdon Press, 1958. 109 pp. (P) Subtitled, "A Letter to a Young Minister," the book is heavy on reminiscences and advice. The perspective is that of a retired, liberal minister.   128

Thielicke, Helmut, ed.
Encounter With Spurgeon. Philadelphia: Fortress Press, 1963. 283 pp. (P) A popular German preacher and theologian selects and abbreviates some of Spurgeon's lectures and sermons. In one chapter he enthusiastically identifies his own homiletics with Spurgeon's. Book is by Spurgeon; introductory chapter by Thielicke.   129

Valentine, Ferdinand, O.P.
The Art of Preaching. Westminster, Md.: The Newman Press, 1952. 224 pp. (C) More a commentary from past experience in preaching than a textbook, with suggestions on connected topics such as the methods of conducting group discussions on religious themes.   130

Veuillot, Pierre
The Catholic Priesthood. Westminster, Md.: The Newman Press, 1958. 638 pp. (C) A collection of all papal documents

bearing on the priestly vocation, from Pope Pius X to Pius XII —and thereby a source for material suitable for priest retreats and recollections. In addition, it brings together all the recent papal pronouncements on preaching—valuable for discovery of the norms for Catholic preaching. 131

Volbeda, Samuel
The Pastoral Genius of Preaching. Grand Rapids: Zondervan Publishing House, 1960. 85 pp. (P) Edited homiletics lecture notes of a late professor at Calvin Seminary. Disjointed and uneven reading. 132

Von Allmen, Jean-Jacques
Preaching and Congregation. Richmond: John Knox Press, 1962. 65 pp. (P) An examination of what happens when we preach, how to bridge the gap between the source of preaching and those to whom it is addressed, preaching's place in worship, how to prepare sermons, and the ecumenical implications. 133

Ward, Ronald A.
Royal Sacrament: The Preacher and His Message. London: Marshall, Morgan & Scott, 1958. 182 pp. (P) A New Testament scholar defines preaching and discusses the relationship of the preacher to theology, literature, biblical problems, the church, and the divinity school. 134

Wesley, John
John Wesley on Pulpit Oratory. Rev. and abridg. by Ross E. Price. Kansas City: Beacon Hill Press, 1955. 21 pp. (P) A few selections from Wesley's writings on preaching. 135

Whitesell, Faris D.
The Art of Biblical Preaching. Grand Rapids: Zondervan Publishing House, 1950. 160 pp. (P) An apologetic for biblical preaching, together with its essentials, its methods, and biographies of contemporary practitioners. 136

Williams, Jerome O.
The Gospel Preacher and His Preaching. Nashville: Broadman Press, 1949. 84 pp. (P) A survey written in simple and direct language especially for Southern Baptist preachers with limited higher education. 137

Wright, James
A Preacher's Questionnaire. Edinburgh: St. Andrew's Press, 1958. 90 pp. (P) The Warrack Lectures for 1956. General

reflections on forty years of preaching. The "why, what, to whom, how, and with what results" approach.   **138**

Preaching and Theology

Augustine, St.
On Christian Doctrine. Trans. by J. F. Shaw. ("Great Books Series.") Chicago: Encyclopedia Britannica, 1952. 698 pp. (C) The fourth book, "Christian Instruction," seeks to transfer the principles of rhetoric to revelation; valuable for general tenets of homiletics as well as for the treatment on style.   **139**

Baab, Otto J.
Prophetic Preaching: A New Approach. Nashville: Abingdon Press, 1958. 159 pp. (P) Similarities in issues and approach between the situation of the modern preacher and the ancient prophets. The prophetic preacher's passion, problem, purpose, power, perspective, proclamation, and promise.   **140**

Baillie, Donald M.
The Theology of the Sacraments. New York: Charles Scribner's Sons, 1957. (P) Lecture VI, "The Preaching of the Christian Doctrine," recommends the teaching of Christian doctrine from the pulpit by means of the incidental method, the "times and seasons" method, and by courses of sermons on great doctrines. Gives examples of how a sermon on doctrine may spring out of the scriptures and how doctrine may be related to problems of everyday life.   **141**

Barth, Karl
The Preaching of the Gospel. Trans. by B. E. Hooke. Philadelphia: The Westminster Press, 1963. 94 pp. (P) An interpretation of preaching as God speaking through our words, in the context of the church, through the medium of doctrine and the Bible, with some notes on the preparation of the sermon. A reissue of Barth's 1918 lectures.   **142**

Theology and Church. New York: Harper & Row, 1962. (P) Lectures V and VI carry an exposition of Freidrich Schleiermacher's theories of the role of the preacher as virtuoso, prophet, mediator, priest, and hero. Emphasis here is on the mediator role. Refers to Schleiermacher's distinction between poetic, rhetorical, and didactic speaking, but stresses the poetic. In Lecture VI, Barth discusses Schleiermacher's definition of preaching as the "self-communication" of the preacher.   **143**

The Word of God and the Word of Man. New York: Harper & Row, 1957. (P) In chapter IV, "The Need and Promise of Christian Preaching," Barth analyzes the basic expectation of the congregation as the answer to the question, Is it true? All activity of the Sunday ritual except the Word as brought by the preacher merely "puts off" the answer to the question. This chapter brings into view the awesome responsibility of the preacher in answering the crucial question of his hearers. A reprint of his 1928 work. **144**

Brightman, Edgar S.
Person and Reality. New York: The Ronald Press Company, 1958. (P) In Part II, "Categories of Being," communication, for Brightman, is a category of being which presupposes nonidentical persons in an interpersonal relationship, without which "there is no meaning in society, public verification, scientific and philosophical discussion, in any socially directed questions or in any answers." In chapter 14, Brightman describes communication as a "sharing of thought and purpose and feeling between persons. . . . One can be aware of what another means, what he purposes, what he feels and commit himself to like meaning, purposes, and feeling." **145**

Browne, Robert E. C.
The Ministry of the Word. London: SCM Press, 1958. 125 pp. (P) The ministry of the Word. Studies in ministry and worship. The theological and apologetic dimensions of preaching. **146**

Brunner, Emil
The Christian Doctrine of God. Vol. I. Philadelphia: The Westminster Press, 1950. (P) Appendix to Prolegomena, "Apologetics and Eristics," and "Missionary Theology." Discusses apologetics as the "intellectual discussion of the Christian Faith in the light of ideologies of the present which are opposed to the Christian message." Missionary theology requires use of the inductive method to make an intellectual presentation of the gospel from the starting point of the spiritual situation of the hearer. **147**

Bultmann, Rudolf
Jesus Christ and Mythology. New York: Charles Scribner's Sons, 1958. (P) In chapter III, "The Christian Message and the Modern World-View," Bultmann explains his theory of "Christian preaching as kerygma, that is, a proclamation addressed not to theoretical reason, but to the hearer as self." His way of bringing the Word of God to modern man is to de-mythologize

the Scriptures. The method of de-mythologizing—exegesis—is explained in chapter IV, "Modern Biblical Interpretation and Existential Philosophy." Of interest to the preacher are Bultmann's suggestions for interpreting the Bible for the hearer by beginning with the question, "How is man's existence understood in the Bible?"   148

Theology of the New Testament. Vols. I & II. New York: Charles Scribner's Sons, 1951. (P) Bultmann's contention that Christian preaching is kerygma—a proclamation addressed not to the theoretical reason, but to the hearer as a self—pervades both volumes. Although there are no explicit rules for homiletical interpretation of the New Testament, the explications of the Christian message as presented by Jesus, the apostles, and the early Church teachers make these volumes of interest as resource books for the pulpit speaker.   149

Cairns, David S.
A Gospel Without Myth? Bultmann's Challenge to the Preacher. London: SCM Press, 1960. 232 pp. (P) Discussion of the problem of how to preach the demythologized biblical theology of Rudolph Bultmann. The author, professor of practical theology at Christ's College, Aberdeen, believes preaching can only be nourished on a richer, deeper kind of theology.   150

Casserly, J. V. Langmead
Apologetics and Evangelism. Philadelphia: The Westminster Press, 1962. 183 pp. (P) This rather short work contains a thorough analysis of the interrelationships among the elite and nonelite of the Christian and non-Christian world; between the theologian and apologist, and in turn the apologist and the pastor. In analyzing all the relationships, Casserly recognizes the basic problem of content, responsibility and methodology of communication. As the title would suggest, he is most concerned with the communicative function of the apologists.   151

Clowney, Edmund P.
Preaching and Biblical Theology. Grand Rapids: Wm. B. Eerdmans Publishing Co., 1961. 124 pp. (P) After careful definition of biblical theology the work proceeds to a consideration of biblical theology and the authority, character, and content of preaching. The emphasis is on the recovery of the authority of the written Word of God. A short bibliography is useful as a guide to the important recent works on the subject of biblical theology. 152

Coggan, Frederick D.
The Ministry of the Word. London: Canterbury Press, 1946. 127 pp. (P) The New Testament concept of preaching and its relevance for today.   153

Come, Arnold B.
An Introduction to Barth's Dogmatics for Preachers. Philadelphia: The Westminster Press, 1963. 243 pp. (P) This work is a preacher's guide to the reading of Barth's *Dogmatics*. Of particular interest to the preacher as communicator are the explanations of Barth's method of analogy in chapter V and in VI through IX, which are directly concerned with the preacher, his biblical sources, interpretations, and his theological and humanistic responsibilities.   154

Daniélou, Jean
Christ and Us. New York: Sheed & Ward, 1961. 236 pp. (C) Chapter VII ("Word, Sacraments, Mission") contains an excellent coverage of recent scholarship on the theology of preaching, in particular the efficacy of the Word and the prophetical aspect of proclamation.   155

DeWolf, L. Harold
The Religious Revolt Against Reason. New York: Harper & Bros., 1949. (P) Chapter IV, "Objections to Irrationalism," includes a critique of such communicative devices as the paradox, analogy, example, and testimony as rational means of winning belief. DeWolf is herein rejecting the idea that revelation must be an offense to the understanding, affirming the need for reasoned communication of the Christian message.   156

Dodd, C. H.
The Apostolic Preaching. New York: Harper & Row, 1950. 96 pp. (P) A significant turning point in Protestant homiletical thought. An English biblical scholar's analysis of the importance of kerygma in the primitive church. Originally published in 1935.   157

Farmer, Herbert H.
The Servant of the Word. New York: Charles Scribner's Sons, 1942 (reprinted by Fortress Press in 1964). 109 pp. (P) The importance of both preacher and listener in effective preaching. Keen insights into the theology of preaching.   158

Forsyth, P. T.
Positive Preaching and the Modern Mind. Grand Rapids: Wm. B. Eerdmans Publishing Co., 1964. 258 pp. (P) The 1907 Lyman

Beecher Lectures. The place of preaching in the modern
world; strangely relevant half a century later.   **159**

Grasso, Domenico, S. J.
*Proclaiming God's Message: A Study in the Theology of Preach-
ing.* Notre Dame: University of Notre Dame Press, 1965. 272 pp.
(C) It is hard to estimate the importance of this book, probably
the most significant publication in English at this time on the
theology of preaching. Grasso considers all the crucial questions
(essence and nature of preaching; its object, subject, efficacy,
dimensions; role of the preacher; adaptation) with a profound
theological insight. An ideal text for the introductory course in
preaching and indispensable reading for all interested in the
ministry of the Word.   **160**

Henry, A. M.
A Mission Theology. Notre Dame: Fides Publishers, 1962. 197
pp. (C) This short volume has become one of the most important recent contributions to the study of the apostolate of
preaching in the various ecclesial contexts: missionary, catechetical, pastoral. Indispensable for all seriously interested in the
theology of preaching.   **161**

Hitz, Paul, C.SS.R.
To Preach the Gospel. New York: Sheed & Ward, 1963. 209 pp.
(C) Solid treatment of the theology of preaching, from the
scriptural, historical, and pastoral points of view, leading up to a
renewal of mission preaching. This translation of the French
version (1954) is one of the most significant and influential
contributions to the *aggiornamento* of American preaching.   **162**

Hofinger, Johannes, S.J.
*The Art of Teaching Christian Doctrine: The Good News and
Its Proclamation.* Notre Dame: University of Notre Dame Press,
1957. 278 pp. (C) One of the true pioneer contributions to the
renewal of preaching in American Catholicism—the earliest extensive treatment of scholarship from the modern catechetical
movement accessible in English. Of general interest because of its
thorough examination of the content and structure of the Christian message, it has special relevance for catechetical preaching. **163**

Jenkins, Daniel T.
The Strangeness of the Church. New York: Doubleday & Com-
pany, 1955. (P) See chapter VIII, "The Word of God and the
Church." Although the entire chapter treats of the preacher's

functions, Jenkins' interpretation of the nature of oral communication leads him into contradictions and generalizations. In one paragraph Jenkins states, "The congregation is not an audience." In the same paragraph he insists that the congregation should listen to the sermon responsibly "with a realization that it is meant to make a difference to their life together and should not go either unheeded or, if need be, unchallenged." Although Jenkins seems to see the preacher as one who persuades the unbeliever and reinforces the belief of the faithful, he contends that the expository sermon should be the norm. **164**

Tradition, Freedom, and the Spirit. Philadelphia: The Westminster Press, 1951. (P) See chapter X, "Tradition, Freedom and the Worship of the Church." The presupposition of all preaching is that there is a Word from God. The preacher's first task is to discover the Word through critical study of the Scriptures. Secondly, he must help the congregation reach the place where they can hear God speaking for themselves. Thirdly, the preacher must not obtrude himself between the Word of God and his people. As the title might suggest, this work attempts to reconcile traditional life and activity of the church with the condition of modern man. So it is with Jenkins' interpretation of the function of the sermon. **165**

Joly, Eugene
What Is Faith? New York: Hawthorn Books, 1959. 144 pp. (C) With every type of preaching working as it does in the service of faith, it is absolutely essential that preachers understand thoroughly the final product, the goal, and purpose of their ministry; this book answers that need admirably. **166**

Jungmann, Josef A., S.J.
The Good News, Yesterday and Today. New York: William H. Sadlier, 1962. 228 pp. (C) An adapted translation of Jungmann's *Die Frohbotschaft* (1936), one of the most significant works ever published on the proclamation of the faith. It considers the history of Christian proclamation and the task of renewal facing preachers today; an indispensable study for anyone interested in the theology of preaching. **167**

Kahmann, J., C.SS.R.
The Bible on the Preaching of the Word. De Pere, Wis.: St. Norbert Abbey Press, 1965. 117 pp. (C) Excellent treatment, in a very succinct fashion, of the basic elements of a theology of preaching—its meaning and content, its power and efficacy. **168**

Kantonen, T. A.
   The Theology of Evangelism. Philadelphia: Muhlenberg Press, 1954. 98 pp. (P) A neat summary of the theology of preaching attached to the articles of the Apostles' Creed.   **169**

Kelly, Balmer Hancock
   A Theology for Proclamation. Richmond: Union Theological Seminary in Virginia, 1954. 23 pp. (P) An inaugural address which relates biblical to kerygmatic preaching and discusses the implications of the relationship.   **170**

Kerr, Hugh T.
   Positive Protestantism. Philadelphia: The Westminster Press, 1950. 147 pp. (P) The thesis of this book is that the essence of Christianity is to be found in the gospel straightforwardly and unequivocally proclaimed. This reaffirmation needs to be reflected in what the author calls a "new preaching."   **171**

Knox, John
   The Integrity of Preaching. Nashville: Abingdon Press, 1957. 96 pp. (P) Presentation of the meaning of "biblical preaching." Analysis of the difference between preaching that "sounds" biblical and that which is truly a proclamation of the Word. Excellent ideas on the personal nature of preaching and on its setting in worship, of the necessity of the participation of the worshiper in the sermon. Incidental: shrewd suggestions on sermon preparation and construction.   **172**

Kraemer, Hendrik
   The Communication of the Christian Faith. Philadelphia: The Westminster Press, 1956. 128 pp. (P) Analyzes psychological, sociological, and cultural breakdown of communication and offers suggestions for solutions. The problems are approached from biblical, historical, and cultural perspectives.   **173**

Lehmann, H. T.
   Heralds of the Gospels. Philadelphia: Muhlenberg Press, 1953. 76 pp. (P) Rejecting a fundamentalistic view of the Bible, the author feels the Word of God and the words of man in the Bible cannot be identified. Stresses the importance of knowing *what* to preach rather than *how* to preach. Suggestions for self-improvement. Purpose of book and conclusions not entirely clear.   **174**

Lüthi, Walter; Eduard Thurneysen
   Preaching. Confession. The Lord's Supper. Richmond: John Knox Press, 1960. 121 pp. (P) Essays by two Swiss theologians,

calling for a rediscovery of the essence of Protestantism and to
an awakening of our unity with European Christians. A stimulating exposition of the meaning of preaching. 175

McNeill, Robert B.
Prophet, Speak Now. Richmond: John Knox Press, 1961. 92 pp.
(P) A call for prophetic preaching in the Old Testament tradi-
tion to help purify today's church. 176

Mascall, E. L.
Existence and Analogy. London: Longmans, Green & Co., 1949.
(P) See chapter V, "The Doctrine of Analogy." Review of literature on use of doctrine of analogy in making it possible to talk
about God. ". . . the question of analogy does not arise at all
in the mere proof of the existence of God; it arises only when
having satisfied ourselves that the existence of a finite being
declares its dependence upon self-existent being, we then appre-
hend that no predicate can be attributed to finite and to self-
existent being univocally." Thorough exposition of analogy
duorum ad tertium and analogy *unius ad alterum*. Doctrine of
Analogy is central to Mascall's theory of communication about
God and appears in all his works. 177

He Who Is. London: Longmans, Green & Co., 1958. (P) See
chapter III, "Experience and Revelation." Examines the difficulty
of communicating religious experience in human language.
". . . it is impossible adequately to describe it to anyone else and
so make it the basis of an argument." 178

Words and Images. London: Longmans, Green & Co., 1957. (P)
See chapter V, "Knowledge and Communication." Raises the
question of the relation of theological thought and knowledge
to its communication. Differentiates between communication of
concepts and "contuition" through the employment of images.
Reviews uses and limits of analogy in theological discourse. 179

Miller, Donald G.
Fire in Thy Mouth. Nashville: Abingdon Press, 1954. 160 pp.
(P) A presentation of biblical preaching as redemptive event
dealing with the role of the Bible, the preacher as biblical interpreter, the values and implications of biblical preaching. The
first chapter contains an interesting discussion of the definition of
preaching. 180

Morris, Frederick M.
Preach the Word of God. New York: Morehouse-Gorham Co.,
1954. 157 pp. (P) Stresses the responsibility of the congregation

in producing preaching. Advocates instructing the congregation about the true nature of preaching and preaching on the subject of believing.   181

Mounce, R. H.
The Essential Nature of New Testament Preaching. Grand Rapids: Wm. B. Eerdmans Publishing Co., 1960. 159 pp. (P) An excellent theological treatise intelligently utilizing the Greek roots of words for preaching.   182

Mouroux, Jean
I Believe. New York: Sheed & Ward, 1959. 109 pp. (C) Full appreciation for the nature of faith is indispensable for an activity like preaching, working, as it does, in the service of faith. This study is one of the best available; an important contribution for the theology of preaching.   183

Murphy-O'Connor, Jerome, O.P.
Paul on Preaching. New York: Sheed & Ward, 1964. 314 pp. (C) A very scholarly treatise on Paul's doctrine concerning preaching, extremely valuable for understanding of the theology of preaching; including consideration of the efficacy of the Word, prophetical nature of preaching, necessity for sanctity in the preacher, and other timely topics.   184

Newman, John H.
An Essay in Aid of a Grammar of Assent. Garden City, N. Y.: Image Books, 1955. 396 pp. (C) This classic will be of interest to anyone concerned with the study of the theology of preaching; its treatment of real assent, Christocentric content, and imagery is extremely relevant today.   185

The Idea of a University. New York: Longmans, Green & Co., 1947. 413 pp. (C) In the precise and thorough Newman fashion, the lecture "University Preaching" presents the essential qualities of all preaching, while considering specifically the mode of treating sermon subjects for university hearers.   186

Niebuhr, H. Richard
The Responsible Self. New York: Harper & Row, 1963. (P) The appendix to this book contains passages of the Earl Lectures on "Metaphor and Morals" and "Responsibility and Christ." The thesis of the first lecture is that men in "isolating, defining, understanding, describing, explaining their life as agents, their moral existence, have made a manifold use of simile, metaphor and symbol." The term "responsibility" is metaphoric in itself; thus

the second lecture shows how the Christian may interpret his moral acts through the metaphor of "responsibility." The discussion of decision-making in this lecture is particularly useful to the pulpit speaker.   187

Niles, Daniel T.
The Preacher's Task and the Stone of Stumbling. New York: Harper & Bros., 1958. 125 pp. (P) Presents Christianity in its encounter with the other major religions of the world. Stresses the need for the preacher to be obedient to the historic faith of the church in Jesus Christ. Concludes with a helpful statement of the context of preaching. Emphasizes that Christian preaching is proclamation.   188

Preaching the Gospel of the Resurrection. Philadelphia: The Westminster Press, 1953. 93 pp. (P) Four inspirational lectures on preaching as the signature of hope, death, love, and life.   189

Ott, Heinrich
Theology and Preaching. Philadelphia: The Westminster Press, 1965. 156 pp. (P) An argument for the unity of theology and preaching by Barth's successor at Basel. Theology is the conscience of the sermon; the sermon is the conscience of theology. Theology is whole; preaching, "we-sided." Theology is reflective; preaching, immediate, but they are the same basic task.   190

Philibert, Michel
Christ's Preaching and Ours. Trans. by David Lewis. Richmond: John Knox Press, 1963. 55 pp. (P) The author examines the preaching of Christ and shows its implications for modern preaching. He feels that the Sunday sermon is often a substitute for the example given by Christ, in which preaching was an instrument for the instruction of the disciples who then did the real preaching.   191

Phillips, Harold Cooke
Bearing Witness to the Truth. Nashville: Abingdon-Cokesbury Press, 1949. 219 pp. (P) The Lyman Beecher Lectures. The six chapters of the book are expositions of the title: what the author means by truth, the ways of knowing truth, the sermon as a means of interpreting truth, the preacher and truth, and Jesus as the incarnate revelation of truth.   192

Ritschl, Dietrich
A Theology of Proclamation. Richmond: John Knox Press, 1960. 190 pp. (P) An admittedly one-sided approach to preaching

exegetically from a passage of scripture without attempting to relate this to contemporary life, in the faith that the Holy Spirit will reveal to each hearer its relevance for his own life. Using Barth's concept of the three forms of the Word, Ritschl asserts the primary form of the Word is the preached form and that it is Christ himself who speaks through the preacher. He states that Christ is really present when his Word is proclaimed by his messenger.   193

Rock, Augustine, O.P.
Unless They Be Sent. Dubuque, Iowa: William C. Brown Company, Publishers, 1953. 208 pp. (C) A penetrating and scholarly discussion of the theology of preaching; highly useful material for the introductory level of the course work in preaching; concentrates on the concept and nature of preaching and its precise purpose.   194

Schroeder, Frederick W.
Preaching the Word with Authority. Philadelphia: The Westminster Press, 1954. 128 pp. (P) An elementary treatment of the nature and purpose of preaching.   195

Semmelroth, Otto, S.J.
The Preaching Word: On the Theology of Proclamation. New York: Herder and Herder, 1965. 256 pp. (C) A translation of the German publication of 1962, which treats the general nature of the Word of God, the way this is communicated through the church, and the manner in which it exercises its divine power upon the Christian. Extremely scholarly and sometimes compelling, the work concentrates on determining the effectiveness of the Word in relation to the effectiveness of the sacraments; other crucial points in the theology of preaching, however, receive little attention, and the style is consistently arid.   196

Sizoo, Joseph R.
Preaching Unashamed. Nashville: Abingdon Press, 1949. 132 pp. (P) Lectures dealing with the centrality of the cross in the reconciling work of preaching the gospel. A book with strong convictions about the relevance of preaching which is true to its nature as kerygma.   197

Sleeth, Ronald E.
Proclaiming the Word. Nashville: Abingdon Press, 1964. 142 pp. (P) An attempt to relate biblical preaching to the human situation as advocated in Tillich's method of correlation.   198

Smith, Charles W. F.
Biblical Authority for Modern Preaching. Philadelphia: The Westminster Press, 1960. 176 pp. (P) An up-to-date approach to biblical preaching encouraging an ordered use of the Bible in the pulpit. A good treatment of biblical preaching which maintains the tension between content and life-situation, stressing the Christian year but also the group dynamics in which both preacher and people are involved. **199**

Smith, Roy L.
Preach the Word. Nashville: Abingdon Press, 1947. 128 pp. (P) Lectures dealing with the relevance of the Word as the word of prophets, scholars, apostles, and believers. The style is narrative-analytic, and the lectures seem designed to inspire more than to enlighten. **200**

Stewart, James S.
A Faith to Proclaim. London: Hodder & Stoughton, 1953. 160 pp. (P) The Lyman Beecher Lectures for 1952 dealing with a theology for preaching. The cardinal doctrines of faith are treated with evangelical fervor. Considered a classic by many, it is a good presentation from within the Reformed heritage. However, it may leave some readers uneasy with its failure to face the crucial problems of the modern secular mind. **201**

Stott, John R. W.
The Preacher's Portrait. Grand Rapids: Wm. B. Eerdmans Publishing Co., 1961. 124 pp. (P) New Testament concepts of the preacher—steward, herald, witness, father, servant. **202**

Thompson, Claude H.
Theology of the Kerygma: a Study in Primitive Preaching. Englewood Cliffs, N. J.: Prentice-Hall, 1962, 174 pp. (P) Lectures to acquaint preachers with the centrality of theology in apostolic preaching. Asserts that sound theology and effective preaching are inseparable. Gives brief introduction to major concepts of biblical theology for those who may not know its ability to enrich the preaching enterprise. **203**

Tillich, Paul
Systematic Theology. Vol. I. Chicago: University of Chicago Press, 1959. 32-33 pp. (P) The introduction discusses how "practical theology" becomes a bridge between the Christian message and the human situation. Points to the nontheological resources for practical theology. Pages 54-55 contain stipulations for semantic clarity in explaining the Christian faith. **204**

Systematic Theology. Vol. II. Chicago: University of Chicago Press, 1958. 108-13 pp. (P) Stresses the importance of distinguishing between the empirically historical, the legendary, and the mythological elements in using biblical stories to relay the Christian message. **205**

Systematic Theology. Vol. III. Chicago: University of Chicago Press, 1963. (P) On pages 57-72 of Part IV, "Life and the Spirit," Tillich discusses the role of language in thought, act, communication, and culture. On pages 193-96 the function of practical apologetics and evangelistic preaching in the church are distinguished. **206**

Weatherspoon, Jesse Burton

Sent Forth to Preach. ("Studies in Apostolic Preaching.") New York: Harper & Bros., 1954. 180 pp. (P) A book written to strengthen the kinship of the modern preacher to the apostles and other first-century preachers. **207**

Wedel, Theodore O.

The Pulpit Rediscovers Theology. New York: The Seabury Press, 1957. 177 pp. (P) Encouragement and help are given to utilize intelligently the recent renewal of biblical theology for preaching. **208**

Wilder, Amos N.

The Language of the Gospel: Early Christian Rhetoric. New York: Harper & Row, 1964. 136 pp. (P) A scholarly, but readable study of the various rhetorical forms (story, dialogue, etc.) in the New Testament and their implications for communicating the Christian faith. **209**

Wingren, Gustaf

The Living Word. A Theological Study of Preaching and the Church. Philadelphia: Muhlenberg Press, 1960. 215 pp. (P) Theological analysis of the function of preaching in creating and identifying the Christian church. Writing is heavy, probably due to difficulties of translation from the Swedish. Repays serious study. **210**

The Word: Readings in Theology. New York: P. J. Kenedy & Sons, 1964. 301 pp. (C) A compilation by students of the Canisianum, Innsbruck, of recent valuable contributions by European scholars (e.g., K. Rahner, D. Grasso, E. Schillebeeckx). Studies include investigation of the Old and New Testament revelation; the Word and Preaching; the efficacy of the Word. **211**

Topics of Preaching

Abbey, Merrill R.
Living Doctrine in a Vital Pulpit. Nashville: Abingdon Press, 1965. 202 pp. (P) A helpful discussion of doctrinal preaching built on Abbey's principle of "double analysis."   212

Baker, Eric W.
Preaching Theology. London: The Epworth Press, 1954. 67 pp. (P) A collection of articles previously published in England and intended to suggest "useful lines of approach which preachers might develop" in preaching on the doctrines of God, man, hope, the cross, temptation, suffering, pride, communion of the saints, etc. Solid, suggestive, stimulating. Emphasis on subject matter rather than method.   213

Baughman, Harry F.
Preaching from the Propers. Philadelphia: Muhlenberg Press, 1949. (P) Lectures by a Lutheran who advocates expository preaching as the best way to "feed the church." He illustrates from selected days in the liturgical calendar.   214

Blackwood, Andrew W.
Doctrinal Preaching for Today. Nashville: Abingdon Press, 1946. 224 pp. (P) Part I deals with making doctrine personal and gives sample outlines on doctrinal subjects. Part II is an adaptation of homiletical principles to doctrinal presentations.   215

Expository Preaching for Today: Case Studies of Bible Passages. Nashville: Abingdon Press, 1953. 224 pp. (P) Goals and methods of expository preaching. Passages and outlines. Suggestions on organization, style, and delivery.   216

Preaching from Prophetic Books. Nashville: Abingdon Press, 1951. 224 pp. (P) Deals with the pulpit use of the prophetic writings and focuses on preaching values rather than exegesis.   217

Duffield, Guy P.
Pentecostal Preaching. New York: Vantage Press, 1957. 100 pp. (P) Foursquare Church minister delivers a Bible College alumni association lectureship on preaching, emphasizing the theme of holiness.   218

Enslin, Morton Scott
Preaching from the New Testament: An Open Letter to Preachers. Privately printed by the author, 1952. (P) A plea by a noted liberal to utilize higher criticism in preaching.   219

Farmer, Herbert H.
The Bible and Preaching. Birmingham, England: Berean Press,
1952. 24 pp. (P) Joseph Smith Memorial Lectures. The importance of the Bible and of preaching from it alone.   220

Ford, Douglas W. C.
An Expository Preacher's Notebook. New York: Harper &
Bros., 1960. 220 pp. (P) Largely sample sermons, but with a
helpful preface on the content and technique of expository
preaching.   221

Johnson, Howard Albert, ed.
Preaching the Christian Year. New York: Charles Scribner's
Sons, 1957. 235 pp. (P) Lectures by theologians and preachers
presenting theological analyses of liturgical themes.   222

Kemp, Charles F.
Life Situation Preaching. St. Louis: The Bethany Press, 1956.
224 pp. (P) A rationale for preaching to life's problems, together with model sermons and biographies of their preachers.   223

Knox, John
Criticism and Faith. Nashville: Abingdon-Cokesbury Press,
1946. (P) Chapter VI, "Historical Criticism and Preaching,"
examines the relationship between the historical critic of the
Bible and the homiletical interpreter. Suggests how the preacher
may make use of biblical criticism and where the emphasis on
it should lie in the sermon.   224

Kulandran, Sabapathy
The Message and the Silence of the American Pulpit. Boston:
The Pilgrim Press, 1949. 203 pp. (P) A critique and appreciation
of the American pulpit. American Protestant preaching needs to
deal less with social issues and political reforms and emphasize
biblical interpretation and Christian theology as it is vitiating
its influence at home and abroad. Author's ideas may help those
wishing to question the efficacy of their own preaching.   225

Leavell, Roland Q.
Prophetic Preaching Then and Now. Grand Rapids: Baker
Book House, 1963. 96 pp. (P) Building on Moses and Jesus as
supreme examples of prophetic preaching, the author discusses
seven kinds of preaching which he feels should exemplify the
prophetic tradition.   226

Menzies, Robert
Preaching and Pastoral Evangelism. Edinburgh: St. Andrew's Press, 1962. 153 pp. (P) The Warrack Lectures for 1961 encouraging and informing the parish minister in evangelistic preaching.　　　　227

Miller, Donald G.
The Way to Biblical Preaching. Nashville: Abingdon Press, 1957. 160 pp. (P) A substantial discussion of the nature of expository preaching along with a consideration of such matters as structure, proportion, purpose, recreation of mood, and studying a passage and determining its content.　　　　228

Montgomery, Richard Ames
Expository Preaching. Westwood, N. J.: Fleming H. Revell Co., 1939. 90 pp. (P) Four lectures. A vigorous apologetic and methodology for expository preaching.　　　　229

Myers, Sidney
The Old Testament and Present-Day Preaching. London: The Independent Press, 1953. 63 pp. (P) Three lectures, largely for lay preachers, comprising arguments for preaching from Old Testament texts and examples of sermonic treatment.　　　　230

Patton, Carl S.
The Use of the Bible in Preaching. New York: Willett, Clark and Co., 1936. 268 pp. (P) A plea for the use of the insights derived from modern historical study of the Bible in preaching. Though there have been advances in this field since that time, many of the principles advocated are still valid. Author feels that the critical study of the Scriptures has made of the Bible a new book for preaching and has made available a wealth of new material. Examples are given of sermonic studies of biblical passages, growing out of various types of biblical criticism.　　　　231

Pickell, Charles N.
Preaching to Meet Men's Needs. New York: Exposition Press, 1958. (P) The meaning of The Acts of the Apostles as a guide for preaching today.　　　　232

Poteat, Gordon
We Preach Not Ourselves. New York: Harper & Bros., 1944. 185 pp. (P) The author discusses the loss of authority in much modern preaching and asks if the preacher can use the Bible as the background and basis for preaching today and still be faithful to the scientific method.　　　　233

Ray, Jefferson Davis
Expository Preaching. Grand Rapids: Zondervan Publishing
House, 1940. 123 pp. (P) A lightweight apologetic and method-
ology, written in folksy style. 234

Roach, Corwin C.
Preaching Values in the Bible. Louisville: Cloister Press,
1946. 299 pp. (P) The author discusses preaching on the difficulties of the Bible, preaching on the Bible as a whole, on
the books of the Bible, the ideas of the Bible, the persons,
archaeology, and geography of the Bible, on contradictions and
combinations of the Bible, preaching with the help of the
biblical languages, and miscellaneous approaches to biblical
preaching. 235

Robinson, James H.
Adventurous Preaching. Great Neck, New York: Channel
Press, 1956. 182 pp. (P) The Lyman Beecher Lectures for 1955.
A discussion of racio-religious problems as related to preaching.
The book presents much thought-provoking material. 236

Sangster, W. E.
Doctrinal Preaching: Its Neglect and Recovery. Birmingham,
England: Berean Press, 1953. 22 pp. (P) An apologetic for and
a critique of contemporary doctrinal preaching. A single
lecture. 237

Short, Roy H.
Evangelistic Preaching. Nashville: Tidings Press, 1946. 112
pp. (P) A strong plea for evangelistic preaching by a Methodist pastor and published by the General Board of Evangelism
of The Methodist Church. A conventional approach which may
be somewhat out of touch with the needs and temper of the
present day. 238

Stanfield, V. L.
Effective Evangelistic Preaching. Grand Rapids: Baker Book
House, 1965. 78 pp. (P) A Southern Baptist evangelist and
seminary professor theorizes about preaching to win converts
and presents six "model" evangelistic sermons. 239

Stevenson, Dwight E.
Preaching on Books of the New Testament. New York:
Harper & Row, 1956. 268 pp. (P) A helpful methodology for
preaching a sermon on an entire biblical book; illustrated for
each unit with introductory material and homiletical helps. 240

Preaching on Books of the Old Testament. New York: Harper & Row, 1961. 262 pp. (P) A sequel to his treatment of New Testament books.   241

Stibbs, Alan M.
Expounding God's Word. London: Inter-Varsity Fellowship, 1960. 112 pp. (P) A treatment of principles and methods of expository preaching, clearly written and helpfully illustrated with outlines and sample sermons.   242

Toombs, Lawrence E.
The Old Testament in Christian Preaching. Philadelphia: The Westminster Press, 1951. 186 pp. (P) An excellent, up-to-date, and biblical treatment of the difficult task of finding Christian truth in pre-Christian Scripture.   243

Whitesell, Faris D.
Evangelistic Preaching and the Old Testament. Chicago: Moody Press, 1947. 206 pp. (P) How to preach for conversions utilizing various units of Scripture found in the Old Testament. Ideas are amply illustrated.   244

Preaching on Bible Characters. Grand Rapids: Baker Book House, 1955. 150 pp. (P) The case for preaching on biblical personalities, together with copious examples of sermonic approaches.   245

Williamson, G. B.
Preaching Scriptural Holiness. Kansas City: Beacon Hill Press, 1953. 80 pp. (P) The preaching possibilities in the doctrine of holiness.   246

The Preacher

Boylan, M. Eugene
Spiritual Life of the Priest. Westminster, Md.: The Newman Press, 1949. 161 pp. (C) In a short, straightforward chapter ("Preaching"), Boylan emphasizes the necessity for a preacher to have a deep spiritual life. The preparation of the man is more important than the preparation of the sermon; it is through the preacher's own spirituality that God works.   247

Calkins, Raymond
The Romance of the Ministry. Boston: The Pilgrim Press, 1944. 253 pp. (P) The pastor for thirty years of the First Church in Cambridge, Mass., (Congregational) shares his mature and prophetic wisdom on the joys and disciplines of the

pastoral ministry, including preaching. Remarkable felicity
of style and perception. **248**

Clarke, James W.
Dynamic Preaching. Westwood, N. J.: Fleming H. Revell
Co., 1960. 126 pp. (P) A Scottish-American homiletician discusses the glory of preaching, the preacher and his message,
and the supreme dynamic of preaching—his devotional life. **249**

Humbert of Romans
Treatise on Preaching. Westminster, Md.: The Newman Press,
1951. 160 pp. (C) Without being a technical treatise on theory,
this work from the thirteenth century is filled with wise observations on the whole life and activity of the preacher. **250**

Jarvis, E. D.
If Any Man Minister. London: Hodder & Stoughton, 1950.
94 pp. (P) The 1950 Warrack Lectures dealing with the
preacher as evangelist, craftsman, teacher, minister, and man. **251**

Jeffrey, George J.
This Grace Wherein We Stand. New York: Charles Scribner's
Sons, 1949. 96 pp. (P) A series of lectures dealing with the
preaching resources, the travail of preparation, sermon delivery,
the minister's devotional life, and the level of his own character.
Written in a warm, personal style, easily read, with many illustrations. **252**

Jenkins, Daniel T.
The Gift of Ministry. London: Faber & Faber, 1947. 184 pp.
(P) A treatment of the work of the ministry in the modern
world; the urgent problem of the means of communication between minister and people; the manner of man the minister
must be and his particular function as a separate individual in
the world of today. The dialectic of humble service and authoritative proclamation is woven into the pattern of the whole
book. **253**

John Chrysostom, St.
On the Priesthood. New York: The Macmillan Company,
1955. 133 pp. (C) Books IV and V deal specifically with preaching, with the necessity for preachers to be virtuous and eloquent;
a classic worthy of every preacher's careful reading. **254**

Keighton, Robert Edward
The Man Who Would Preach. Nashville: Abingdon Press,
1956. 128 pp. (P) The book's purpose is to bring to the man

who preaches and the man preparing to preach a fuller comprehension of his own soul and intellect. Because the preacher is limited by what he actually is, this book is for those who have a concern for their task and its limitations as well as its ceaseless challenge. 255

Kennedy, Gerald H.
Who Speaks for God? Nashville: Abingdon Press, 1954. 139 pp. (P) Consists of four lectures to preachers which could also pertain to laymen as those who are under compulsion to take a stand for persons, for the spiritual, for freedom, for hope. Fluent, informal style. 256

Macgregor, W. M.
The Making of a Preacher. Philadelphia: The Westminster Press, 1946. 96 pp. (P) Develops an ideal of ministry by considering the characteristics of our Lord's ministry. Then discusses the making of a preacher through knowledge of God and knowledge of man and the enriching of a preacher through reading. Finally, he considers the theme and quality of preaching which should ensue. 257

MacLennan, David A.
A Preacher's Primer. New York: Oxford University Press, 1950. 113 pp. (P) Five lectures: the preacher as interpreter, prophet, therapist, a workman unashamed, and as spiritual athlete. 258

Manning, Henry
The Eternal Priesthood. Westminster, Md.: The Newman Press, 1950. 286 pp. (C) Chapters 8 and 14 contain an inspiring treatment of the necessity and responsibility of preaching, with recommendations for conscientious sermon preparation and presentation. 259

Melton, W. W.
The Making of a Preacher. Grand Rapids: Zondervan Publishing House, 1953. 150 pp. (P) The introduction for young ministers to the life and work of preaching by a Southern Baptist minister. 260

Morrison, John A.
The Preacher of Today. Anderson, Ind.: Warner Press, 1937. 136 pp. (P) General reflections by an experienced professor of homiletics. 261

Niles, Daniel T.
The Preacher's Calling to Be Servant. London: Lutterworth Press, 1959. 139 pp. (P) The Warrack Lectures for 1958. Focus is on the preacher's attitudes. Written in a strongly biblical and inspirational mood.   262

O'Donnell, Thomas
The Priest of Today. Dublin: Browne & Nolan, 1946. 459 pp. (C) Chapter XVI offers some insights on preaching.   263

Pearson, Roy M.
The Preacher: His Purpose and Practice. Philadelphia: The Westminster Press, 1962. 242 pp. (P) A broad survey of the minister's relationship as preacher to the church of today.   264

Smart, James D.
The Rebirth of Ministry: A Study of the Biblical Character of the Church's Ministry. Philadelphia: The Westminster Press, 1960. 184 pp. (P) A case for the ministry as integration of the roles of biblical preacher, teacher, pastor, theologian, and evangelist—as the only way to be true to the ministry of Jesus.   265

Stewart, James S.
Heralds of God. London: Hodder & Stoughton, 1946. 222 pp. (P) Promotes the thesis that "preaching exists . . . for the proclamation of the mighty acts of God." The 1943 Warrack Lectures on preaching from the perspective of the Reformed tradition. It deals with the preacher's world, theme, study, technique, and inner life. A recognized classic, strongly evangelical, intense, and exceedingly practical.   266

Tizard, Leslie James
Preaching, the Art of Communication. New York: Oxford University Press, 1959. 106 pp. (P) Deals with the preacher as a speaker of God's Word. Concise, can serve particularly as an evaluative review for practicing preachers.   267

The Congregation

Abbey, Merrill R.
Preaching to the Contemporary Mind. Nashville: Abingdon Press, 1963. 192 pp. (P) Preaching in relation to contemporary culture. An analysis of current attitudes and the preaching opportunities they present.   268

Benard, Edmund I.
The Appeal to the Emotions in Preaching. Westminster, Md.:
The Newman Press, 1944. 45 pp. (C) A clear and sound statement of the philosophical basis of the emotional appeal in
preaching.   269

Doniger, Simon, ed.
The Application of Psychology to Preaching. Great Neck,
N. Y.: Pastoral Psychology Press, 1952. (P) A helpful anthology.   270

Garrison, Webb B.
The Preacher and His Audience. Westwood, N. J.: Fleming
H. Revell & Co., 1954. 285 pp. (P) The reasons and methods
by which a preacher can communicate to the audience. The
audience and communication process are studied from a psychological viewpoint.   271

Hughes, Thomas H.
Psychology of Preaching and Pastoral Work. New York: The
Macmillan Company, 1941. 266 pp. (P) An English free church-
man applies psychological insights to the minister's work.   272

Jackson, Edgar N.
A Psychology for Preaching. Great Neck, N. Y.: Channel
Press, 1961. 191 pp. (P) Deals with the importance of linking the
new insights of modern psychology, the new techniques of intimate personal counseling with the old tradition of authoritative preaching. Discusses ways of making the sermon a
dialogue, rather than a monologue, while still keeping the
primacy of worship in the church in mind. A thoughtful, perceptive, well-balanced and informing book.   273

How to Preach to People's Needs. Nashville: Abingdon Press,
1956. 191 pp. (P) A practical handbook relating the understanding of recent psychological insights to the art of preaching. Each of the seventeen chapters deals with an emotional
problem, an introductory section analyzing the problem, a
résumé of sermons, and a concluding explanation of how the
sermon accomplished its purpose.   274

Luccock, Halford E.
Christianity and the Individual in a World of Crowds. Nashville: Parthenon Press, 1937. 165 pp. (P) A large portion of the
book deals with the psychology of people in today's world.
One section treats specifically and insightfully the kind of
preaching involvement with people demands.   275

McNeil, Jesse Jai
The Preacher-Prophet in Mass Society. Grand Rapids: Wm. B. Eerdmans Publishing Co., 1961. 116 pp. (P) Deals with understanding the times in which we live, the problems of communicating with mass man, and the preacher's conception of his own calling, life, and ministry. Presents an analysis of the breakdown in communication between the preacher-prophet and mass man. 276

Niles, Daniel T.
The Context in Which We Preach. Geneva: John Knox House, 1956. 15 pp. (P) A keen analysis of the contemporary culture in the world community. 277

Sellers, James E.
The Outsider and the Word of God. Nashville: Abingdon Press, 1961. 235 pp. (P) Subtitled: "A Study in Christian Communication." Heavy on the mass media, but with helpful insights on preaching. Focus is on preaching to the person who does not know the language of faith. 278

Teikmanis, Arthur L.
Preaching and Pastoral Care. Englewood Cliffs, N. J.: Prentice-Hall, 1964. 144 pp. (P) A vigorous assertion, abundantly supported, that preaching and pastoral care are "dynamically and inseparably bound together." 279

Ziegler, Edward K.
Rural Preaching. Westwood, N. J.: Fleming H. Revell Co., 1954. 153 pp. (P) An application of general preaching principles to the rural context. 280

The Setting—Liturgical

Coffin, Henry Sloane
Communion Through Preaching. New York: Charles Scribner's Sons, 1952. 124 pp. (P) Coffin's main purpose here is "to encourage sacramental sermons which enable God to have face to face communion with his people." The four chapters deal with the relationship of the Word and sacraments, preaching which is recognized as demonstration of the Spirit and of power, preaching which is part of worship as living sacrifice, and the craftsmanship of "the monstrance." The book is rich in expository material for a large number of texts and contains the mature wisdom of one of America's most notable preachers. 281

Fuller, Reginald
What Is Liturgical Preaching? London: SCM Press, 1957. 64 pp. (P) A brief defense of preaching's place in the (Anglican) liturgy—its relation to the Scripture reading and the Eucharist.   282

Keir, Thomas H.
The Word in Worship. London: Oxford University Press, 1962. 150 pp. (P) An expansion of the Warrack Lectures for 1960. The preacher's task, his difficulties and his opportunities, the relationship of Word, worship, and sacrament, and the part played by language and verbal imagery. Especially valuable to ministers of the Reformed tradition.   283

Macleod, Donald
Word and Sacrament: A Preface to Preaching and Worship. Englewood Cliffs, N. J.: Prentice-Hall, 1960. 176 pp. (P) Presents the problems which confront the contemporary preacher. Provides a historical presentation of the Reformed liturgical tradition. Points out how preaching can come into its own in the context of worship.   284

Martimort, A. M. et al.
The Liturgy and the Word of God. Collegeville: Liturgical Press, 1959. 183 pp. (C) This collection of papers from the Strasbourg Congress of 1958 brings together in scholarly fashion the theory of liturgical preaching largely responsible for the current teaching of the Catholic Church, as delineated in the Constitution on the Liturgy of Vatican II. An extremely significant contribution.   285

Priest's Guide to Parish Worship. Washington, D. C.: Privately Printed, 1964. 185 pp. (C) Printed by the Liturgical Conference to assist priests in interpreting the teaching and guidance of the Council in its Constitution on Christian Worship, this volume contains, in particular, an excellent chapter on liturgical preaching (Chapter III: "The Minister of the Word"), which explains in easy style the precise meaning, purpose, and structure of the homily; there are also some fine points made on reading the Word to the assembly.   286

Stewart, James S.
Exposition and Encounter: Preaching in the Context of Worship. Birmingham, England: Berean Press, 1957. 16 pp. (P) A single lecture delivered before the Friends' Institute in Birmingham, England, setting forth the thesis that "the purpose

of exposition is encounter, that encounter with God in Christ which is of the essence of worship."

287

The Setting—Special Occasions

Baillargeon, Anatole, O.M.I., ed.
Handbook for Special Preaching. New York: Herder and Herder, 1965. 192 pp. (C) The first of two proposed volumes on the various forms of special preaching; includes essays on the Bible Service, conferences to Sisters, Cana conferences, weekend retreats, days of recollection, married couples' retreats, exercises for a liturgical week, preaching to non-Catholics, and parish missions. Somewhat uneven in quality, it remains a good supplementary reference for anyone involved in these preaching situations.

288

Carter, G. Emmett
The Modern Challenge to Religious Education. New York: William H. Sadlier, 1961. 422 pp. (C) In Bishop Carter's study we have one of the best basic texts on catechetical preaching; a comprehensive survey of the whole field—historical analysis, essence of the Christian message, and the method of presentation.

289

Daniels, Earl
The Funeral Message. Nashville: Cokesbury Press, 1937. 108 pp. (P) The significance of preaching at funerals, consideration of different kinds of sermons for different occasions, and a decalogue for funeral sermons.

290

Drinkwater, F. H.
Telling the Good News. London: The Macmillan Company, 1960. 228 pp. (C) This is a collection of articles, already published, on matters catechetical. It is not a textbook for teachers, but random reflections by the author upon his long and rich association with the catechetical movement in England. The book is perhaps most commendable for its not disinterested observations about religious thinking in the Anglo-Catholic community over the past fifty years.

291

Dubay, Thomas M., S.M.
Sisters' Retreats. Westminster, Md.: The Newman Press, 1963. 226 pp. (C) Helpful pointers for preachers of sisters' retreats, based on solid research. Directives of lasting value on source material, problems of the retreat master as well as the needs of sisters.

292

Gordon, Gladys P.
Let's Be Catechists. Paris: National Center of Religious Education, 1962. 158 pp. (C) This is a handbook used by French catechists to train aspirants, grouping together with fair success what is necessary for training as an effective catechetical preacher.

293

Hennessy, Thomas C., S.J., ed.
The Inner Crusade. Chicago: Loyola University Press, 1965. 187 pp. (C) Helpful and informative essays on various aspects of the closed retreat in the U. S.

294

Hofinger, Johannes, S.J., ed.
Teaching All Nations. New York: Herder and Herder, 1961. 421 pp. (C) This collection contains the now-famous Eichstatt study week papers, of supreme importance for missionary and catechetical preaching; many of the insights will be of interest to all interested in preaching, especially Grasso's essay on the kerygmatic features of the communication of the Christian message to nonbelievers.

295

Hofinger, Johannes, S.J.; William J. Reedy
The ABC's of Modern Catechetics. New York: William H. Sadlier, 1962. 119 pp. (C) This booklet treats the current trend in catechetical preaching, the meaning of the Christian message, and the method of presentation. Eminently practical, it contains solid theory and discussion of the principles, plus concrete exemplification.

296

Hofinger, Johannes, S.J.; Theodore Stone, eds.
Pastoral Catechetics. New York: Herder and Herder, 1964. 287 pp. (C) In this study is found a collection of essays on the final purpose of all preaching: faith. Following the biblical concept of faith as a personal encounter between God and man in Christ, the work is divided into three parts: God meeting man (divine revelation); man meeting God in faith (the response to the call); and the actual transmission of God's message. A fine compilation of solid scholarship.

297

Iparraguirre, Ignatius, S.J.
How to Give a Retreat. Westminster, Md.: The Newman Press, 1959. 188 pp. (C) A practical handbook for all retreat masters. The author shows with valuable clarity and concrete suggestions how the spiritual exercises of St. Ignatius can be adapted to present-day situations.

298

Jungmann, Josef A., S.J.
Handing on the Faith. New York: Herder and Herder, 1959. 445 pp. (C) This volume has resulted from Jungmann's catechetical lectures at Innsbruck; a comprehensive manual exploring all phases of catechetical preaching. 299

Lance, Derek
Till Christ Be Formed: Teaching Religion as the History of Salvation. London: Darton, Longman & Todd, 1964. 144 pp. (C) Excellent study of the principles of modern catechetics, addressed to teachers, with special emphasis on the presentation of doctrine within the context of salvation history. 300

Link, Mark J., S.J., ed.
Faith and Commitment. Chicago: Loyola University Press, 1964. 309 pp. (C) This compilation of twenty-six essays from the pages of *Lumen Vitae*, considering the fact of the Christian mystery, man's response to God's message of love, and the principles of transmitting God's message to others, assembles some of the most significant studies yet done in the area of catechetical preaching. 301

McNamara, William, O.C.D.
Manual for Retreat Masters. Milwaukee: The Bruce Publishing Co., 1960. 94 pp. (C) This manual stresses the vital role of the retreat master as spiritual director, showing that competent direction is the key to effective retreat work. It contains valuable retreat material, especially for teen-agers, and should serve as a helpful guide for those engaged in the retreat apostolate. 302

MacNutt, Sylvester F., O.P.; Dalmatius Madden, O.P.
Teach Us to Love: Sisters' Conference Needs. St. Louis: B. Herder Book Co., 1963. 82 pp. (C) A handy booklet containing useful notes on the psychology of women, a choice of sermon topics, and the problems of preachers of sisters' retreats. 303

Madson, Norman A.
Preaching to Preachers. Mankato, Minnesota: Lutheran Synod Book Company, 1952. 208 pp. (P) A collection of sermons to preachers, many of which contain helpful insights on preaching. 304

Motte, Jean-Français, O.F.M.; Medard Dourmap, O.F.M.Cap.
The New Parish Mission: The Work of the Church. Chicago: Franciscan Herald Press, 1962. 109 pp. (C) An important pastoral work, describing recent developments of mission preaching

in France. Stress is placed on the underlying principles rather than on technical details.

305

Mussner, Franz

The Use of Parables in Catechetics. Notre Dame: University of Notre Dame Press, 1965. 107 pp. (C) Compact, modern source of supplementary reading for those concerned with communicating the Christian message to various audiences, offering assistance for the preacher's exegetical task.

306

Nebreda, Alphonso M., S.J.

Kerygma in Crisis? Chicago: Loyola University Press, 1965. 140 pp. (C) Extremely important study of the role of preevangelization, that primary task of preaching which seeks to dispose the hearer for the message of God, without which the seed of the Word will never take root.

307

Powell, John, S.J., ed.

The Retreat Master Faces the Nun in the Modern World. St. Mary's, Kansas: St. Mary's College, 1965. 89 pp. (C) Proceedings of an institute held in 1964, with interesting and provocative insights on preaching to sisters.

308

Sharp, John K.

Our Preaching. Philadelphia: Dolphin Press, 1936. 279 pp. (C) A study of special homiletics (preaching for specific occasions) —applying the principles of general homiletics to differing materials and situations.

309

Sheed, Frank J.

Are We Really Teaching Religion? New York: Sheed & Ward, 1953. 35 pp. (C) In this short pamphlet, which has already secured for itself a reputation in religious education circles, the author considers the various ramifications of communicating the key doctrines of Christianity, in particular: Spirit, God, man, Christ, union, and mystery.

310

Sheed, Frank J.; Maisie Ward

Catholic Evidence Training Outlines. London: Sheed & Ward, 1954. 288 pp. (C) Informative study of street preaching— principles, content, method.

311

Sloyan, Gerard S., ed.

Modern Catechetics. New York: The Macmillan Company, 1962. 379 pp. (C) A second volume (see *Shaping the Christian*

Message) of essays on the Christian message and the method of presentation in religious formation; of particular interest for catechetical preaching. **312**

Shaping the Christian Message. New York: The Macmillan Company, 1959. 327 pp. (C) An excellent collection of essays on various phases of Christian proclamation, with specific ramifications for catechetical preaching. Especially noteworthy for preachers will be the contributions of Father Coudreau (on the pedagogy of faith) and Canon Drinkwater (on the style and language requisite for communication). **313**

Van Caster, Marcel, S.J.
The Structure of Catechetics. New York: Herder and Herder, 1965. 253 pp. (C) Scholarly and comprehensive treatment of the principles of catechetical preaching; overall effect mitigated by cumbersome style, which at times reads like class notes. **314**

The Sermon

Arderne, James
Directions Concerning the Matter and Style of Sermons. London: Basil N. Blackwell, 1952. 30 pp. (P) Reprint of the brief 1671 classic by the Dean of Chester, edited by John Mackay. **315**

Blackwood, Andrew W.
Planning a Year's Pulpit Work. Nashville: Abingdon Press, 1942. 231 pp. (P) A classic treatment of the minister's task of long-range planning. He favors a loose honoring of the church year. **316**

The Preparation of Sermons. Nashville: Abingdon Press, 1948. 272 pp. (P) A more extensive discussion of sermon construction, fixing attention on preparing for the pulpit, "not on the theory of preaching or on the personality of the preacher." **317**

Browne, Benjamin P.
Let There Be Light. Westwood, N. J.: Fleming H. Revell Co., 1956. 157 pp. (P) Primarily examples of sermon illustrations, together with some principles. **318**

Bryan, Dawson
The Art of Illustrating Sermons. Nashville: Abingdon-Cokesbury Press, 1938. 272 pp. (P) A discussion of the art and

method of illustrating sermons. Not a collection of illustrations, although some are contained within the discussion.   319

Caldwell, Frank H.
Preaching Angles. Nashville: Abingdon Press, 1954. 126 pp. (P) Discussion of thirty different angles of approach to preaching aimed at enriching the variety of a minister's sermons. Angles of textual excavation, biography, approach through books, art and music, and rhetorical technique are considered with references to examples in contemporary preaching.   320

Cooke, J. B. Deaver
The Carpenter's Method of Preaching. Philadelphia: The Seabord Press, 1953. 96 pp. (P) Sermon construction compared to the methods of Jesus, the carpenter—mainly an analogy to the way one builds with wood.   321

Elliott, L. R.
The Efficiency Filing System. Nashville: Broadman Press, 1959. 67 pp. (P) Helpful insights for preserving sermonic materials.   322

Faw, Chalmer
A Guide to Biblical Preaching. Nashville: Broadman Press, 1962. 198 pp. (P) Methods of dealing with various units of Scripture: atoms, sentences, paragraphs, books, etc.   323

Foster, John
The Preacher's Use of Church History. Birmingham, England: Berean Press, 1958. 23 pp. (P) A plea for preaching about the church and for using church history as illustrative material.   324

Garrison, Webb B.
Creative Imagination in Preaching. Nashville: Abingdon Press, 1960. 175 pp. (P) New ideas for sermons and illustrations, and how to find them.   325

Gibson, George Miles
Planned Preaching. Philadelphia: The Westminster Press, 1954. 140 pp. (P) Planned preaching may be the successful element in effective preaching. Suggestions for long-range preaching plans.   326

Hastings, Robert J.
A Word Fitly Spoken. Nashville: Broadman Press, 1962. 122 pp. (P) A how-to-do-it book on illustrating sermons, amply demonstrated.   327

Jones, E. Winston
Preaching and the Dramatic Arts. New York: The Macmillan Company, 1948. 123 pp. (P) An appeal for the use of the arts of presentation to make truth effective, showing the limitations of the intellect and the role of the imagination. Demonstrates by example, both negative and positive, the "how" of effective preaching. To help the preacher avoid dullness and acquire a technique of appealing construction.   328

Jordan, G. Ray
You Can Preach. Westwood, N. J.: Fleming H. Revell Co., 1951. 256 pp. (P) A practical presentation of the essentials of effective preaching. Attempts to trace the birth, growth, and end of a sermon but is weak on delivery. Offers suggestions for selecting sermon topics and for building them into "well-constructed" sermons.   329

Littorin, Frank
How to Preach the Word with Variety. Grand Rapids: Baker Book House, 1953. 157 pp. (P) A practical book of sermon craftsmanship written with a fundamentalist orientation.   330

Luccock, Halford E.
In the Minister's Workshop. Apex ed. Nashville: Abingdon Press [1944]. 254 pp. (P) Treatment of a great variety of subjects vital to the minister: literary forms, reading, writing, the alert eye and ear, study habits, preaching as two-way traffic. Specific and concrete help in the craftsmanship of the making of sermons.   331

Macartney, Clarence E.
Preaching Without Notes. New York: Abingdon Press, 1946. 186 pp. (P) This book represents over forty years of Macartney's preaching experience and considers such subjects as illustration, preaching without notes, Bible biographical preaching, and getting ready for the pulpit.   332

McCracken, Robert
The Making of the Sermon. New York: Harper & Bros., 1956. 104 pp. (P) A brief treatment of the types of sermons, preaching as an art, long-range preparation, and the construction of the weekly sermon. A personal and practical treatment arising out of the author's presentation of the Stone Lectures at Princeton Seminary.   333

Macleod, Donald, ed.
Here Is My Method: The Art of Sermon Construction. West-wood, N. J.: Fleming H. Revell Co., 1952. 191 pp. (P) Thirteen preachers present brief statements about their method of con-structing a sermon, and one sermon of each preacher appears fol-lowing his statement of method. Henry Sloane Coffin, James Gordon Gilkey, Gerald Kennedy, John A. Redhead, Jr., and Ralph W. Sockman are among the preachers.   **334**

Macpherson, Ian
The Art of Illustrating Sermons. Nashville: Abingdon Press, 1964. 215 pp. (P) An excellent treatment of the subject by a British preacher. One of few books in the field.   **335**

Mark, Harry C.
Patterns for Preaching. Grand Rapids: Zondervan Publishing House, 1954. 178 pp. (P) A description of forty methods of organizing materials.   **336**

Matthews, G. C.
The Craftsmanship of the Preacher. London: The Faith Press, 1955. 52 pp. (P) A capsule refresher course for practicing Angli-can clergy built around six specialized types of sermons.   **337**

Matthewson, Lester
The Illustration in Sermon, Address, Conversation and Teach-ing; a self-correcting course in the illustration covering every phase and branch of their origin and use. Westwood, N. J.: Fleming H. Revell Co., 1936. 368 pp. (P)   **338**

Morgan, G. Campbell
Preaching. London: Marshall, Morgan, and Scott, 1955. 87 pp. (P) A revision of Morgan's 1925 lectures in which he describes his sermon-preparation methods.   **339**

Nichols, Sue
Words on Target. Richmond: John Knox Press, 1963. 86 pp. (P) A witty treatment of the style of preaching and writing in the church. One of few books, in any age, on style.   **340**

Perry, Lloyd M.
A Manual for Biblical Preaching. Grand Rapids: Baker Book House, 1965. 215 pp. (P) A how-to-do-it book on sermon con-struction. A highly developed system of sermon types; step-by step methods for sermon building; extensive lists of resources,

criteria, texts, and sermonic ideas. Especially valuable are the
suggestions for preaching on special occasions.   341

Prideaux, Sherburne Povah Tregekes
  The Making of Sermons. New York: Morehouse-Gorham Company, 1947. 99 pp. (P) A summary of twenty years of classroom
lectures on homiletics by an Anglican.   342

Rhoades, Ezra
  Case Work in Preaching. Westwood, N. J.: Fleming H. Revell
Co., 1942. 159 pp. (P) This is a radically different book on
homiletics, written by a professor who feels that "the usefulness
of most ministers could be multiplied if they would eliminate
apparently trivial errors, eccentricities and inhibitions." He
seeks to help them do this by a series of semifictional letters
to former students, each of which is followed by a series of
questions to be answered by the reader concerning his own
preaching.   343

Robbins, Howard Chandler
  Preaching the Gospel. New York: Harper & Bros., 1939. 151
pp. (P) The book offers a plan for a year's preaching related to
the seasons of the Christian year and to the Episcopal lectionary.
Suggestions are given which may help readers get out of the
rut of conventional preaching.   344

Roddy, Clarence S.
  *We Prepare and Preach; The Practice of Sermon Construction
and Delivery.* Chicago: Moody Press, 1959. 190 pp. (P) A
helpful anthology of sermon construction techniques and sample
sermons. Eleven evangelical preachers contribute.   345

Rossin, Donald F.; Palmer Ruschke
  Practical Study Methods for Student and Pastor. Minneapolis:
T. S. Denison & Co., 1956. 173 pp. (P) An extremely helpful
book on filing and indexing sermonic materials.   346

Sangster, W. E.
  The Craft of Sermon Construction. Philadelphia: The Westminster Press, 1951. 208 pp. (P) A very simple treatment of
sermon craftsmanship dealing in some detail with the classifica-
tion of sermons by subject matter, structural type, and psychological method. Tending to be wordy and to lack depth, the book
nevertheless contains Sangster's usual commonsense advice.   347

  The Craft of Sermon Illustration. Philadelphia: The Westminster Press, 1950. 125 pp. (P) A simple and commonsense

approach to the matter of choosing, collecting, filing, and using sermon illustrations. 348

The Craft of the Sermon. Philadelphia: The Westminster Press, 1950, 1951. 322 pp. (P) *The Craft of Sermon Construction* and *The Craft of Sermon Illustration,* bound in one volume. 349

Smithson, Robert J., ed.
My Way of Preaching. London: Pickering and Inglis, 1956. 176 pp. (P) Contributions of fourteen British preachers. Each chapter contains a monograph on sermon preparation and a representative sermon by a different minister. Such format does not allow for much depth but does give a sampling of various approaches to preaching. 350

Sollitt, Kenneth W.
Preaching from Pictures. Boston: W. A. Wilde, 1938. 150 pp. (P) "A handbook for worship leaders explaining and illustrating with twelve complete services of worship the preaching power of pictures." Part I of the book consists of pictures and worship resources; part II deals with the psychological value of preaching from pictures, the choice and use of pictures, and the psychology of effective preaching. 351

Unger, Merrill F.
Expository Preaching. Grand Rapids: Zondervan Publishing House, 1955. 252 pp. (P) A comprehensive, detailed study based on dispensational theology with considerable hermeneutical material. 352

White, Douglas
He Expounded. Chicago: Moody Press, 1952. 159 pp. (P) An apologetic, a set of principles, and techniques for expository preaching. 353

Whitesell, Faris D.
Power in Expository Preaching. Westwood, N. J.: Fleming H. Revell Co., 1963. 149 pp. (P) A comprehensive survey of expository preaching: a strong rationale and a well-developed methodology. 354

Sixty-Five Ways to Give an Evangelistic Invitation. Grand Rapids: Zondervan Publishing House, 1945. 116 pp. (P) A unique book that focuses on the conclusion of sermons to evangelize. Of use to preachers who wish to secure an overt response to their preaching. 355

Whitesell, Faris D.; Lloyd M. Perry
Variety in Your Preaching. Westwood, N. J.: Fleming H. Revell
Co., 1954. 211 pp. (P) A manual of methods to help insure
variety. Many checklists.   356

Wood, A. Skevington
Heralds of the Gospel. Grand Rapids: Zondervan Publishing
House, 1963. 126 pp. (P) A survey of the preaching task, with
emphasis on details of sermon preparation.   357

Delivery

Brack, Harold A.
Effective Oral Interpretation for Religious Leaders. Englewood
Cliffs, N. J.: Prentice-Hall, 1964. 176 pp. (P) Helpful principles
and techniques for oral Bible reading and conduct of worship. 358

Craig, William Charles; Ralph Raphael Sokolowsky
The Preacher's Voice. Columbus, Ohio: Wartburg Press, 1945.
132 pp. (P) A brief, somewhat technical book with practical
suggestions.   359

Kirkpatrick, Robert White
The Creative Delivery of Sermons. New York: The Macmillan
Company, 1944. 235 pp. (P) A practical book on sermon delivery; does not deal with sermon construction. Considers the
mechanics of delivery in some depth and concentrates on the
"creative spirit" which must use the mechanics at the moment of
preaching. Reveals wide acquaintance with speech disciplines. 360

Lamar, Nedra Newkirk
How to Speak the Written Word. Westwood, N. J.: Fleming
H. Revell Co., 1959. 175 pp. (P) Aims at unaffected naturalness
in reading. Includes exercises, explanation of diacritical mark-
ings, an answer book. Useful for all who read aloud. One section
deals with how to read the Bible.   361

Phillip, Frank
Manual of Elocution for the Ministry. New York: Charles
Scribner's Sons, 1948. 116 pp. (P)   362

Sangster, Paul E.
Speech in the Pulpit. New York: Philosophical Library, 1958.
84 pp. (P) A helpful treatment of the preacher's voice and its
use. Some attention also to bodily action.   363

Stevenson, Dwight E.; Charles F. Diehl
Reaching People from the Pulpit. New York: Harper & Row,
1958. 172 pp. (P) A very practical and helpful book on the
physiological, psychological, and methodological aspects of communicating the gospel, created by the collaboration of a professor of homiletics and a professor of speech. 364

White, Richard C.
The Vocabulary of the Church. New York: The Macmillan
Company, 1960. 178 pp. (P) A guide to pronunciation of words
used in sermons. 365

History—Individual Preachers

Attwater, Donald
St. John Chrysostom: Pastor and Preacher. London: Harvill
Press, 1959. 192 pp. 366

Baur, Chrysostomos
John Chrysostom and His Time. London: Sands & Co., 1960.
399 pp. A scholarly treatment of one of the most famous
preachers of all time and the forces which influenced his life
and ministry. 367

Beecher, Lyman
Autobiography. Ed. by Barbara M. Cross. 2 vols. Cambridge:
Harvard University Press, 1961. 418 and 487 pp. (P) First pub-
lished in 1864, this is a fascinating story of a scion of preachers. 368

Belden, Albert David
*George Whitefield—The Awakener: A Modern Study of the
Evangelical Revival.* New York: The Macmillan Company, 1953.
302 pp. (P) 369

Broadhurst, Allan R.
He Speaks the Word of God. Englewood Cliffs, N. J.: Prentice-
Hall, 1963. 91 pp. (P) A study of the themes of Norman
Vincent Peale's sermons, arising out of a doctoral dissertation
using the "content analysis" technique. 370

Clark, James M.
*Meister Eckhardt: An Introduction to the Study of His Works
with an Anthology of His Sermons.* London: Thomas Nelson &
Sons, 1957. 267 pp. 371

Crocker, Lionel
Henry Ward Beecher's Speaking Art. Westwood, N. J.: Fleming
H. Revell Co., 1937. 243 pp. (P) A perceptive analysis by a well-
known speech professor, a Baptist layman.   372

Doan, Gilbert E., Jr., ed.
The Preaching of F. W. Robertson. Philadelphia: Fortress
Press, 1964. 205 pp. (P) A biography and selected sermons.   373

Doughty, William
John Wesley, Preacher. London: The Epworth Press, 1955.
213 pp. (P) An interesting biography which throws light on
Wesley's preaching ministry. Copious quotations from his
journal, his sermons, and from listeners.   374

Handy, Francis J.
Jesus, the Preacher. Nashville: Abingdon Press, 1949. 137 pp.
(P) An appreciation of Jesus' preaching, both content and
method.   375

Holmes, John Haynes
I Speak for Myself. Boston: Beacon Press, 1959. 308 pp. (P)
The autobiography of a preacher who suggests a return to im-
passioned oratory in the pulpit.   376

Hoogstra, Jacob T., ed.
John Calvin, Contemporary Prophet. Grand Rapids: Baker
Book House, 1959. 257 pp. (P) A memorial book, compiled as a
symposium of fourteen authors who view Calvin as theologian,
ecclesiastical leader, and prophetic preacher.   377

Howard, G.
Walkin' Preacher of the Ozarks. New York: Harper & Bros.,
1944. 273 pp. (P) The experiences of a preacher in a unique
ministry.   378

Kiessling, Elmer C.
*The Early Sermons of Luther and Their Relation to Pre-
Reformation Sermons.* Grand Rapids: Zondervan Publishing
House, 1935. 155 pp. (P) A doctoral dissertation which broke
new ground in the study of Reformation preaching.   379

Lee, Umphrey
The Lord's Horseman. Nashville: Abingdon Press, 1954. 220
pp. (P) A moving biography of that great little man who felt
compelled to preach the Word of God everywhere, to all men.

Interestingly written, including little-known incidents which give new insight into John Wesley's search for God, his orderly habits, his universal interests.   380

Lewis, A. J.
Zinzendorf, the Ecumenical Preacher. Philadelphia: The West-minster Press, 1962. 208 pp. (P) A study of the Moravian contri-bution to Christian mission and unity, written in a picturesque style. Particularly interesting in the light of the modern concern for ecumenicity.   381

McGlynn, Robert H.
The Incarnation in the Sermons of St. Peter Chrysologus. Mundelein, Ill.: St. Mary on the Lake Seminary, 1956. 150 pp. (C)   382

MacGregor, Geddes
The Thundering Scot: A Portrait of John Knox. Philadelphia: The Westminster Press, 1957. 240 pp. (P) The intriguing story of the most famous Scottish preacher.   383

McLean, Archibald
Alexander Campbell as a Preacher. Grand Rapids: Baker Book House, 1955. 46 pp. (P) A reprint of the 1908 edition.   384

McLoughlin, William G., Jr.
Billy Graham: Revivalist in a Secular Age. New York: The Ronald Press Company, 1960. 269 pp.   385

Billy Sunday Was His Real Name. Chicago: University of Chicago Press, 1955. 325 pp.   386

Miller, Perry
Jonathan Edwards. New York: William Sloane, 1949. 348 pp. (P) The definitive biography of the greatest of the Puritan preachers.   387

Nixon, Leroy
John Calvin: Expository Preacher. Grand Rapids: Wm. B. Eerdmans Publishing Co., 1950. 136 pp. (P) Half given to Calvin's homiletical theory; half to reproduction of twelve sermons.   388

Parker, Thomas H. C.
The Oracles of God. London: Lutterworth Press, 1947. 175 pp. (P) An introduction to the preaching of John Calvin.   389

Reidy, Maurice F., S.J.
Bishop Lancelot Andrewes, Jacobean Court Preacher: A Study in Early Seventeenth-Century Religious Thought. Chicago: Loyola University Press, 1955. 237 pp. (C)   390

Rigell, William Richard
Prophetic Preaching. Nashville: Broadman Press, 1936. 139 pp. (P) A study of the ministry of John the Baptist for modern prophets.   391

Stearns, Raymond Phineas
The Strenuous Puritan: Hugh Peter, 1598-1660. Urbana: University of Illinois Press, 1954. 463 pp. (P) A lively account of a vigorous Puritan preacher.   392

Turnbull, Ralph G.
Jonathan Edwards, the Preacher. Grand Rapids: Baker Book House, 1958. 192 pp. (P) A careful analysis and appreciation of Edwards and especially his preaching. Movingly written and carefully documented.   393

Van der Meer, F.
Augustine, the Bishop. New York: Sheed & Ward, 1961. 679 pp. (C) Contains a fine chapter on Augustine the preacher, delineating his principles and discussing his own characteristics as a preacher.   394

Wagner, Don M.
Expository Method of G. C. Morgan. Westwood, N. J.: Fleming H. Revell Co., 1957. 128 pp. (P) An appreciation and analysis of a skilled biblical preacher.   395

Walker, Granville T.
Preaching in the Thought of Alexander Campbell. St. Louis: The Bethany Press, 1954. 272 pp. (P) A doctoral dissertation on the preaching of the founder of the Disciples of Christ.   396

Welsby, Paul A.
Lancelot Andrewes, 1555-1626. London: SPCK, 1958. 298 pp. (P)   397

History—Groups

Blackwood, Andrew W.
Preaching in Times of Reconstruction. Great Neck, N. Y.: Pulpit Press, 1945. 63 pp. (P) Thirteen biographical and critical

studies of great preachers of the past and present who excelled in preaching in a time of reconstruction.   398

Calkins, Harold L.
Master Preachers, Their Study and Devotional Habits. Washington, D. C.: Review and Herald Publishing Association, 1960. 121 pp. (P) Eleven British, five American, and four contemporary American preachers are surveyed.   399

Davies, Horton
Varieties of English Preaching, 1900-1960. London: SCM Press; and Englewood Cliffs, N. J.: Prentice-Hall, 1963. 276 pp. (P) Following an introductory chapter on trends and varieties of English preaching, 1900-1960, Davies considers distinguished representatives of eight kinds of preaching heard in this period, giving biographical background, analysis, and evaluation of the preacher's work. Fourteen preachers are included.   400

Gammie, A.
Preachers I Have Heard. London: Pickering and Inglis, 1945. 200 pp. (P) Personal impressions of the author on the preaching and persons of the outstanding preachers he listened to.   401

Goodpasture, B. C.; W. T. Moore, eds.
Biographies and Sermons of Pioneer Preachers. Nashville: Privately printed, 1954. 589 pp. (P) Reprint of Moore's *The Living Pulpit of the Christian Church* (1867).   402

Gray, Joseph M. M.
Prophets of the Soul. Nashville: Abingdon Press, 1936. 267 pp. (P) Biographical sketches of eight preachers in "the progress of liberal thought in American Protestantism."   403

Harris, Muriel (Eutychus, pseud.)
Pulpits and Preachers. London: Methuen and Co., 1935. 215 pp. (P) Brief biographical sketches of fifty-two British preachers.   404

Higgins, Paul
Preachers of Power. New York: Vantage Press, 1950. 72 pp. (P) Biographies of Beecher, Brooks, and Rauschenbusch.   405

Howes, Raymond F., ed.
Historical Studies of Rhetoric and Rhetoricians. Ithaca, N. Y.: Cornell University Press, 1961. 446 pp. Includes such essays as "Classical rhetoric and the mediaeval theory of preaching";

"Whateley and his rhetoric"; "George Whitefield, commoner evangelist"; "Samuel Taylor Coleridge in lecture-box and pulpit." **406**

Jones, Edgar DeWitt
Lords of Speech; Portraits of Fifteen American Orators. Chicago: Willett, Clark & Company, 1937. 250 pp. (P) Beecher, Brooks, and Bryan are included, among other famous speakers. **407**

The Royalty of the Pulpit. New York: Harper & Bros., 1951. 477 pp. (P) A survey and appreciation of the Lyman Beecher Lectures on preaching. Presents distinctive features of the content of the lectures and the context and pattern of their times. A reference book for the homiletician with copious biographical material. **408**

Macartney, Clarence E.
Six Kings of the American Pulpit. Philadelphia: The Westminster Press, 1945. 210 pp. (P) Biographies of Whitefield, Simpson, Beecher, Brooks, Talmage, and Bryan. **409**

McGraw, James
Great Evangelical Preachers of Yesterday. Nashville: Abingdon Press, 1961. 143 pp. (P) Twenty-four chapters of biographical material, without sermons. Range is Wycliffe to Jowett. **410**

McLoughlin, William G., Jr.
Modern Revivalism: Charles Grandison Finney to Billy Graham. New York: The Ronald Press Company, 1959. 551 pp. **411**

Petry, Ray C.
No Uncertain Sound: Sermons That Shaped the Pulpit Tradition. Philadelphia: The Westminster Press, 1948. 331 pp. (P) A collection of noteworthy and pivotal sermons in the history of preaching. **412**

Pollard, Arthur
English Sermons. London: Longmans, Green & Co., 1963. 60 pp. (P) A study of twenty preachers whose sermons were of high literary merit. From Latimer to Liddon. **413**

Roy, Ralph Lord
Apostles of Discord. Boston: Beacon Press, 1953. 437 pp. (P) "A study of organized bigotry and disruption on the fringes of Protestantism." Critical evaluations of contemporary preachers who are involved in right-wing movements. **414**

Webber, F. R.

A History of Preaching in Britain and America. Including the biographies of many princes of the pulpit and the men who influenced them. 3 vols. Milwaukee: Northwestern Publishing House, 1952. 2,063 pp. (P) Groups its biographies into the context of theological and ecclesiastical history. Gives short characterizations of preaching styles, with limited quotations in example. Strong final chapter on evangelical preaching. A fundamentalist orientation.   **415**

Weisberger, Bernard A.

They Gathered at the River. The Story of the Great Revivalists and Their Impact upon Religion in America. Boston: Little, Brown and Company, 1958. 345 pp. An excellent historical survey with special attention to Lyman Beecher, Charles G. Finney, Dwight L. Moody, and Billy Sunday.   **416**

History—Periods

Blench, J. W.

Preaching in England in the Late Fifteenth and Sixteenth Centuries. New York: Barnes & Noble, 1964. 349 pp. (P) Revision of a doctoral dissertation.   **417**

Brigance, William Norwood, ed.

A History and Criticism of American Public Address. Vols. 1 & 2. New York: Russell & Russell Publishers, [1943] 1960. 992 pp. (See Hochmuth for vol. 3.) The classic work of its kind sponsored by the Speech Association of America. Included among great American speakers are Jonathan Edwards, Theodore S. Parker, Henry Ward Beecher, and Phillips Brooks. Extensive bibliographies on periods and persons.   **418**

Brilioth, Yngve

A Brief History of Preaching. Philadelphia: Fortress Press, 1965. 216 pp. (P) A recent translation of an excellent work, limited largely to continental preaching.   **419**

Landmarks in the History of Preaching. London: SPCK, 1950. 39 pp. (P) Donellan Lectures in Dublin, 1949. Deals with the form of the sermon in the ancient, medieval (scholastic), and Reformed periods.   **420**

Dargan, Edwin Charles

A History of Preaching. Grand Rapids: Baker Book House, 1959. 1,178 pp. (P) A reprint in one volume of the two-volume classic first published in 1904. Heavy on continental preaching.   **421**

Foster, John
After the Apostles: Missionary Preaching of the First Three Centuries. London: SCM Press, 1951. 128 pp. (P) Contemporary pictures of the evangelists at work, so that the reader may "listen in" to bits of early missionary preaching. Study of the second- and third-century apologists with copious quotations from their sermons. Lectures, originally. 422

George, Charles H.; Katherine George
The Protestant Mind of the English Reformation, 1570-1640. Princeton: Princeton University Press, 1961. 452 pp. The effect of Protestant preaching and writing on the English Reformation. 423

Herr, Alan Fager
Elizabethan Sermon. Philadelphia: University of Pennsylvania Press, 1940. 169 pp. (P) A thorough survey and an extensive bibliography written as a doctoral dissertation. 424

Hochmuth, Marie et al. eds.
A History and Criticism of American Public Address. Vol. 3. New York: Russell and Russell Publishers, [1955] 1965. 530 pp. (See Brigance for vols. 1 & 2.) Among other famous speakers are included Dwight L. Moody and Harry Emerson Fosdick. Extensive bibliographies on periods and persons. 425

Hudson, Winthrop S.
The Great Tradition of the American Churches. New York: Harper & Row, 1953. 282 pp. (P) Two perceptive chapters on the role of the pulpit in church history. A sharp puncturing of some of the idealistic writing on Beecher, Brooks, *et al.* 426

Johnson, Charles A.
The Frontier Camp Meeting. Dallas: Southern Methodist University Press, 1955. 319 pp. (P) The fascinating account of the trans-Allegheny West between 1800 and 1840 when revivalistic preaching moved the country. Extensive notes and bibliography. 427

Kerr, Hugh T.
Preaching in the Early Church. Westwood, N. J.: Fleming H. Revell Co., 1942. 235 pp. (P) Relates the content and character of important early Christian teachers and preaching with the needs of the contemporary church. Keeps the responsibilities of the modern preacher in mind. Deals with various homiletical problems, such as liberties with literal meaning, problems of reading sermons, and makes a plea for biblical and theological preaching. 428

Levy, Babette May

Preaching in the First Half Century of New England History.
Hartford, Conn.: The American Society of Church History, 1945.
215 pp. A calm, detached appraisal of early American sermons
and preachers, aiming to encourage preachers today who might
look back, believing these to be the "brave days of old."   429

Mackerness, Eric David

*Heeded Voice; Studies in the Literary Status of the Anglican
Sermon, 1830-1900.* London: W. Heffer & Sons, 1959. 155 pp. (P)
A literary analysis of nineteenth-century sermons.   430

Maclure, Millar

The Pauls' Cross Sermons, 1534-1642. Toronto: University of
Toronto Press, 1958. 174 pp. (plus 82 pages of Notes and
Register.) (P) Revision of doctoral dissertation on the "outdoor sermon, addressed to all estates in a place of public assembly
[which is] a medieval institution of great historical importance."   431

Miller, Perry

The New England Mind: From Colony to Province. Cambridge: Harvard University Press, 1953. 513 pp. (P) A scholarly
and interestingly written book which contains an analysis of
Ramistic rhetoric on Puritan preaching.   432

Niebuhr, H. Richard; Daniel D. Williams, eds.

The Ministry in Historical Perspectives. New York: Harper &
Row, 1956. 318 pp. (P) Although not directly instructive in the
preacher's communicative role in the church, the nine essays in
this book are descriptive of what kinds of communication between preachers and their congregations have taken place
through the centuries.   433

Oliver, Robert T.

History of Public Speaking in America. Boston: Allyn and
Bacon, 1965. 553 pp. An excellent survey of the field. The influence of the pulpit is noted throughout and especially in
chapter 10, "The Expanding Influence of the Pulpit—1800-1920."
Extensive bibliographies of both periods and preachers.   434

Owst, Gerald R.

The Destructorium Victorum of Alexander Carpenter. London:
SPCK, 1952. 40 pp. (P) A lecture to supplement Owst's *Literature and Pulpit,* describing a new document opening new insights
to medieval popular preaching.   435

Literature and Pulpit in Medieval England. New York: Barnes & Noble, 1961. 614 pp. (P) Deals with the influence of the preaching of the medieval church on English literature, considers "The Preaching of Satire and Complaint," "Sermon and Drama," and "A Literary Echo of the Social Gospel." 436

Preaching in Medieval England. London: Russell and Russell, 1965. 381 pp. (P) An introduction to sermon manuscripts of the period c. 1350–1450. 437

Petry, Ray C.
Preaching in the Great Tradition. Philadelphia: The Westminster Press, 1950. 122 pp. (P) The book is a discussion of neglected chapters in the history of preaching and particularly a commentary upon pre-Reformation preaching. The author reminds us of the sense of responsibility of pioneer preachers and our Christian heritage. He relates preaching to Christian teaching, to the ministry to the common life, and to the ministry of worship as it was conceived by early preachers. Lectures. 438

Pipes, William H.
Say Amen, Brother! New York: William Frederick Press, 1951. 210 pp. (P) Old-time Negro preaching: a study in American frustration. 439

Smyth, Charles
The Art of Preaching. New York: The Macmillan Company, 1940. 257 pp. (P) "A practical survey of preaching in the Church of England 747-1939." Carefully documented and written in a delightful style. The lectures are addressed to parish clergy. Sharp emphasis on the language of the pulpit. 440

Sweet, William Warren
Revivalism in America. New York: Charles Scribner's Sons, 1944. 188 pp. (P) The origin, growth, and decline of evangelistic preaching. An excellent selective bibliography. 441

Thompson, Ernest Trice
Changing Emphases in American Preaching. Philadelphia: The Westminster Press, 1943. 234 pp. (P) Uses five American preaching notables to illustrate its title. They range from Bushnell "and the beginning of American Liberalism" to Rauschenbusch "and the challenge of the Social Gospel." Easy to read, clear, and concrete. Biographies are fully drawn so that the meaning of the preacher's pulpit product is understandably drawn out. 442

Teaching

Lundquist, Carl
The Teaching of Preaching in Baptist Theological Seminaries of the United States. St. Paul, Minn.: Privately published by the author at Bethel College, 1960. 363 pp. (P) A doctoral dissertation in which the Baptist seminary homiletics instructional programs are compared to those of eighteen other seminaries. 443

Stasheff, Edward; Kenneth E. Andersen
A Study of Current Developments in the Teaching of Preaching in America and the United Kingdom. Indianapolis: Indiana Area of The Methodist Church, 1963. 117 pp. (P) An empirical study of the preparation for preaching made available to theological students at Methodist seminaries and centers for continuing education. Much statistical material arising from questionnaires and interviews. 444

Wallace, Karl R., ed.
A History of Speech Education in America. New York: Appleton-Century-Crofts, 1954. 673 pp. A project of the Speech Association of America, this landmark volume of twenty-eight chapters covers American speech education from colonial times to about 1925. Much helpful material on early preachers and their training. 445

Bibliography

Cleary, James W.; Frederick W. Haberman
Rhetoric and Public Address: A Bibliography, 1947-1961. Madison: University of Wisconsin Press, 1964. 487 pp. An extremely valuable research tool. Over 8,000 entries are carefully indexed and cross-indexed. Entries include approximately 4,300 articles and monographs, 2,700 books, and 900 doctoral dissertations. Extensive inclusion of preachers and homiletical theorists. 446

ARTICLES

Abbey, Merrill R.
"Ecumenical Outlook as Pulpit Guide," *Religion in Life,*
Autumn, 1945, pp. 499-507. A successful minister and teacher
points up the significant advantages of the ecumenical spirit in
preaching. **447**

Agius, Ambrose, O.S.B.
"So That Christ Be Preached," *Clergy Review,* September,
1945, pp. 402-7. Practical instructions on preaching, using the
preaching of Christ as a model, with additional help from the
preaching of St. Paul. **448**

App, A. J.
"Do Collegians Like Your Sermons?" *Homiletic and Pastoral
Review,* April, 1962, pp. 600-605. Many pros and cons on topics
that collegians were able to recall and some which they preferred. **449**

Arisian, Khoren, Jr.
"The Sermon and the Man," *The Pulpit,* March, 1964, pp. 7-9.
The article touches lightly on each phase of sermon preparation. **450**

Babson, Roger W.
"Give 'em Both Barrels," *Church Management,* November,
1936, p. 68. The minister's responsibility to exhibit strong leadership through his preaching. **451**

Bachman, John V.
"Rhetoric in the Ministry," *Today's Speech,* September, 1959,
pp. 3-5. This article outlines the application of rhetorical theory

to the work and practice of the preacher. It provides a useful guide to the nature of the preparation of the minister.   452

Baer, Dallas C.
"Preaching in a Difficult and Fault-Finding Age," *Pulpit Digest,* June, 1938, pp. 5-11. An insightful ordination sermon.   453

Bailey, Bede, O.P.
"Parochial Sermons," *Life of the Spirit,* October, 1958, pp. 162-66. The purpose and need for parochial sermons.   454

Barrett, J. D.
"Fruitful Vine or Barren Fig Tree?" *Furrow,* October, 1952, pp. 524-26. A positive approach in preaching is more fruitful than a negative one.   455

Bartlett, Gene E.
"When Preaching Becomes Real," *Pastoral Psychology,* October, 1963, pp. 17-25. A divinity school president asserts that preaching can be real when two qualities are present. The first is the faith that God is acting in the sermon-event. The second is the "act of correspondence"; this is explained in some detail and involves the concretizing of revelation in human experience.   456

Bedoyere, Michael De La
"From the Pew," *Life of the Spirit,* October, 1958, pp. 166-71. A layman speaks out about preaching. The Sunday sermon should be an instruction on the spirit and teaching of the Mass with practical applications to everyday Christian living.   457

Blackwood, Andrew W.
"Marks of Great Evangelical Preaching," *Christianity Today,* November 12, 1956, pp. 3-6. Defining preaching as "God's way of meeting the needs of sinful men," the author finds the following marks of greatness in the preaching of past generations: preaching from the Bible doctrinally, preaching to the unsaved, to the followers of Christ, and to common people; and preaching with authority and under divine constraint.   458

"The Minister's Workshop: Five Marks of an Evangelical Preacher," *Christianity Today,* May 8, 1964, p. 43. The five marks indicated relate to the content or major thrust of the sermon.   459

Bodo, John R.
"The Sermon in the Minister's Task," *The Pulpit,* May, 1960, pp. 6-8, 14. Attempts to clarify ambiguities about preaching and the place of the sermon.   460

Bradley, J. Chapman
"Ecclesiastical Public Relations: The Preaching Function,"
Pastoral Psychology, April, 1952, pp. 40-45. A layman-editor sug-
gests that the psychological principles of salesmanship be applied
to preaching, so that preachers' product (the gospel) will "sell."
His canons of presentation are "The Primer, The Picture, The
Persuader, The Proof, The Penalty, The Pledge."   461

Bristol, Lee H., Jr.
"Check-List for Preachers," *Pulpit Digest*, November, 1952, pp.
15-16. A layman offers suggestions for present-day preaching. The
layman looks for the preacher who gives the historic faith with
simple directness, truly knows his product, believes that the
gospel really is good news, and knows the importance of well-
chosen stories.   462

Brzegowy, Chester A., C.R.
"Youth Evaluates the Preacher," *Homiletic and Pastoral Review*, February, 1945, pp. 333-39. Three elements—the preacher's
voice, the manner in which he presents the material, and the
material he presents—play an equally important part in the
sermon.   463

Buell, Harold E.
"Pulpit Communication," *Journal of Communication*, Fall,
1954, pp. 89-93; also *The Pulpit*, June, 1960, pp. 26-27. A minister makes practical suggestions for preparation and presentation
of sermons utilizing principles of communication.   464

Bullough, Sebastian, O.P.
"Dominican Congress on Preaching: 1957," *Life of the Spirit*,
December, 1957, pp. 277-84. Seventh centenary of the death of
St. Hyacinth; commemorative congress discussing historical,
theoretical, and practical aspects of Dominican preaching.   465

Burkhart, Roy A.
"The Limitations of Preaching," *Church Management*, April,
1952, pp. 9-10, 14. The need to place the sermon in its proper
perspective and role in the total program of the church.   466

Butman, Harry R.
"Sermons I Wish I Had Heard," *Minister's Quarterly*, August,
1952, pp. 3-6. People appreciate competent craftsmen as preachers
but hunger for the great and unforgettable. Sermons of other
generations as well as sermons found in literature might be read
profitably.   467

Callan, Charles J., O.P.
"Neglect of Preaching," *Homiletic and Pastoral Review,* June,
1936, pp. 923-26. Gives the situation, results of neglect, causes,
and remedies. Some of his ideas are in vogue today.   468

Campbell, Paul E.
"The Priest in the Pulpit," *Homiletic and Pastoral Review,*
July, 1946, pp. 800-804. A short article of ideas on the sermon, its
qualities, some abuses, the development of material, the source
of material, and general background on the duty of preaching. 469

Casey, Donal
"The Sunday Sermon," *Furrow,* October, 1955, pp. 610-19. Consideration of the directives for sermon content in force at that
time.   470

Cass, John
"The Preaching of Christ," *American Ecclesiastical Review,*
August, 1940, pp. 113-30. This article goes through much of
Christ's preaching and teaching, illustrating the simplicity, logic,
and concrete examples used in the Gospels.   471

Chamberlain, Stephen R.
"Preaching and the Covenant," *The Pulpit,* October, 1955, pp.
2-4. Preaching in the context of the congregation.   472

Chanter, William G.
"The Foolishness of Preaching," *Religion in Life,* Summer,
1937, pp. 406-19. An appeal to make preaching more effective by
making it "foolish" in the sense that Paul and Jesus did.   473

Clark, William K.
"The Fusion Approach to Preaching," *The Pulpit,* June, 1962,
pp. 24-26. Description of various approaches to preaching with a
suggested eclectic solution.   474

Clasby, Michael
"The Canonical and Moral Aspects of Preaching the Divine
Word," *Homiletic and Pastoral Review,* May, 1946, pp. 588-95.
The author talks about the legislation, extra-diocesan preachers,
preaching obligation of the pastoral clergy, catechetical method
of teaching, preaching program, qualifications of the preacher,
preparation, frequency, omission of Sunday sermons.   475

Copenhaver, Charles
"The Craft of Preaching," *Minister's Quarterly,* Fall, 1965,
pp. 1-5. A Reformed Church pastor discusses preaching in the

categories of construction, clarity, conviction, change of pace, and compassion.

476

Corbett, Edward P. J.
"The Sagging Pulpit," *Homiletic and Pastoral Review,* June, 1959, pp. 821-26. This article is written by a qualified Catholic layman. His recommendations on how to improve one's preaching extend to both a balanced criticism of present seminary training and also to concrete suggestions on technique. Well worth reading.

477

Coughlan, John
"Are We Failing Our People?" *The Priest,* May, 1952, pp. 358-60. Preparation to preach—reflection, meditation, prayer—presented in simple, clear prose. The overwhelming importance must be on *what* we preach.

478

De Lamotte, Roy C.
"Why Can't Our Eggheads Preach?" *The Pulpit,* June, 1957, pp. 4-5, 10. Suggestions on how to be scholarly, honest, and still be an effective preacher.

479

Eccles, Robert S.
"Should the Preacher Also Be a Teacher?" *The Pulpit,* June, 1952, pp. 2-4. Preaching as it meets the needs and relates to Christian education.

480

Edenhofer, Romuald, O.S.B.
"Homiletic Glimpses," *Homiletic and Pastoral Review,* November, 1943, pp. 129-32. There is, the author contends, need for both theory and practice, in order to preach effectively.

481

Eldon, Magdalen
"Sermons I Should Like to Hear," *Clergy Review,* March, 1962, pp. 152-58. Third in a series of comments by lay people on the Sunday sermon. In addition to practical recommendations about the length of the sermon, crying children, etc., the writer suggests needed topics: God's personal love for us, Christ living in us, the doctrine on grace, especially the continuing sacramental grace of marriage. She stresses also the need for a living language and, above all, for genuine love of God in the preacher himself.

482

Ellis, E. Earle
"The Quest for the Mind: Communicating the Gospel to a Secular World," *Christianity Today,* August 28, 1961, pp. 35-36.

This article grapples with the problem of communication and suggests that the form, or how we communicate the gospel, is as important as the content. That form demands dialogue with the world in language it understands. 483

Esler, David
"The Preaching Ministry," *The Pulpit,* September, 1958, pp. 6-8. The preaching ministry is primarily one of witness. 484

Farmer, Franklin
"Make Your Speech Effective," *Church Management,* December, 1964, pp. 36-37. A threefold methodology presented. 485

Farmer, Herbert H.
"The Preacher and Persons," *Review and Expositor,* October, 1946, pp. 403-18. As part of a series of lectures on preaching, this well-known author points out how failure to think of members of congregations as individuals militates against effective preaching. 486

Fennell, Desmond
"What I Miss in Sermons," *Doctrine and Life,* October, 1964, pp. 471-81. Candid and pertinent critique of contemporary preaching. 487

Fenton, Joseph Clifford
"Apologetics and Preaching." *American Ecclesiastical Review,* February, 1945, pp. 130-38. An attempt to decide whether (or which parts of) classic apologetics have a place in the sermon. Double role of apologetics as defense and explanation. In this last sense a necessary subject of the sermon. While not devoid of some insights, this article is of limited relevance in the present theological atmosphere of renewed liturgy and catechetics. 488

Ferré, Nels F. S.
"The Place of Preaching in the Modern World," *The Pulpit,* December, 1962, pp. 7-10. What kinds of preaching are called for in today's situation. 489

Fischer, Balthasar
"The Congregation Speaks Up," *Lumen Vitae,* October–December, 1960, pp. 635-47. This is the report of suggestions made by a panel of laymen to the Wurzburg Conference on Homiletics in 1960. Fourteen suggestions (seven on content; seven on delivery) present areas of discussion. Father Fischer comments on the suggestions, correlating them with traditional homiletic teaching and modern preaching needs. 490

Fleming, Frederick S.
"Shall We Have a Moratorium on Preaching?" *Pulpit Digest,*
September, 1936, pp. 58-61. An oft-quoted title of an article which
is really a loose-jointed criticism of popular preaching and a plea
for a reexamination of the forms of church life.   **491**

Fosdick, Harry Emerson
"What Is the Matter with Preaching?" *College of the Bible
Quarterly,* October, 1952, pp. 5-18. A minister and homiletics
professor suggests that preaching often fails because it is centered
on subjects and ideas, instead of on people and their problems, to
which the gospel is addressed. He urges that a real sermon is alive
and interesting because it deals with real issues in peoples' experience. The article is reprinted from *Harpers,* July, 1928.   **492**

Fox, Thomas, C.S.P.
"The Pulpit Keeps Its Appeal," *American Ecclesiastical Review,* September, 1941, pp. 161-75. This article laments the fact
that many sermons are losing their effect because of the lack of
interest many priests display in presenting their sermons; it encourages the priest to look deeper into "age old" dogmas and see
the many openings that present themselves for making effective
sermons.   **493**

Freshley, Dwight L.
"The Theory of Communication in Preaching," *Journal of
Communication,* June, 1959, pp. 59-67. A clear description of the
salient features of modern homiletic theory as a unique form of
oral communication.   **494**

Fridy, Wallace
"Preaching Is Important," *The Pulpit,* April, 1961, pp. 20-22.
Why preaching is important.   **495**

Frost, S. B.
"The Direction of Our Preaching," *The Preacher's Quarterly,*
March, 1955, pp. 101-6. Preaching contemporizes the Word of
God. Four factors provide this contemporary character: the occa-
sion, the preacher, the hearer, and the sermon. Hence the one-
time-ness of any sermon.   **496**

Garrison, Webb B.
"Twelve Baskets of Fragments," *Church Management,* September, 1960, pp. 24-26. Argues that vitality and power in the
pulpit depend upon the preacher's relationship to the Bible.   **497**

Gibbs, Walter C.
"On Preaching," *College of the Bible Quarterly,* July, 1946, pp. 26-33. An emeritus professor of church history discusses preaching for the Disciples of Christ under three headings: the preacher himself, his message, his method. A continuing emphasis throughout is his desire that preaching be person-centered, rather than subject-centered.   498

Giere, Verne
"Pastoral Christian Stewardship," *Church Management,* February, 1946, pp. 44-47. Preaching and sermon preparation seen as important stewardship responsibilities of the pastor.   499

Graham, Billy
"Evangelism: Message and Method," *Christianity Today,* August 3, 1959, pp. 3-5. Mr. Graham deals with preaching from several perspectives: the cross must be the center of one's message; a decision should be sought; and a teaching ministry is essential for follow-up.   500

Green, Oscar F.
"The Three Factors in Preaching," *Religion in Life,* Autumn, 1944, pp. 578-85. A minister suggests that modern preaching has failed to develop a technique. He suggests three essential elements: the gospel, the art of rhetoric, and the Holy Spirit.   501

Guilbert, Edward S.
"The Preacher's Five Words," *Minister's Quarterly,* November, 1952, pp. 22-24. The preacher must be his own critic and strive in the preparation and delivery of the sermon to remain faithful to his craft. The article is a brief and useful reminder to preachers who have been away from the seminary for a number of years.   502

Hagedorn, Ivan H.
"Wise-Cracking Parsons," *Church Management,* March, 1941, pp. 340-42. Denounces the tendency of preachers to yield to the times and become "wise-crackers" in the pulpit.   503

Haislip, Homer W.
"Must We Have Sermons?" *Church Management,* April, 1941, pp. 408-10. Conclusion: We must have *good* sermons and plenty of them.   504

Halton, Thomas
"The Changing Sermon," *Furrow,* December, 1962, pp. 687-93. A short, practical treatise on preaching, considering the con-

gregation, preacher, and the necessity of a good beginning and
delivery.   505

Harper, John C.
"The Pews Talk Back," *The Pulpit,* May, 1959, pp. 6-8, 20.
What laymen expect of a sermon.   506

Harper, Ralph W.
"Preach for Man in the Back Pew," *Church Management,*
November, 1946, p. 38. The minister's message should always be
aimed at helping, healing, or inspiring.   507

Harris, Glendon E.
"Laymen, Spare That Preacher," *Christianity Today,* June 7,
1963, pp. 6-7. The author is a layman, a former minister, and an
editor, who writes to tell other laymen that the chief reason they
are not hearing good sermons is that they will not allow their
ministers the time they need to prepare them. There is also
helpful material here for the preacher, particularly where the
author describes how he learned to preach from his courses in
journalism and homiletics.   508

Hartman, Lewis O.
"Preacher of the Gospel," *Pulpit Digest,* May, 1950, pp. 19-22.
Effective preaching must be Christ-centered in preparation,
content, and presentation. To accomplish this the clergyman
need ask himself, "To whom am I preaching?" "For what
purpose am I preaching?" "What am I preaching?" and "How
am I preaching?"   509

Hastings, Cecily
"Sermons I Should Like to Hear," *Clergy Review,* January,
1962, pp. 24-28. First article in a series in which six lay people,
three men and three women, express what they need to hear
from preachers. Topics mentioned here are the doctrine of the
Trinity, the Mass, Christian life in the modern world, Mary,
the sacraments, the need to read Scripture. Even more revealing
is the manner of preaching recommended, i.e., joyful, positive,
and truly theological rather than apologetic and juridical.   510

Henry, H. T.
"Pedagogic Homiletics," *Homiletic and Pastoral Review,* December, 1941, pp. 223-30. The author suggests resemblances between preaching and teaching.   511

"Pentecostal Preaching," *Homiletic and Pastoral Review,* May, 1940, pp. 825-33; June, 1940, pp. 929-37; July, 1940, pp. 1068-76. This article treats of the complaints and the problems both of the faithful as hearers of the gospel and of the preachers in the pulpit.   512

"The Rhetorical Preacher," *Homiletic and Pastoral Review,* January, 1936, pp. 346-53. An exploration of the true meaning of rhetoric in the light of two contrasting views.   513

Herbst, Winfred, S.D.S.
"On Preaching the Word," *Pastoral Life,* May–June, 1960, pp. 24-29. Here is a brief treatment on sermon regulations: the quality, topic, delivery, sources, composition, and purposes of the sermon.   514

Hope, Norman V.
"I Still Believe in Preaching," *Church Management,* January, 1955, pp. 7-8, 19. Argues for the importance of preaching and discusses what constitutes good preaching.   515

"What Makes Preaching Interesting," *Church Management,* May, 1957, pp. 13-14. Four characteristics of interesting sermons discussed.   516

Howe, Reuel L.
"Overcoming Barriers to Communication," *Princeton Seminary Bulletin,* May, 1963, pp. 44-52; also *Pastoral Psychology,* October, 1963, pp. 26-32. The director of the Institute for Advanced Pastoral Studies avers that communication is interrelation between persons. He identifies some of the barriers to communication and places them under the rubric "monologue" while suggesting that real communication must be dialogical.   517

"The Recovery of Dialogue in Preaching," *Pastoral Psychology,* October, 1961, pp. 10-14. The director of an institute for advanced pastoral study suggests that preaching often fails because the preacher is thinking about theology instead of about people. This causes his failure to listen for, and to ask for, their response, their opinions, etc. which could make preaching "dialogical."   518

Hudson, Peter
"Effective Evangelism: Striking at the Modern Dilemma," *Christianity Today,* November 7, 1960, pp. 3-5. The author grapples with the dilemma of preaching to a society in which reason is declining while the gospel demands individual under-

standing and response. In the light of the dilemma he suggests methods that are necessary for today's effective preaching.   **519**

Hudson, R. Lofton
"The Dynamics of a Sermon," *Review and Expositor,* April, 1948, pp. 169-77. In an effort to answer the question, "What makes a really effective sermon?" the writer points out a need for vitality—for live material, as opposed to mechanics. Effective sermons are based on the "experience level" of the congregation. An excellent appraisal of a significant approach to sermonizing.   **520**

Hudson, Thomas Franklyn
"The Preparation and Delivery of the Sermon," *Pulpit Digest,* October, 1954, pp. 15-19. Helpful suggestions are given to assist the young pastor in his sermon preparation and delivery. Sources of sermonic material, the selection of a text, and the organization of the sermon are briefly dealt with, as well as the techniques of accents, enunciation, gestures, and mannerisms.   **521**

Ice, Orva Lee
"Preaching Where the People Live," *Church Management,* July, 1954, pp. 47-48. Preach to be heard and understood by the common people.   **522**

Irwin, John C.
"Is Preaching an Art?" *Religion in Life,* Spring, 1952, pp. 241-51. A significant study in which the author concludes that the preacher is an artist who interprets the Christian understanding of life for his day.   **523**

James, A. Gordon
"The Art of Communication," *The Preacher's Quarterly,* March, 1959, pp. 71-76. Focus is upon communication within the context of an act of worship. Unity, sincerity, relationship with God are named as essentials. Timely in some ways.   **524**

James, Stanley B.
"The Catholic Pulpit Today," *Homiletic and Pastoral Review,* March, 1937, pp. 604-9. A fair presentation of the differences between sermon qualities of 1937 and past ages.   **525**

John XXIII, Pope
"To the Lenten Preachers at Rome," *Furrow,* April, 1961, pp. 228-32. A translation of an address delivered to the Lenten

preachers of 1961. It contains three points for consideration: the sources of preaching, preaching itself, and the theme proposed for preaching during Lent.   526

Johnson, L. D.
"Let Us Preach to the Limit of Our Vision," *Review and Expositor,* July, 1950, pp. 285-300. The title of the article succinctly sums up the message of this vivid urging by a pastor. He calls for a continual search for a higher vision and preaching unaltered by the personal sophistic temptations and the wishes of the "pillars" of the congregation.   527

Johnson, Robert Inman
"Speech Personality in Effective Preaching," *Review and Expositor,* October, 1938, pp. 391-408. A long-time seminary speech teacher discusses three elements of effective preaching: the message, the audience, and the man; and the relationship of speech training to each.   528

Kearns, Conleth, O.P.
"Christ as Preacher," *Furrow,* April, 1961, pp. 208-22. Using sacred Scripture, the author shows how Christ must have preached, i.e., his posture, words, form, and style.   529

Kelliher, M. G.
"Preach My Gospel to Everyone," *Pastoral Life,* May–June, 1961, pp. 19-22. The priest in the rural areas is presented with frequent opportunities for spreading the knowledge and love of Jesus Christ. There are other means available besides the pulpit.   530

King, Howard W.
"Prayer and Preaching," *Church Management,* February, 1960, pp. 22-24. Comments on the profound consequences of prayer on preaching.   531

Knapp, Charles C.
"Preaching Dynamics," *Church Management,* December, 1962, pp. 7-9. A pastor shares his convictions about the ways to more effective preaching.   532

Lacour, Lawrence L.
"If Aristotle Could Hear You Preach" (in two parts) , *Pastoral Psychology,* October, 1965, pp. 9-17; November, 1965, pp. 43-52. A masterly integration of Aristotle's *Rhetoric* to contemporary preaching theory and practice.   533

Lantz, John Edward
"Speaking in the Church," *Religion in Life*, Summer, 1945, pp. 384-88. A minister, who is also a speech instructor, makes some timely suggestions for improving religious communication.　534

Lebreton, Dagmar R.
"Sermons That Stick," *Homiletic and Pastoral Review*, July, 1949, pp. 785-90. The writer estimates that the average adult aged fifty has heard about two thousand sermons. How many of these really stick with him? She goes on to recollect sermons that have stuck with her during the past fifty years, offering her analysis of their effectiveness. An interesting article, filled with a layman's candid reflections.　535

Lelen, J. M.
"On the Duty of Preaching," *Homiletic and Pastoral Review*, April, 1946, pp. 499-501. Fair presentation of reasons from the Gospels and from the church on the duty of preaching.　536

Lenski, Gerhard E.
"Twenty Worst Preaching Faults," *The Pulpit*, October, 1958, pp. 6-8, 22. Faults of preaching; discusses delivery, construction, personality.　537

Lewis, Richard W.
"What Is a Good Sermon?" *Pulpit Digest*, December, 1941, pp. 16-18. One man's list of the seven requirements he sees for effectiveness in preaching.　538

Linn, Edmund H.
"What's Wrong with Preaching?" *Minister's Quarterly*, August, 1951, pp. 9-13. An analysis of the contemporary weaknesses in preaching together with a proposal to revive the true bases for writing and delivering a sermon. While the writer pays some attention to theological failings, his main contention is that "thorough speech training" is the vital need for the day.　539

Luchs, Fred E.
"Now We See Through a Glass Darkly," *Church Management*, April, 1960, pp. 46-49. Discusses some reasons for lack of sermon clarity.　540

McCarthy, John
"Ministry of the Word," *Furrow*, April, 1951, pp. 223-29. Competent treatment of the obligation to preach.　541

MacDonnell, K. G. T.

"Sermons I Should Like to Hear," *Clergy Review,* June, 1962, pp. 368-74. Last in a series of six comments by lay people on the Sunday sermon. The author calls for strong preaching on the love of neighbor, especially as that love includes human institutions and communities and as it respects the perfection of these institutions and communities in their own order. He appeals also for preaching on love for the men and women in these institutions, whether they be Christian or not, whether they be believers or not.   542

McGarry, J. G.

"Round the Reviews," *Furrow,* July, 1953, pp. 385-88. An announcement of a meeting of the French Congress of the Union des Oeuvres Catholiques at Montpellier whose theme will be "preaching" and the questionnaire submitted to the clergy and the laity.   543

McGlon, Charles A.

"Communicating Through the Arts," *Review and Expositor,* Summer, 1964, pp. 123-30. This article is an introduction to a series of articles on contemporary arts and communication of the gospel. The writer presents concepts applicable to communication of the Christian message from several arts. Some are covered more fully in subsequent articles.   544

McKenna, David L.

"The Jet-Propelled Pulpit," *Christianity Today,* June 4, 1965, pp. 5-9. A description of the diffident man of contemporary society and a plea for an up-to-date pulpit to speak to him understandably.   545

Macleod, Donald

"The Creative Preacher," *Princeton Seminary Bulletin,* January, 1962, pp. 26-39. Our age needs a creative church to reform the world. It is a creative ministry that leads to such a church. Ideas presented here on what makes a creative preacher.   546

"Is Modern Preaching Out of Shape?" *The Pulpit,* September, 1959, pp. 6-8. Deals with the form of the sermon and of the context of preaching.   547

"The Marks of Effective Preaching," *Princeton Seminary Bulletin,* January, 1959, pp. 33-38. Opinions on what makes preaching effective or ineffective.   548

"Preaching with Understanding," *Interpretation*, July, 1950, pp. 298-310. A call for the preacher to preach sermons that better meet the needs of modern man.   549

MacMahon, Bryan
"A Letter to Father Joe," *Furrow*, April, 1953, pp. 179-86. A layman, in letter form to a priest, gives his criticism of several aspects of the sermon involving content and technique.   550

Manning, Richard L.
"Has Evangelism Become 'Offbeat'?" *Christianity Today*, September 11, 1961, pp. 5-7. While the thrust of this article deals with evangelism within the present Presbyterian Church of America, the author suggests that there is a place for the evangelistic service. He then describes the kind of preaching which is most effective and biblical.   551

Manton, Joseph C., C.SS.R.
"Success in Preaching," *The Priest*, May, 1962, pp. 413-17. The rhetorical arts of the preacher form the center for a discussion of sermon preparation and delivery. The basic concerns are the word pictures used in the communication and the techniques of delivery which aid in reaching the audience.   552

Marsh, Thomas H.
"An Approach to Preaching Through Classical Rhetoric," *Religion in Life*, Autumn, 1950, pp. 567-77. A speech teacher in a theological school demonstrates the relationship of classical rhetorical theory to preaching.   553

Marshall, John
"Sermons I Should Like to Hear," *Clergy Review*, April, 1962, pp. 226-31. Fourth in a series of comments by lay people on the Sunday sermon. Starting from the split in modern man between daily living and the spiritual life, Dr. Marshall calls for preaching that reintegrates the things of the world with the things of God. Specifically he mentions a positive preaching on the mystical body, the Mass, Catholic education, the practical use of Scripture, etc., which will integrate doctrine, liturgy, history, and practical morals, and make Sunday's sermon relate to Monday's service in the world.   554

Maser, Frederick E.
"The Preacher—a Bridge Builder," *Religion in Life*, Winter, 1947, pp. 23-28. The author sets forth three essentials for effective preaching: mastery, simplicity, and passion.   555

Moeller, Charles
"Initiation to Prayer and Liturgy," *Lumen Vitae,* January–March, 1952, pp. 17-20. Some notes on themes and manners of preaching. 556

Moorehead, Lee C.
"How Free Is the Pulpit," *The Pulpit,* April, 1959, pp. 6-8, 21. What should and should not limit preaching. 557

Newman, Leslie
"The Future of Preaching," *The Preacher's Quarterly,* June, 1965, pp. 97-104. The writer believes preaching has a future. However, he takes certain necessary considerations into account: the revolution in communication media, a proper balance between preaching and teaching, the core of preaching as creative truth. Good solid thinking on very plausible premises. 558

Nogosek, Robert J., C.S.C.
"For a Renewal of Preaching," *Worship,* April, 1964, pp. 283-88. This excellent study insists that to be effective preaching must be practical, concrete, kerygmatic, interesting, prophetic, and liturgical. 559

Nord, Kermit; David H. W. Burr; Henry Kinzenga
"A Symposium on Preaching," *Princeton Seminary Bulletin,* May, 1958, pp. 24-32. Three preachers give personal reflections on various aspects of preaching. 560

Oates, Wayne
"Plato and Preaching," *Review and Expositor,* July, 1944, pp. 270-77. The author notes that the modern preacher can receive help from Plato in matters of explanation, argumentation, illustration, application, and style. 561

O'Riordan, Sean
"Round the Reviews," *Furrow,* July, 1951, pp. 374-80. A review of some articles dealing with sermons and sermon delivery, appearing in important continental periodicals. 562

"Round the Reviews," *Furrow,* November, 1951, pp. 660-68. A summary of the July, 1951 issue of the *Italian Clergy Review* (*Revista del Clero Italiano*), which was devoted to the general subject of preaching. 563

Ortmayer, Roger
"The Novelist Needs the Preacher—and Vice Versa," *Religion in Life,* Spring, 1944, pp. 274-84. Both the novelist and the

preacher are admonished to look for truth in the vast crop of facts available.   564

Park, John Edgar
"The Folklore of Preaching," *Religion in Life,* Autumn, 1939, pp. 606-14. A perceptive description of dangers and weaknesses commonly found in the "folklore" of preaching.   565

Parker, T. L. *et al.*
"Preaching: Its Purpose and Qualities Today," *Month,* November–December, 1942, pp. 433-49. A symposium whose purpose is to study the position of the preacher today, to examine his problems and opportunities, and to see how he may treat his material.   566

Phillips, Harold Cooke
"The Gospel and the Preacher," *Review and Expositor,* July, 1953, pp. 279-97. A popular preacher of long standing reports in this article one of his lectures on preaching. He discusses some basic processes relating the gospel, the preacher, and the hearers.   567

Pius XII, Pope
"Documents," *Furrow,* April, 1957, pp. 252-63. An address of Pius XII to those taking part in the Sixth Italian Week of Revision in Pastoral Practice in Rome, Sept. 14, 1956. The address states the proposition that the preaching of the Word of God in the community finds its scope and its ultimate direction in Christ's preaching, in that of the church.   568

"Preaching Station or Church?" *Church Management,* October, 1956, pp. 5-6. An editorial placing preaching in a proper perspective to the totality of the church's program.   569

Presley, Horton
"Preaching in Perspective," *Christianity Today,* July 5, 1963, p. 37. The "vague pomposity" that arises from many pulpits could be avoided if the preacher would carefully minister to the congregation's needs and capabilities.   570

"Pulpit and Pew: An Appraisal," *Christianity Today,* October 29, 1956, pp. 20-22. A layman looks at the pulpit and feels that preaching has tended to complicate the gospel message. Biblical preaching and teaching which meet people in their points of need are desired. The layman has a right to expect simplicity, authority, power, urgency, and a call for decision from the pulpit.   571

Rees, Paul S.
"A Homiletical Checkup," *Christianity Today*, May 7, 1965, p. 41. A reminder that sermons must be authentic, specific, and catholic.   572

"The Minister's Workshop: Form and Freedom," *Christianity Today*, January 3, 1964, p. 29. The author faces the tension between form and freedom and shows that these belong together and are not antithetical to one another.   573

"The Minister's Workshop: Power in Preaching," *Christianity Today*, March 13, 1964, p. 35. The author grapples with what is meant by power in preaching. He suggests that it is linked with content, pertinence, rapport, conviction, and overtones.   574

"The Minister's Workshop: Preaching That Confronts the Times," *Christianity Today*, April 10, 1964, p. 35. The article discusses *relevance* as a crucial issue that may be costly to the preacher in its accomplishment.   575

Reid, Clyde H.
"Preaching and the Nature of Communication," *Pastoral Psychology*, October 1963, pp. 40-49. A professor of practical theology asserts that much preaching fails because it is monologue. Building on modern communications theory, he suggests ways of making preaching "dialogical" and reports an experimental study in which his approach is statistically validated.   576

Ridpath, Ben Morris
"How to Conduct a Preaching Mission," *Church Management*, April, 1946, pp. 17-18. The preaching mission as the successor to the revival meeting. A methodology on how to conduct such a mission.   577

Roche, Stephen J.
"A Plea for Better Preaching," *The Priest*, July, 1953, pp. 523-28. Comparing the parish priest and his Scottish Presbyterian counterpart, Roche stresses some of the causes behind the better preaching of the Presbyterian.   578

Samarin, William J.
"A Layman Speaks to the Pulpit," *Christianity Today*, June 5, 1964, pp. 5-6. The author states that there is a "famine of the Word" because communication is poor which can only

be improved as both the Bible and the people truly speak to and through the preacher. **579**

Schnepp, Alfred, S.M.
"A Plea for Intellectual Preaching," *Homiletic and Pastoral Review,* November, 1937, pp. 141-49. This article stresses the need for intellectual preaching that appeals to the mind rather than the sermon that moves its hearers merely emotionally and suggests ways of making an intellectual sermon effective. **580**

"Wanted: Spiritual Sermons," *Homiletic and Pastoral Review,* January, 1940, pp. 375-80. **581**

Schoonover, Vic R.
"Interview with an Empty Pew," *Pastoral Psychology,* April, 1963, pp. 21-28. A minister describes, humorously, some of the problems of communicating with his people. The pew speaks about preachers, preaching, and listening. **582**

Seidenspinner, Clarence
"Contemporary Literature and Preaching," *Religion in Life,* Summer, 1942, pp. 444-51. A prominent minister analyzes the essential values of contemporary literature and preaching. A perceptive and scholarly study. **583**

Shafer, Floyd Doud
"Prophets: Speak for Man," *Christianity Today,* July 5, 1963, pp. 11-12. Here is a plea for preaching on behalf of man and to man, showing that the only way to true human fulfillment is in a life that glorifies God. **584**

Sheed, Rosemary
"Sermons I Should Like to Hear," *Clergy Review,* February, 1962, pp. 90-96. Second in a series of comments by lay people on the Sunday sermon. The writer suggests preaching the difference between essentials and inessentials in the church, the church as mystical body, morality and justice in human society, the good faith and good works of those outside the church, the Mass as a community prayer, and the dignity and theological aspect of sex. Overall motif: vital necessity of Sunday preaching in the communication of divine truth. **585**

Sheerin, John B., C.S.P.
"The American Mentality," *Homiletic and Pastoral Review,* April, 1948, pp. 481-86. Sympathetic awareness of the attitudes of others is necessary to convince and persuade. With this in mind,

the author speaks about applying this especially to the secular-istic mentality prevalent today. **586**

"In Your Neighbor's Shoes," *Homiletic and Pastoral Review,* February, 1948, pp. 321-26. A novel way of portraying sermon deficiencies. **587**

"The Plight of Preaching," *Homiletic and Pastoral Review,* September, 1946, pp. 913-17. This article contains thoughts on the sermon, its depreciation among priests, its place as an in-tegral part of the Mass, its theory and practice, reasons for its decay, and means of developing better preachers. **588**

"This Above All," *Homiletic and Pastoral Review,* September, 1944, pp. 881-85. There is a need for definiteness of object—to give a definite spiritual good to hearers—and definite audience, topic, and personality of the preacher. **589**

Sheridan, John D.
"Laymen and Preaching," *Furrow,* April, 1951, pp. 205-12. Candid and helpful comments from a professional author, espe-cially relevant for style and delivery techniques. **590**

Siekmann, T. C.
"Pastoral Reflections: Preaching Christ," *Pastoral Life,* July–August, 1954, pp. 39-40. In a short selection, the author points out that a safe way to inspire persons to practice virtue is to hold up for imitation the person of Christ. **591**

Sinclair, Paula
"From Pew to Pulpit," *Orate Fratres,* May, 1941, pp. 295-97. The main point of this article is to indicate that lay people do not want philosophical sermons; they are looking for things that will help them in their ordinary lives. **592**

Sizoo, Joseph R.
"The Recovery of Preaching," *Religion in Life,* Spring, 1939, pp. 259-65. A well-known preacher gives his analysis of the ele-ments necessary for the revival of great preaching: compas-sionate understanding of the world, the gospel message, personal experience, and technique of preaching. **593**

Skoglund, John E.
"The Minister as Preacher," *The Pulpit,* January, 1961, pp. 24-29. Thoughts on developing a philosophy of preaching. **594**

Smith, Burkett L.
"The Power of Preaching," *Christianity Today*, April 9, 1965,
p. 15. A pastor's reflection on easily found substitutes for
preaching the gospel.   **595**

Smith, Fred
"Homil-ethics," *Church Management*, June, 1953, pp. 55-56.
Ethics in the pulpit.   **596**

Smith, Horace G.
"Why Doesn't Someone Talk Back to That Man?" *Church
Management*, May, 1960, pp. 28, 30. Several types of responses
which a congregation gives to preaching.   **597**

Smith, Stanford
"What the Layman Expects from His Minister," *Religion
in Life*, Summer, 1955, pp. 361-72. A prominent Methodist
layman gives a perceptive analysis of the congregant's expectations.   **598**

Sockman, Ralph W.
"The Future of Parish Preaching," *Pulpit Digest*, May, 1964,
pp. 13-18. The lessening influence of the pulpit may be
due to the loss of the Sunday sermon from a central place in
the thinking of church members, the increasing conviction that
sermons do not change many lives, and the fact that pressure
groups are attacking the freedom of the ministry. To correct
this crucial situation there must be changes in the concept of
the preaching office, more emphasis on teaching, and more
laity involvement.   **599**

**Sockman, Ralph W.; Ilion T. Jones; Reuel L. Howe; James D.
Smart**
"What Is the Minister's Real Task?" *Religion in Life*,
Summer, 1955, pp. 323-60. Preaching is at the center of the
minister's task. Each of these prominent clergymen defines that
task from his personal experience.   **600**

Soper, Donald O.
"The Future of Preaching," *The Preacher's Quarterly*, March,
1965, pp. 12-18. One of London's most indomitable Christians
and colorful preachers sets down his convictions about preaching in this age of doubt and speculation. He believes in preaching and its efficacy. Moreover, he is convinced of its necessity
in this age. A good article for any preacher suffering from sagging morale.   **601**

Spahr, William

"What I Like to Hear in the Pulpit," *Pulpit Digest,* February, 1937, pp. 44-45. A layman's challenge to clergy to preach courageously.

602

Stanikowski, E., O.F.M.

"The Homiletic Meeting of Wurzburg," *Lumen Vitae,* July–September, 1958, pp. 551-54. A summary of the topics and conclusions of the Second Congress of the Homiletic Union of Germany, in April, 1958. The major items of discussion: the nature of preaching, the relation of preaching and systematic theology, the theology of preaching. There is little more than a summary given.

603

Stevenson, Dwight E.

"The Way to the Pulpit Leads Across a Study Desk," *College of the Bible Quarterly,* October, 1947, pp. 9-18. A professor of homiletics insists that preaching requires diligent, disciplined study. Through study, the preacher is prepared over the long haul, and the sermon is prepared as a short-term goal. But the success of both rests on careful planning of time to study and good use of that time. Specific helps are offered for the latter.

604

Still, William

"The Holy Spirit in Preaching," *Christianity Today,* September 23, 1957, pp. 8-10. The author suggests several conditions which must be met if the Holy Spirit is to make Christ manifest in preaching. The preacher must believe that the Bible, in all its parts, is the Word of God; he must be completely dedicated as a servant of Jesus Christ, and the sermon itself must be the Word of God.

605

Strawson, William

"Preaching in an Age of Unbelief," *The Preacher's Quarterly,* December, 1961, pp. 330-37. Contemporary preaching cannot hide from an age of unbelief; it must face the difficulties and problems with courage. Only thereby will the pulpit gain respect. Much substance well expressed.

606

Sullivan, Frank J.

"A Listener's Lament," *Pastoral Life,* September–October, 1954, pp. 30-31. A layman airs a pet peeve regarding sermons and preaching: being talked-down-to.

607

Tavard, George H., A.A.
"The Liturgy of the Word," *Worship,* November–December, 1964, pp. 620-25. An insightful examination of some recent Protestant publications about preaching.   **608**

Taylor, Vernon L.
"The Classical Approach to Homiletics," *The Pulpit,* September, 1961, pp. 24-26. Theory of preaching, its origin in classic rhetoric, and what it means.   **609**

Terrien, Samuel L.
"The Old Testament and the Christian Preacher Today," *Religion in Life,* Spring, 1946, pp. 262-71. An excellent analysis of Christian attitudes about the Old Testament and its significance for the preacher.   **610**

Tillich, Paul
"Communicating the Gospel," *Pastoral Psychology,* June, 1956, pp. 10-16. A theology professor argues that the gospel presentation, properly made, demands decision for or against. He feels the presentation is too seldom properly made, and therefore the real opportunity is not extended. He suggests that proper communication involves understanding man where he is and participating in his situation on behalf of the gospel.   **611**

Todd, H. M.
"Sermons I Should Like to Hear," *Clergy Review,* May, 1962, pp. 288-95. Fifth in a series of comments by lay people on the Sunday sermon. The writer calls particularly for sermons on the dignity of the married state, on the need for Christian unity, on the mystery of the Passion and Resurrection, and on the layman's concern in the choice of bishops. The emphasis suggested is strongly theological, liturgical, and scriptural.   **612**

Tralle, Henry E.
"Pedagogy and Preaching," *Review and Expositor,* January, 1935, pp. 63-72. The author shows how pedagogical processes may assist the preacher in his task of transformation of life. Several functions of the learning process are discussed and related to the preaching task. The author displays a keen insight into preaching as being meaningful as it functions in life.   **613**

Tralle, Millicent
"If I Were a Preacher," *Church Management,* October, 1960, pp. 52-53. A laywoman offers some practical advice to preachers.   **614**

"What Makes Soul-Gripping Sermons," *Church Management,* January, 1960, pp. 40-41. We need more soul-gripping sermons in today's churches. The best sermons satisfy the mind, warm the heart, and feed the soul. These sermons are helped by good public speaking techniques. The minister's textbook for a soul-gripping sermon is the Bible.   **615**

Valentine, Ferdinand, O.P.
"The Pulpit Presentation of the Faith," *Life of the Spirit,* October, 1958, pp. 151-62. The priest is a teacher; the pulpit is an instrument for stimulating the mental activity of the faithful in the parochial apostolate.   **616**

"The Views of the Congregation," *Furrow,* April, 1961, pp. 223-24. Ten laymen make requests to preachers to improve the form and content of their sermons.   **617**

Walker, Alan
"Preaching for a Verdict," *The Pulpit,* September, 1956, pp. 4-7. Preaching should relate people to Christ.   **618**

Watermulder, David B.
"Learning from the World," *The Pulpit,* January, 1960, pp. 4-6, 22. Principles of communication used by news magazines can help the preacher communicate more effectively.   **619**

Weisiger III, Cary N.
"Preaching on the Edge of Desperation," *Christianity Today,* December 10, 1956, pp. 13-14, 34. The author suggests a realistic approach to effective preaching in the face of multiplicity of responsibilities in the parish.   **620**

White, Richard C.
"For God's Sake, Say Something," *The Pulpit,* April, 1964, pp. 8-11; also *College of the Bible Quarterly,* July, 1962, pp. 11-23. A homiletics professor suggests that many sermons say nothing because they "generalize" in language and are hackneyed in theme, development, illustration, and imagery. He indicates some negative results of such generalizing and offers some constructive solutions.   **621**

Winder, J. M.
"Personal Activity of the Preacher," *Homiletic and Pastoral Review,* July, 1939, pp. 1061-63. The author speaks of the complete and adequate communication of the Word as the preacher's

personal responsibility. Preaching has a quasi-sacramental character, and its preparation demands the conveyance of exact symbols to express ideas and the ability to make a psychologically successful appeal.   622

Wright, Robert Roy
"Kerygma, Class, and Communication," *The Pulpit,* July–August, 1965, pp. 8-11. The sociological barriers the preacher must cross to communicate the gospel.   623

Preaching and Theology

Alsobrook, Aubrey
"Toward a Theology of Proclamation," *Christianity Today,* May 22, 1964, pp. 14-15. Here is an emphasis on biblical preaching with frequent reference to contemporary writings in support of the thesis.   624

"Ambassadors, Not Diplomats," *Christianity Today,* January 19, 1962, p. 3. The article states that the pulpit must proclaim a message from God, not reflect the problems of the society.   625

Arnold, Franz
"The Act of Faith, a Personal Commitment," *Lumen Vitae,* April–September, 1950, pp. 251-55. A brief history of the meaning of faith in a Christian context with a plea that preaching restore true faith to the Christians of today.   626

Atkins, Gaius Glenn
"Thus Saith the Lord," *Religion in Life,* Summer, 1950, pp. 345-55. A thoughtful study of the need for authoritative "prophetic" preaching.   627

Beauchesne, Richard, O.M.I.
"Preaching, Mystery and Ministry," *Worship,* August–September, 1965, pp. 412-17. The author insists that preaching, working as it does in the service of faith, must have a similar threefold quality: personal in content, historical in approach, testatory in character.   628

Beenken, Gilbert M.
"Is Preaching Important?" *Christianity Today,* February 12, 1965, pp. 47-50. This is a sermon delivered to the author's congregation in which half deals with unimportant preaching and the other half with important preaching that must be biblically based.   629

Bell, L. Nelson
"A Layman and His Faith," *Christianity Today*, February 17, 1958, p. 19. A layman pleads for a simple presentation of the basic truths of the Bible, centered around the person of Christ and applied practically to life's problems.   630

"The 'Prophetic Ministry' of the Church," *Christianity Today*, September 12, 1960, p. 19. Here is a layman's plea for a prophetic ministry that aims at changed men through the work of Christ which ultimately transforms society.   631

Boylan, Patrick A.
"Scripture and Preaching," *Furrow*, April, 1961, pp. 199-207. It is the priest's task to study the Word of God, gathering from it the outlines of God's redemptive plan and the stages of its accomplishment so that he may be able to convey this message to his people.   632

Braaten, Carl E.
"The Interdependence of Theology and Preaching," *Dialog*, Winter, 1964, pp. 12-20. A comparison and contrast of Ott and Ebeling, contemporary European theologians with much to say about the theology of preaching. They agree that "theology without preaching is empty and preaching without theology is blind."   633

Bunting, John J., Jr.
"Demythologizing in the Pulpit," *Religion in Life*, Summer, 1962, pp. 387-93. The author argues his case for demythologizing in the pulpit.   634

Carr, Aidan, O.F.M.Conv.
"Preaching Is Teaching," *Pastoral Life*, January–February, 1954, pp. 24-27.   635

Cass, John
"The Bible: The Handbook of Preaching," *American Ecclesiastical Review*, January, 1941, pp. 47-51. This article presents some very good and informative reasons for using the Scriptures in preparing sermons.   636

Coates, Kenneth A.
"Are We Preaching the Gospel?" *Minister's Quarterly*, Autumn, 1959, pp. 36-37. Preaching, too long concerned with ethics, needs to return to its Reformation roots and proclaim God's forgiving love in Christ as the basis for Christian ethics. A

timely return to a reexamination of the traditional Protestant understanding of preaching.

637

"Conclusions of the Montpellier Congress," *Furrow,* April, 1961, pp. 225-27. A summary of nine conclusions pertaining to the essence and nature of preaching.

638

Copeland, E. Luther
"The Propagation of the Faith," *Review and Expositor,* July, 1958, pp. 300-10. The author presents an interesting interrelationship of *kerygma, diakonia,* and *koinonia* as integral obligatory parts of effective propagation of the gospel.

639

"Crisis in the Pulpit," *Christianity Today,* June 4, 1965, pp. 24-25. A sharp editorial retort to those who assert that preaching is dead. A plague is called down upon the houses of both the action-oriented liberal and the other worldly orthodox.

640

Curley, Francis X., S.J.
"The Secret of the Sermon," *American Ecclesiastical Review,* June, 1957, pp. 382-93. The secret of the sermon lies in the Scriptures. According to the unanimous opinion of the ancient and medieval authors, a sermon should be brief, humble, and suited to the congregation.

641

Davis, Charles
"The Theology of Preaching," *Clergy Review,* September, 1960, pp. 524-45. One of the great contemporary articles on preaching. Davis confronts and attempts to illuminate the foremost theological issues with respect to preaching: its place in the church; comparison with the sacraments; its foundation in orders and jurisdiction; its intrinsic efficacy; the type of grace mediated, etc. Valuable also for the excellent bibliography that follows the article.

642

Delepierre, J., S.J.
"Theology and Preaching," *Furrow,* March, 1954, pp. 140-51. The author distinguishes between the theology of preaching and the preaching of theology.

643

Doerffler, Alfred
"The Protestant Minister as a Gospel Preacher," *Church Management,* June, 1960, pp. 35, 37. The minister is exhorted to preach the gospel continually in all its fullness as a message of great joy.

644

Dulles, Avery, S.J.
"The Protestant Preacher and the Prophetic Mission," *Theological Studies,* December, 1960, pp. 544-80. In this extremely important and timely article, the author discusses the efficacy of Protestant preaching in the light of the traditional argument (with its restrictive interpretation); Dulles' answer, strongly ecumenical in tone, suggests that Protestant preachers can effectually serve as God's instruments for grace, being made fruitful by means of charisms of prophecy and teaching. 645

Eldersveld, Peter H.
"What Is Preaching? The Pulpit and Our World," *Christianity Today,* June 7, 1963, pp. 3-5. After reviewing several dim views of preaching expressed by modern preachers and theologians, the author suggests that the sermon must be an exposition of the Word of God. 646

"The Word for This World," *Christianity Today,* January 21, 1957, pp. 13-15, 25. Concerned with the content of preaching, the author submits that there must be a return to the true gospel of the sovereignty of God if preaching is to be penetrating. 647

Fuller, Carlos Greenleaf
"How to Preach with Power," *Christianity Today,* January 5, 1959, pp. 3-4. Dissatisfied with the lack of spiritual power in the American pulpit, a retired pastor suggests that the reason lies in the content of preaching. 648

Furnish, Victor Paul
"Prophets, Apostles, and Preachers," *Interpretation,* January, 1963, pp. 48-60. A study of the biblical concept of preaching under the headings of "What is the word to be preached?" "By what authority is this word preached?" and "To what end is the word preached?" 649

Graf, Ernest, O.S.B.
"The Bible and the Preacher," *Homiletic and Pastoral Review,* April, 1946, pp. 517-22. The author lays down the biblical background for preaching. 650

Grounds, Vernon
"The Theologian and the Preacher," *Christianity Today,* June 9, 1958, pp. 15-18. Even with his many responsibilities, it is the minister's primary responsibility to answer the agonizing questions of his people in the light of the biblical message. It is his divinely assigned task to be a theologian. 651

Haddaway, Klein K.
"Theology Basic to Preaching," *The Pulpit,* July, 1954, pp. 2-4.
Importance and relationship of theology to preaching.   652

Hall, Clyde C.
"But Where Is the Substance?" *Christianity Today,* November
6, 1964, pp. 6-7. Here is an incisive indictment of preacher and
people who do not get involved in the real task of the church
after the sermon has been delivered.   653

Harrisville, Roy A.
"The Word Is Near You," *Dialog,* Winter, 1964, pp. 36-41.
The author explains the reason for the irrelevance of today's
pulpit and offers an approach to hermeneutics which may provide the solution.   654

Heinecken, Martin
"The Primacy of the Word," *Dialog,* Winter, 1964, pp. 21-26.
The author asserts that it is in actual proclamation that the
church lives. He tries to make clear in what sense and why the
"Word" should be regarded as the "sole" means of grace.   655

Henry, H. T.
"Misapplied Scripture," *Homiletic and Pastoral Review,* January, 1941, pp. 353-61. The author comments on the preacher's
use of Scripture for his own assertion when the inspired writer
had a different point in mind.   656

"The Scriptural Preacher," *Homiletic and Pastoral Review,*
January, 1942, pp. 327-34. Some hints on the exact and correct
use of Scripture.   657

"Search the Scriptures," *Homiletic and Pastoral Review,* January, 1940, pp. 353-60. Outdated ideas on sacred Scripture.   658

Hitz, Paul, C.SS.R.
"Theology and the Ministry of the Word," *Theology Digest,*
Winter, 1958, pp. 3-7. Improvement in preaching will follow
only when a suitable basis is given it in proper theological understanding of the Word.   659

Hofinger, Johannes, S.J.
"Our Message," *Lumen Vitae,* April–September, 1950, pp. 264-
80. An outline of a complete kerygmatic approach to teaching
and preaching.   660

Holmer, Paul L.
"The Logic of Preaching," *Dialog*, Summer, 1965, pp. 205-13.
An argument against false definitions of preaching, followed by
the assertions that (1) to preach is one way to be a Christian, (2)
a sermon must be theological, and (3) the sermon is constrained
by what it must do for the hearer. The relationship of preaching
and theology pervades the article.   661

"Preachers and Theology," *The Pulpit*, June, 1962, pp. 7-9.
Relationship between preaching and theology.   662

Hoover, J. Edgar
"Communist Propaganda and the Christian Pulpit," *Christianity Today*, October 24, 1960, pp. 5-7. The author suggests that the
Christian pulpit is the center of one of the heaviest of the communist attacks. The attack is threefold: to undermine, hood-
wink, and exploit the pulpit for its own ends. In describing a
solution to the problem, Mr. Hoover states that the Christian
pulpit is one of America's most formidable barriers against
communism.   663

"How We Communicate the Christian Message," *The New
Christian Advocate*, May, 1959, p. 12. "Real communication has
to do with participating or, better, making others participate, in
the reality and meaning of the given—the Christian message."   664

Ice, Harry L.
"Why Preach?" *College of the Bible Quarterly*, October, 1945,
pp. 4-10. A college director of ministerial training offers some
random suggestions concerning the reasons for preaching in the
current situation. Somewhat disconnected and rudimentary.   665

"The Joy of Preaching the Gospel of Jesus Christ," *Christianity
Today*, October 24, 1960, pp. 22-23. The reason for the joy of
preaching the gospel is observed in the changed lives it produces. 666

Jungmann, Josef A., S.J.
"Christ's Place in Catechesis and Preaching," *Lumen Vitae*,
October–December, 1952, pp. 533-42. A general article on the
importance of centering Christian teaching and preaching on the
good news of Christ.   667

Kik, J. Marcellus
"Strengthening the Pulpit," *Christianity Today*, August 3,
1959, pp. 13-15. The strength of the pulpit lies in greater depth

theologically and biblically in the content of the sermons
preached. A more effective evangelism will also result.   **668**

Killinger, John
"Existential Preaching," *Princeton Seminary Bulletin*, April,
1962, pp. 44-52. Implications of existentialism for preaching.
Fairly good summary.   **669**

Knutson, Kent S.
"New Wine for Fresh Skins," *Dialog*, Winter, 1964, pp. 42-47.
"We need to examine the skins of the age in which God has
placed us to make sure that the wine is not lost. The gospel is
always new wine, but we may be preaching it to fit only old
skins. New wine needs fresh skins."   **670**

Kugelman, R., C.P.
"Preaching and the Word of God," *Bible Today*, October,
1964, pp. 845-51. Source and subject of preaching must be God's
written Word, understood, interpreted, and applied by the
church.   **671**

Lantz, John Edward
"The Power of Preaching," *The Pulpit*, October, 1957, pp. 24-
27. Our concept of preaching is an important factor in shaping
our efforts. Preaching is a means of releasing God's power.   **672**

Lantz, William Carson
"Rhetoric and Theology: Incompatible?" *Western Speech
Journal*, March, 1955, pp. 77-82. This paper investigates the
techniques and assumptions of each of these disciplines and tries
to determine whether the theologian can honestly utilize the
techniques of the rhetorician. It is a very stimulating study.   **673**

Lawrence, Emeric A., O.S.B.
"Faith in the Word of God," *Worship*, February, 1963, pp. 177-
84. Outstanding study of the crucial necessity for preachers to
have the correct outlook and attitude towards the Word they
proclaim.   **674**

Leitch, Addison H.
"The Primary Task of the Church," *Christianity Today*,
October 15, 1956, pp. 11-13, 18. The primary task of the church
is to bring men into relationship with Jesus Christ by ministering the Word and the Spirit through preaching and sacraments. **675**

Liege, André, O.P.
"The Ministry of the Word: from Kerygma to Catechesis,"
Lumen Vitae, March, 1962, pp. 21-36. The principle that the
ministry of transmitting the Word "must reproduce . . . the very
forms in which God revealed Himself," forms the presupposition
for this examination of the purposes of preaching and catechizing.
The relation between the gospel Word and Christian teaching is
introduced with an examination of the mystery of God's Word
and the prophetical office of the church. The relation of evangelization and catechesis is considered in the closing pages.   676

McCollough, Thomas E.
"Preaching's Rediscovery of Theology," *Review and Expositor,*
January, 1959, pp. 43-55. The author points out that recent
developments in biblical studies, theology, and Christian ethics
have strong relevance to preaching.   677

McCool, Francis J., S.J.
"The Preacher and the Historical Witness of the Gospels,"
Theological Studies, December, 1960, pp. 517-43. This article
attempts to dispel fears of preachers educated before modern
biblical exegetes began to challenge the historicity of the gospels
and thus worried about what they can safely preach to their
people. McCool presents a brief study of the beginnings, principles, dangers, and results of this new critical method, with exemplification from actual texts. This is an important article;
indispensable for preachers interested in authentic biblical
preaching.   678

McKenzie, J. L., S.J.
"The Word of God in the Old Testament," *Theological
Studies,* June, 1960, pp. 183-206. Scholarly treatment of the Israel-
ite idea of Word—a distinct reality charged with power. Important study for the theology of preaching.   679

MacLennan, David A.
"Preaching," *Pulpit Digest,* May, 1952, pp. 17-23. Preaching
has priority over all other functions of the ministry for the following reasons: (1) the New Testament clearly places the
proclamation of the Word as top priority; (2) under God the
church has been built more by the preaching of the gospel than
by any other means; (3) it remains the chief means of communicating the good news; (4) it creates opportunities for both pastoral counseling and the administration of the church; and (5)
it is given primacy by most laymen.   680

Martin, W. B. J.
"Preaching: Poetry in the Pulpit," *Christian Advocate*, August 3, 1961, pp. 12-13. A homiletics professor builds a case for the sermon as "poetry" rather than "argument."   **681**

Massa, Conrad Henry
"Wanted: A Theology of Preaching," *The Pulpit*, February, 1961, pp. 8-10. Need for an adequate theological understanding of the nature and purpose of preaching.   **682**

"Men No Longer Lend Their Ears," *Christianity Today*, June 7, 1963, p. 24. This editorial presents the problem of competition in communication between the preacher and contemporary mass media, but indicates that the Word of God is news that will get a hearing.   **683**

Miller, Donald G.
"Words or a Deed," *Interpretation*, April, 1952, pp. 131-46. Develops the idea that to preach the gospel is "to effect a deed."   **684**

Moorehead, Lee C.
"The Theology of Preaching," *The Pulpit*, January, 1963, pp. 7-9. An appreciation of Forsyth, Farmer, and Barth, for their contributions to the theology of preaching, and some projected effects of preachers and taking them seriously.   **685**

Mueller, J. Theodore
"Return to Reality: Preaching the Gospel of Christ," *Christianity Today*, March 28, 1960, pp. 3-5. Opposing the *"ersatz sermons"* of our day, the author pleads for dedicated preachers who are not ashamed to preach the gospel of Christ—the real preaching.   **686**

Nebreda, Alphonso M., S.J.
"The Theological Problem of Transmission," *Lumen Vitae*, June, 1965, pp. 309-24. A reprint of a talk delivered at the Christopher Study Week (Summer, 1964) on apostolic renewal in the seminary, it is a very fine treatment of the role of pre-evangelization in the context of the human mediations willed by God for the transmission of his message.   **687**

Nord, Kermit
"On Biblical Preaching," *Pulpit Digest*, April, 1959, pp. 17-20. Although a sermon begins with an existential question, the

answer must come from God's Word. We face the challenges of people biblically illiterate and spiritually immature, the need to communicate the authority of our faith, and the scientific advancements of this space age. In response, we must faithfully interpret the gospel to our people.   688

O'Brien, I., O.P.

"Preaching—a Function of Theology," *Irish Ecclesiastical Record,* August, 1963, pp. 80-90. Informative investigation of the mutual dependence and relationship of preaching and theology. 689

Osborn, Ronald E.

"Voice for Mankind," *The Pulpit,* November, 1965, pp. 8-10. A vigorous apologetic for the preaching ministry.   690

Oster, Henri

"God's Plan," *Lumen Vitae,* March, 1962, pp. 37-52. The divine plan of salvation centers on Christ's pasch. The entire Bible is written in testimony to this all important event. The development of this doctrine through the age of the fathers stressed the economy of salvation. But the economy is still active in the world. It must be presented to Christians as being realized in the world now. An analysis of the present necessity for a return to this traditional view, its aims and methods, especially relates the economy of salvation to current pastoral needs.   691

Paterson, John

"The Business of Preaching," *Religion in Life,* Winter, 1937, pp. 62-69. An analysis of sermon and preacher leads to the conclusion that the sermon is "proclamation" and the preacher should be part of it.   692

Pearson, Roy M.

"Determine Why You Are Preaching," *The Pulpit,* October, 1954, pp. 2-4. Valid and invalid reasons for preaching, both conscious and unconscious.   693

"Motive for Preaching," *Pulpit Digest,* February, 1959, pp. 11-17. The purpose of preaching is to speak so that the heathen become Christian and the Christian Christlike. This purpose is accomplished as the sermon becomes a proclamation, a demonstration, and an implantation.   694

"The Purpose of Preaching," *Religion in Life,* Spring, 1963, pp. 267-78. A chapter from Pearson's book, *The Preacher: His*

Purpose and Practice. Outline builds on four biblical phrases, but is not comprehensive.   **695**

Pilch, Wenseslaus, O.F.M.
"Scripture in Your Sermon," *Homiletic and Pastoral Review,* March, 1964, pp. 487-95. The priest is a prophet; his use of Scripture is a must. The author offers some insights on the various senses and usage of the Bible.   **696**

Rees, Paul S.
"The Minister's Workshop: Begin with a High View," *Christianity Today,* May 11, 1962, p. 58. One of the main reasons for the decline of preaching is that preachers allow it a secondary rather than a primary role in their ministries.   **697**

Reumann, John H. P.
"The Kerygma and the Preacher," *Dialog,* Winter, 1964, pp. 27-35. A brilliant critical analysis of the use of "kerygma" in the attempt to understand the nature of New Testament preaching. **698**

Roddy, Clarence S.
"On the Preaching of Theology," *Christianity Today,* August 31, 1959, pp. 5-7. The author shows the necessity of theology by unveiling the errors of those who belittle its importance. The center of theology is at the point of its clearest revelation, namely, in the person and work of Jesus Christ. The cross is the apex of the revelation and therefore must be the pivotal point of preaching.   **699**

Ruopp, Harold W.
"The Authority of the Modern Preacher," *The Pulpit,* December, 1952, pp. 2-4. Sources of the preacher's authority.   **700**

Rust, Eric C.
"Theology and Preaching," *Review and Expositor,* April, 1955, pp. 145-65. A professor of Christian Apologetics sets down a clear relationship between preaching and its theological framework.   **701**

Scherer, Paul
"Preaching as a Radical Transaction," *Review and Expositor,* October, 1957, pp. 560-73. The article is the text of one of a series of three lectures on the contemporary indictments of preaching. This lecture speaks to the criticism that the gospel, as often preached, is too "easy" to be true. In his characteristic

interesting manner, Dr. Scherer graphically presents the challenges of preaching. 702

"Shall We Scrap the Sermon?" *Christianity Today,* April 13, 1962, pp. 28-29. The editor answers his title question with a resounding, No! He supports this from the biblical record and history. 703

Sleeth, Ronald E.

"Theology Versus Communication Theories," *Religion in Life,* Autumn, 1963, pp. 547-52. A keen analysis of the ideological tensions between theologians and communications teachers, with suggestions for rapprochement. 704

Stacey, W. David

"The Authority of Preaching," *The Preacher's Quarterly,* December, 1956, pp. 292-97. Article contends that without authority preaching is useless. Consciousness of a word from God is essential. This consciousness is our authority. Makes good sense. 705

Stanley, David M., S.J.

"The Fonts of Preaching," *Worship,* February, 1963, pp. 164-72. Deeply significant essay on the necessity of biblical orientation for all preaching; shows how failure to rely on sound exegesis has resulted in generations of sermons on the "fringe benefits" of moralistic application. The aim of preaching is to make God's Word relevant; but this must not deteriorate into practical applications that simply fetter the Word of God. 706

Taylor, E. K., C.M.S.

"The Eloquence of Sacred Scripture," *Clergy Review,* December, 1958, pp. 719-26. Splendid article on the eloquence of sacred Scripture as inspiring and forming the eloquence of the preacher. Of special value is the summary of St. Augustine's analysis of the rhetoric of St. Paul in the *De Doctrina Christiana.* 707

Toohey, William, C.S.C.

"Is Preaching Merely Sacred Rhetoric?" *American Ecclesiastical Review,* September, 1961, pp. 152-59. An examination of the relationship between preaching and rhetoric, pinpointing the dangers in thinking that the former is simply public speaking from a pulpit. Toohey shows that the unique quality of the Christian message (supernatural truth) places preaching in a category quite apart from other forms of discourse: the content demands proclamation rich in biblical imagery. 708

Van Dusen, Henry P.
"The Premises of Theology and the Task of Preaching," *Religion in Life,* Spring, 1937, pp. 180-90. An excellent analysis of basic premises to guide both the theologian and preacher. 709

Ward, J. W. G.
"The Primacy of Preaching," *Church Management,* October, 1936, pp. 11-12. Stresses preaching of the gospel as the primary duty of the minister. Calls for increased quality in preaching. 710

Ward, Wayne E.
"Preaching and the Word of God in the New Testament," *Review and Expositor,* January, 1959, pp. 20-30. The author presents a summary of C. H. Dodd's idea of the kerygma and Karl Barth's concept of the Word of God as related to New Testament preaching. Finally the article unifies the two concepts and sets forth a resultant philosophy of preaching. 711

Weber, F. R.
"Why Our Preaching Fails," *Christianity Today,* February 17, 1958, pp. 3-5. The author suggests that preaching is ineffective because the great truths of redemption are omitted, i.e., the law which leads sinners to repentance and the gospel which declares the good news of salvation in Jesus Christ. A variation of life-centered preaching has taken its place. 712

White, Richard C.
"The Newer Preaching," *College of the Bible Quarterly,* January, 1962, pp. 18-29. A professor of homiletics offers an assessment of developments in preaching which have resulted from current emphasis on biblical theology in preaching. He describes the content and method of the "newer preaching" and suggests some dangers inherent in it. 713

Woodburne, A. Stewart
"The Preacher, an Interpreter," *Religion in Life,* Autumn, 1936, pp. 544-51. A professor of theology presents an effective case for the sermon as an explanation of religion and life. 714

Topics of Preaching

Alleman, Herbert C.
"Personal Religion," *Interpretation,* July, 1948, pp. 299-312. A short homiletic analysis of Job, Ecclesiastes, and Psalms. 715

Anderson, William Henry, Jr.

"The Possibility of Biblical Preaching," *Christianity Today,* June 7, 1963, pp. 8-9. An article presenting the predicament of modern preaching in bridging the cultural gap between the contemporary and the biblical worlds. **716**

Arendzen, J. P.

"Attende Doctrinae," *Clergy Review,* May, 1938, pp. 377-86. Excellent article on the doctrinal needs of the faithful and the doctrinal duty of priests, both as teachers and preachers. Stresses the fruitfulness of the doctrinal sermon rather than the mere moral exhortation. **717**

Aubrey, Edwin E.

"The Preacher: A Creative Theologian," *Religion in Life,* Summer, 1938, pp. 392-406. A theologian argues his case for "creative theology" as the material for sermons. **718**

Auchinloss, Hugh

"Fifty Years a Church Tramp," *Christianity Today,* January 2, 1961, pp. 13-15. The author is a Presbyterian layman who, because of his work, has spent ten months out of each year traveling. During his career he made notes of his reactions to the various churches and preachers he visited and he came to the conclusion that there has been a decline in expository preaching. He attributes the cause to a lack of sufficient preparation. Whenever a sermon spoke to his personal need, "invariably it was the expository type." **719**

Balcomb, Raymond E.

"What Is Biblical Preaching?" *The Pulpit,* October, 1962, pp. 7-9. Biblical preaching is not artificially using the Bible, but a genuine wrestling with the meaning of a particular text. **720**

Barackman, Paul F.

"Preaching from the Acts," *Interpretation,* April, 1959, pp. 177-94. Here Professor Barackman gives some pregnant thoughts on preaching from Acts. **721**

"Preaching from Amos," *Interpretation,* July, 1959, pp. 296-315. This article gives many seed thoughts for sermons on Amos. **722**

"Preaching from the Corinthian Epistles," *Interpretation,* October, 1959, pp. 444-61. The main themes of the Corinthian epistles adapted to preaching are set forth. **723**

"Preaching from Numbers," *Interpretation,* January, 1959, pp. 55-70. A very informative article with some practical suggestions on how to preach from the book of Numbers. 724

"Sunday Martyrdom," *Interpretation,* October, 1956, pp. 387-99. A well-written article in expository preaching. 725

Barr, Browne
"Expository Preaching," *Minister's Quarterly,* November, 1955, pp. 13-15. The writer defends the thesis that expository preaching, rightly understood, invariably produces more effective sermons based upon the Word of God. The definition and advantages of expository preaching are ably set forth and merit study. 726

Bjornard, Reidar B.
"Christian Preaching from the Old Testament," *Review and Expositor,* January, 1959, pp. 20-30. As pointed out by the author, the Old Testament has much sub-Christian material, but is a most useful source for preaching today. He sets forth a number of relevant themes that may be drawn from the Old Testament. 727

Blackwood, Andrew W.
"The Minister's Workshop: The God of the Chosen Family," *Christianity Today,* August 3, 1962, p. 35. A series of suggested topics to be preached from the book of Genesis. 728

"The Minister's Workshop: Living for Christ in a Worldly City," *Christianity Today,* December 6, 1963, p. 44. The author gives seed thoughts for doctrinal sermons from the Gospel of John. 729

"The Minister's Workshop: Pastoral Counseling from the Pulpit," *Christianity Today,* April 12, 1963, p. 51. The author gives concrete suggestions for pastoral sermons from the psalms. 730

"The Minister's Workshop: Seeing God in Bible History," *Christianity Today,* June 7, 1963, p. 44. The author illustrates the way sermonizing may be done from I Kings and Bible history by sharing several themes and structures from the book. 731

"Servants of the Word," *Interpretation,* April, 1948, pp. 158-71. This is a plea for more preaching from the prophets, especially expository preaching. Blackwood gives many good suggestions concerning this type preaching. 732

Bowie, Walter Russell
"Some Preaching Values in the Revised Standard Version of the New Testament," *Interpretation,* January, 1950, pp. 51-61. This article lists many instances in which the use of the Revised Standard Version in preaching makes various passages and words clearer than the 1611 translation. 733

Brunsting, Bernard
"Evangelistic Preaching," *Christianity Today,* November 9, 1962, pp. 16-18. The author studies the content and methods involved in effective evangelistic preaching. 734

Calkins, Raymond
"Militant Message," *Interpretation,* October, 1948, pp. 430-43. This article contains a homiletic analysis of the apocalypses of the Old and New Testaments, with the idea of helping the preacher preach from them in a meaningful manner. 735

Carlson, N. Gene
"The Best Way to Preach," *Christianity Today,* June 4, 1965, pp. 9-11. Another statement of the definition and values of expository preaching. 736

Clowney, Edmund P.
"Preaching Christ," *Christianity Today,* March 12, 1965, pp. 5-7. The minister's task is to preach the Word of the Lord so as to reveal the Lord of the Word. 737

Connors, Joseph, S.V.D.
"Science of the Sunday Sermon," *Chicago Studies,* Spring, 1963, pp. 108-18. The author considers four principles for selecting sermon themes (adequate instruction, life situation, liturgical unity, kerygma) which were in vogue prior to the Constitution on the Liturgy. 738

Conrad, Leslie, Jr.
"The Preacher and His Hobbyhorses," *Church Management,* April, 1964, p. 47. The dangers of using overworked sermon themes. 739

Cowling, Dale
"Preaching on Race," *The Pulpit,* November, 1962, pp. 24-26. Principles to consider when preaching on race, written by a minister who is so doing. 740

Curley, Francis X., S.J.
"The Preaching Vocation and Vocational Preaching," (Part I),
American Ecclesiastical Review, July, 1954, pp. 1-11; (Part II)
August, 1954, pp. 81-89. The aim of both articles is to encourage
vocational preaching. There is a very definite need for this type
preaching, and in order to encourage it Father Curley presents
valuable source materials from the popes in the first article and
sources from the Middle Ages in the second.   741

Davis, H. F.
"Grace Explained to the People," *Clergy Review*, March, 1956,
pp. 147-57. Solid and inspiring reflections on the doctrine of grace
in order to help the preacher explain this doctrine to the people.
Argues for the necessity of such preaching even as it offers practical helps and approaches.   742

Dawson, Joseph Martin
"The Preacher and Current Events," *Church Management*,
November, 1942, pp. 46-47. Practical guidelines for preaching on
current events.   743

Dhielly, Joseph
"The History of Salvation in the Bible," *Lumen Vitae*, January–March, 1953, pp. 31-44. The history of salvation is not
presented in the abstract. It is a series of events and personal
meetings; and it is in this way the history of salvation should be
presented. Specific suggestions are given on the manner in which
certain topics may be presented.   744

Doherty, John T.
"Our Paschal Sermons," *The Priest*, March, 1953, pp. 203-6.
Easter sermons should present a truly vital preaching of the
Christian message. How the doctrine of the Resurrection may be
presented from Easter to Pentecost is briefly outlined.   745

Doolan, Aegidius, O.P.
"Doctrine and Preaching," *Furrow*, April, 1951, pp. 230-36.
Urgent plea for a sermon content that is doctrinally lucid.   746

Dunbar, Spence
"Preaching the Social Implications of the Gospel," *Religion in
Life*, Spring, 1951, pp. 245-53. The writer contends that the
preacher is not qualified to preach on the social implications of
the gospel.   747

Fournier, Elie
"A Summary of Pastoral Preaching," *Lumen Vitae,* September, 1961, pp. 508-35. Following *Mediator Dei* and various episcopal preaching directories, the general principles for preaching on the creed during Mass are outlined. These principles are followed by the schematic presentation of a full year's preaching. Each Sunday and major feast is divided into a section on "The Liturgical Language" and "Doctrinal Message."   748

Frost, S. B.
"The Preacher's Address to Children," *The Preacher's Quarter-ly,* June, 1956, pp. 100-107. The children's address is discussed within a worship context. Precautionary suggestions and positive directions are emphasized for greater effectiveness.   749

Furgeson, Earl H.
"The Neglected Merits of Biblical Preaching," *Religion in Life,* Autumn, 1948, pp. 559-68. An analysis of topical and textual preaching weighted in favor of the latter.   750

Garesche, Edward F., S.J.
"What Do We Preach?" *The Priest,* August, 1953, pp. 604-9. To make Sunday sermons lead to action, the preacher should in-struct his audience on the meaning of an active Christian life. 751

Gilmore, J. Herbert
"The Preaching Ministry and the Bible," *Review and Ex-positor,* January, 1960, pp. 58-68. This article concludes that authentic preaching has to be biblical after examining the nature of preaching, the relation of the Bible to preaching, and the current values of biblical preaching. The article draws from several of the better contemporary sources in presenting a strong biblical orientation to preaching.   752

Gossip, Arthur John
"The Whole Council of God," *Interpretation,* July, 1947, pp. 325-40. A plea for more doctrinal preaching, with suggestions on how to make doctrinal preaching better.   753

Graham, Aelred, O.S.B.
"What Do We Preach?" *Clergy Review,* August, 1943, pp. 337-45. Stimulating article on the need for doctrinal preaching and the further need to center this preaching on the two fundamental Christian truths—the Trinity and the Incarnation. Special emphasis on preaching Christ just as he is found in the Gospels,

"letting the narrative speak for itself and its central Figure stand
out as He really was."   754

Graham, Charles L.

"God's Interpreters," *Review and Expositor*, July, 1941, pp.
277-85. This article encourages the minister to speak compassion-
ately to relevant social problems (sins). The author, however,
points out that the preacher must be aligned closely and sacri-
ficially with Christ to be an effective interpreter of God.   755

Green, Michael

"Preaching the Advent: A Contemporary Approach," *Christianity Today*, January 1, 1965, pp. 3-5. The author shows how
preaching the Parousia answers for quests of the human heart.
He does not see Christ's coming as merely a future event but
"coming to us day by day."   756

Greeves, Frederick

"Preaching and Suffering," *The Preacher's Quarterly*, December, 1956, pp. 355-60. Points to lack of sermons of comfort.
Always there is "one broken heart, one terrified mind, one
suffering body among our hearers." The effective preacher has
a sensible philosophy of suffering. Timely observations here.   757

Grider, J. Kenneth

"A Plea for Preaching Christ," *Christianity Today*, March 31,
1958, pp. 13-15. Preaching is still a "holy business" because in it
sinful man is confronted with Jesus Christ. Preaching cannot
simply moralize any more.   758

Halstead, George William

"The Theme of My Preaching 'Christian Obedience.'" *Minister's Quarterly*, Winter, 1961–62, pp. 30-34. A minister, delivering an installation address, maintains that Christian obedience
is the essential message of every sermon and penetrates every
dimension of church life. The argument of the paper is well
stated and consistently developed.   759

Hamaide, Jacques; Pierre Guilbert

"The Message of Salvation in the Acts of the Apostles: Composition and Structure," *Lumen Vitae*, July–September, 1957, pp.
406-17. The preaching recorded in Acts is analyzed and outlined.
The differences in the speaking situations are noted with the
differences in the presentation. The general outlines and concerns of this apostolic preaching are presented with indications
for application in modern times.   760

Harty, Gabriel M., O.P.
"Are We Preaching the Rosary?" *Furrow,* May, 1954, pp. 289-94. Distinction between preaching *on* or *about* the Rosary and preaching the Rosary.　　761

Henry, H. T.
"Christianus Alter Christus," *Homiletic and Pastoral Review,* October, 1942, pp. 10-16. The necessity of preaching about the ontological reality in being a Christian (with bibliographical references).　　762

"Preaching the Epistles," *Homiletic and Pastoral Review,* October, 1941, pp. 1-10. The author suggests an occasional year of sermons based on the epistles of the Sundays and holydays.　　763

"Stray Notes on Panegyrics," *Homiletic and Pastoral Review,* March, 1935, pp. 570-78. Conventional observations on preaching on the saints.　　764

Hermans, Basil, O.Praem.
"The Sunday Instruction," *Furrow,* November, 1953, pp. 626-32. Suggestions for preaching more meaningful sermons based on more important mysteries, commandments, and virtues.　　765

Hickman, Frank S.
"The Regenerative Note in Modern Preaching," *Review and Expositor,* January, 1937, pp. 3-17. The article traces the shift in emphasis away from regeneration in preaching, suggests causes, and offers suggestions for dealing with the trend. The author shows a scholarly perspective as he explains the impact of Calvin, Arminus, religious education, and the findings of the natural sciences.　　766

Hodges, Graham R.
"Homiletical Marksmanship," *Church Management,* September, 1965, pp. 13-14. Argues for the direct-approach type of preaching (if done in Christian love) to meet specific needs.　　767

Hoover, J. Edgar
"Communism: The Bitter Enemy of Religion," *Christianity Today,* June 22, 1959, pp. 3-5. Mr. Hoover states that sermons represent one of the most potent forces for good in the nation today. Thus these must urge a rededication to Christian beliefs in the face of communistic threats to the higher values of human personality.　　768

Howington, Nolan P.

"The Ethical Element in Preaching," *Review and Expositor*, Summer, 1965, pp. 336-50. An exposition of the Christian ethic and a call for biblical preaching that faces squarely contemporary moral problems. 769

"Expository Preaching," *Review and Expositor*, January, 1959, pp. 56-65. The gist of this article is that "in a day of topical preaching when men strive mightily to say something new, there is a need to develop a Bible-centered type of preaching in which men faithfully report the word that is eternally true." The author examines objections to expository preaching and sets forth a methodology. 770

Hudson, R. Lofton

"Therapeutic Preaching," *Review and Expositor*, July, 1952, pp. 295-303. The author, after stating some strong opinions of the field of psychiatry against some types of preaching, describes some themes to develop carefully lest more harm than good is done. Following, the writer suggests some topics for preaching that may be therapeutic psychologically. 771

Hughes, G. Wynne

"Preaching Perfection Today," *The Preacher's Quarterly*, March, 1957, pp. 5-10. Article defines Christian perfection and then instructs us in the best methods of preaching acceptably on it. Ends with a discussion of the values of such a doctrine. Good substance. 772

Hunter, A. M.

"The Proclamation of the Kingdom," *Interpretation*, October, 1960, pp. 440-54. An excellent analysis of several fruitful ways to preach on the parables. 773

Irwin, John C.

"Some Thoughts on Biblical Preaching," *The Pulpit*, September, 1952, pp. 2-3. Distinguishes topical sermons from biblical sermons by the proper use of a text. 774

Kearns, Conleth

"Preaching the Bible," *Furrow*, April, 1953, pp. 193-200. 775

Kelly, Bernard J., C.S.Sp.

"Preaching About Holy Mass," *Irish Ecclesiastical Record*, January, 1963, pp. 12-21. How to give a popular sermon or instruction on the Mass; various approaches are considered. 776

Kemp, Charles F.
"Life-Situation Preaching and Pastoral Work," *Pastoral Psychology,* October, 1956, pp. 35-46. A minister urges that preaching and pastoral work find a common denominator in "life-situation preaching," the insights of pastoral work contributing to preaching, and vice-versa. He suggests that success in doing these two-jobs-in-one depends on the minister's being "person-minded." He also discusses the limitations and possible abuses of his thesis.   777

King, Elisha A.
"Continuous Pastoral Evangelism," *Church Management,* May, 1941, pp. 483-84. The role of preaching in a successful program of evangelism: a methodology.   778

Kirkland, Bryant M.
"Expository Preaching Revitalized," *Pulpit Digest,* July–August, 1965, pp. 9-14. The author points out pulpit giants of the past who were expository preachers and also the weaknesses of topical sermons. Good expository preaching today requires the interpreter to recognize, accept, and accommodate himself to the relativity of words and the force and exemplification of his own life. A challenging article on expository preaching.   779

Koller, Charles W.
"The Minister's Workshop: The Primacy of Expository Preaching," *Christianity Today,* July 3, 1964, p. 29. The author points out several reasons why expository (more scriptural material than other types) preaching is significant, though other types have value.   780

Lantz, John Edward
"Church Co-operation Related to Preaching?" *Church Management,* November, 1963, pp. 22-26. The ecumenical theme in the Southern churches surveyed is manifest in preaching only in the negative for the most part.   781

Lewis, Greville P.
"The Preacher and the Parables," *The Preacher's Quarterly,* December, 1957, pp. 318-22; March, 1958, pp. 40-46; June, 1958, pp. 140-45; September, 1958, pp. 231-37. Expository studies of selected parables as resources for preaching. Some fresh insights although series suffers from brevity.   782

McBriarty, Anthony, C.SS.R.
"Preaching the Eternal Truths: What About Hell?" *American Ecclesiastical Review,* November, 1949, pp. 406-10. In this article

the author decries the fact that the eternal truths, particularly hell, are not subject of more sermons. He blames this on the softness of the times and, of course, the devil. No doubt all priests will agree with the author, but there is the big question of how to preach on hell; and this article fairly well represents the highly questionable negative approach. **783**

McCain, Ray
"Speaking on School Desegregation by Atlanta Ministers," *Southern Speech Journal,* Spring, 1964, pp. 256-62. After presenting a brief analysis of the climate of opinion, the author analyzes a significant number of sermons by Atlanta ministers touching on school desegregation during 1961. These sermons were delivered during a period of concerted effort to sell peaceful desegregation to the public. **784**

McCarthy, Sean, S.M.A.
"Teaching the Mystical Body—a Suggestion," *Furrow,* May, 1953, pp. 269-71. Suggestions on teaching the mystical body doctrine in order to convey its essential meaning and to avoid confusion. **785**

McKeating, H.
"The Preacher and the Apocrypha," *The Preacher's Quarterly,* June, 1964, pp. 219-25; September, 1964, pp. 262-70; December, 1964, pp. 353-59. Preachers are urged to read the Apocrypha not for texts but for illustrations. Recommended as aids to devotion. Concise summaries of books and their message. **786**

McWilliams, Bernard F., C.SS.R.
"That Nasty Subject of Hell," *The Priest,* December, 1957, pp. 981-83. The author feels the sermon on hell in a parish mission can, and should, be given with a positive approach, while not neglecting the fire. **787**

Merrill, Boynton
"The Timeliness of Preaching the Timeless," *Religion in Life,* Spring, 1935, pp. 221-27. A famous preacher supports his conviction that preaching should be directed to the "inward" and "spiritual" rather than the "present crises." **788**

Middleton, Rosemary Sheed
"The Sunday Sermon," *Jubilee,* March, 1961, pp. 37-40. A laywoman's plea for a preaching that satisfies the hunger for theologically sound doctrine. **789**

Muckle, J. Y.
"The Preacher and the Old Testament," *The Preacher's Quarterly*, June, 1960, pp. 165-72; September, 1960, pp. 213-19. A plea for Old Testament preaching and the careful preparation it demands. Value of the literature of the Old Testament for sermon style. Examples of fruitful passages for preaching. Very good material.   790

Nelson, Clifford Ansgar
"The Eschatological Element in Contemporary Preaching," *Religion in Life*, Winter, 1943, pp. 87-99. An analysis of possible positions and an appeal that preachers develop an "Eschatology that will be intellectually respectable, scriptually honest, spiritually sound and relevant to contemporary needs."   791

Penner, Albert J.
"Preaching to Itching Ears," *Minister's Quarterly*, November, 1950, pp. 32-36. In a period of complacency about religion, preachers must return to the biblical sources of their faith for guidance in order to preach the gospel. The writer clearly sees the need to return to the Bible if preaching is to come alive once again.   792

Pitcher, Alvin
"Preaching the Gospel in an Achievement Culture," *The Pulpit*, March, 1962, pp. 7-9. Problem of preaching justification by grace through faith in a culture that stresses justification by works.   793

Pitts, John
"Preaching the Cross of Christ," *Religion in Life*, Spring, 1945, pp. 163-73. A lament on the tendency to preach a "cross-less" Christianity with a dynamic appeal.   794

Poteat, William Louis
"The Prophet Confronts His World," *Review and Expositor*, January, 1937, pp. 18-28. The writer clearly and graphically defines prophetic, contemporary preaching and shows common hindrances to it. The article, quite vivid in current allusion, makes a strong appeal for preaching with relevance to social problems.   795

"Preaching the Cross," *Christianity Today*, March 17, 1958, pp. 20-22. Urges a careful facing of the true meaning of the cross which can easily be clouded by avoiding the offense of the cross.   796

Robinson, J. A. T.
"Preaching Judgment," *The Preacher's Quarterly*, September, 1957, pp. 241-46; December, 1957, pp. 335-40. The idea of judgment in our age. Reasons for its rejection. Rethinking needed so that preaching reflects quality. Worthwhile observations clearly presented.   797

Russell, Daniel
"So Much the Preacher Leaves Unsaid," *Religion in Life*, Spring, 1947, pp. 244-50. A plea for what the author considers fundamentals: God, and love as an active creative force.   798

Sclater, J. R. P.
"Preaching and Prophesying," *Religion in Life*, Summer, 1943, pp. 407-11. The author takes a stand for "doctrinal" preaching as contrasted with "prophetic" preaching.   799

Scott, Earl Striker
"The Children's Sermon," *Church Management*, January, 1938, pp. 215-16. The types of sermon approaches available for addressing children.   800

Sessler, J. J.
"The Preacher in His Pulpit," *Church Management*, October, 1939, pp. 17-21. Deals with the message of the minister.   801

Sheed, Rosemary
"The Sunday Sermon: A Missed Opportunity?" *Life of the Spirit*, February, 1961, pp. 342-49. A sermon should enlarge our rudimentary knowledge of the faith and give us practical guidelines for living. The Mass, sex, Mariology are areas needing homiletic explanation.   802

Sheerin, John B., C.S.P.
"Buried Treasure in the Psalms," *Homiletic and Pastoral Review*, December, 1948, pp. 177-81. The author, as the title suggests, unearths the value of the psalms for sermon usage.   803

"Bypassing the Centers of Resistance," *Homiletic and Pastoral Review*, December, 1944, pp. 168-72. We should preach our dogmas expressing the solid certainty and immutable truth therein. We should preach the dogma straight and direct, firm and paternal-like to obedient members. Yet to counteract resistance, suggestion and indirect statement are good devices.   804

"Dark Before Dawn," *Homiletic and Pastoral Review*, February, 1945, pp. 321-26. In this war (World War II) the fear of death scares, but seldom really reforms, a man and regenerates his life. To a church congregation, death is less imminent. The author proceeds to give many good hints on preaching on death. 805

"On the Brighter Side," *Homiletic and Pastoral Review,* November, 1944, pp. 97-102. This article deals with the care to be taken in delivering moral sermons—a need for much experience and practical knowledge. Preaching that flows in the main stream of the true Christian tradition must be optimistic and positive. 806

"The Pallbearers," *Homiletic and Pastoral Review,* August, 1947, pp. 873-77. Some practical hints on how to counteract the pessimism that many preach concerning the futility of human life and actions. Stresses the importance of human acts as the main means to obtain the happiness of heaven. 807

"Sermons on Sin," *Homiletic and Pastoral Review,* January, 1945, pp. 248-53. A fair approach to the question, but only a partial view in the light of contemporary insights into the theology of sin. 808

Simpson, John E.
"Preaching and Christian Stewardship," *The Pulpit,* April, 1952, pp. 2-3. Suggestions to help preaching on stewardship. 809

Sperry, Willard L.
"Preaching to the Religiously Perplexed," *Religion in Life,* Winter, 1935, pp. 62-73. An excellent case is made for preaching not only to the immediate human situation but to the church of tomorrow. 810

Stanfield, V. L.
"Preaching Values in the Gospel of Matthew," *Review and Expositor,* October, 1962, pp. 512-17. The article points out some practical material in the Gospel of Matthew that can be used to construct sermon materials from Matthew. 811

Turner, J. Clyde
"The Preacher for Such a Time as This," *Review and Expositor,* January, 1943, pp. 38-47. Addressing a wartime audience, the writer urges a distinct position for the minister—cognizant of the issues of the time, courageous and loving enough to speak the principles of the Word of God. 812

Valentine, Foy
"Preaching on Race Relations," *Review and Expositor,* July, 1959, pp. 260-70. After speaking on objections to preaching on

race relations, the author suggests ways of preaching effectively on the topic.　　813

Van Caster, Marcel, S.J.
"Chief Point in Teaching the Mass," *Lumen Vitae*, January–March, 1952, pp. 21-28. Suggestions of themes and organization for a preaching (or course of instructions) on the Mass.　　814

Wade, Wilson
"Biblical Preaching: New Life in the Church," *The Pulpit*, February, 1962, pp. 7-9. Method for genuine biblical preaching.　　815

Weatherspoon, Jesse Burton
"The Evangelistic Sermon," *Review and Expositor*, January, 1945, pp. 59-67. The writer points out that "the evangelistic sermon ought to possess the best qualities of preaching in form and content as well as in spirit."　　816

Wehrli, Allen G.
"Preaching Values in Numbers," *Minister's Quarterly*, Spring, 1965, pp. 13-17. An introduction to the personalities and ideas in an Old Testament book pregnant with value for preaching.　　817

Williamson, R.
"The Preacher and the Epistle to the Hebrews," *The Preacher's Quarterly*, December, 1962, pp. 326-33. A survey of the themes and texts in Hebrews. Helpful as an introductory essay and provides an overall view.　　818

The Preacher

Ashbrook, James B.; Harvey Guthrie
"When Ministers Face Themselves," *The Pulpit*, June, 1960, pp. 8-12. A study of the minister's personal life.　　819

Belford, John L.
"Preachers, Great and Poor—and Just Preachers," *Homiletic and Pastoral Review*, November, 1936, pp. 136-42. Reflections on what a good preacher is.　　820

"Believe What You Preach," *Christianity Today*, January 5, 1962, pp. 24-25. The article faces the concern of the pastor who wonders whether his efforts are futile. The key for the successful minister lies in the faith which he has in the Word which he proclaims.　　821

Black, Binney Simpson
"Preaching with Passion," *Minister's Quarterly,* February, 1949, pp. 3-7. In order that sermons may move men's hearts and alter their lives, the preacher himself must be a man of burning faith who is, like the congregation he serves, constantly in need of salvation. A worthwhile reminder that sermons are from a dying man to dying men.   822

Blackmer, Lewis M.
"Wanted: Shorter Men in the Pulpit," *Church Management,* October, 1959, pp. 80-81. Argues that the pastor should be less of a preacher in order to be more of a minister.   823

Boylan, M. Eugene, O.Cist.R.
"Priest and Pulpit," *The Priest,* June, 1948, pp. 445-48. The sermon betrays the life of the man who gives it; his sermon always springs from his spiritual life. The effective preacher is the humble priest speaking well.   824

Burge, Hollis A.
"The Preacher," *Pulpit Digest,* June, 1941, pp. 9-12. Requisites for good preaching in a clergyman's personal life.   825

Burke, Eugene M., C.S.P.
"The Salvation of the Hearer," *American Ecclesiastical Review,* October, 1945, pp. 288-99. Newman's example illustrates what the basic attitude and approach of the preacher should be. Individuality of hearers is stressed. A generally valuable article for the formation of the preacher's attitude towards his hearers. Modern taste in language and choice of words are, however, not fully taken into account.   826

Carlton, John W.
"Using the Arts in Preaching," *Review and Expositor,* Summer, 1964, pp. 191-205. The article emphasizes primarily the personal values of improving the stature of the preacher through understanding of the arts. The writer draws a parallel between the task of the artist and the minister.   827

Carroll, Thomas P.
"Getting Through from Pulpit to Pew," *Homiletic and Pastoral Review,* February, 1964, pp. 397-402. Fine article on general attitudes one must have in order to fulfill the role of preacher in this present age.   828

Cornforth, G. A. E.
"A Preacher's Temptations," *The Preacher's Quarterly,* December, 1958, pp. 329-34, 376. A discussion of some of the perils of preaching to the preacher's own person: self-display, histrionics, whining, pomposity, laziness, etc. Points are well taken. 829

Coyne, J. J.
"Sacred Eloquence—an Examination of Conscience," *Clergy Review,* August, 1951, pp. 90-96. Not too optimistic estimate of the state of preaching today. Though more negative than positive in tone, it does contain helpful suggestions on the prayer-life of the preacher, proximate preparation, accommodation to the audience. 830

Crocker, Lionel
"The Preacher's Personal Proof," *Central States Speech Journal,* Winter, 1959, pp. 31-34. Since an audience accepts much of what a speaker says because of what he is, the preacher should learn to utilize the strong force of his office and reputation as a persuasive tool. This article helps the minister to recognize the place and importance of personal proof. 831

Cullom, W. R.
"The Minister as Student," *Review and Expositor,* April, 1939, pp. 204-13. The obligation of the minister to be a lifelong student is forcefully presented by the writer. He urges careful, constant contemporizing of information, both religious and secular, as a necessity for valid preaching. 832

"The Minister's Personal Life," *Review and Expositor,* April, 1938, pp. 218-25. The writer urges integrity in the minister's personal life and sums up his arguments with the motto, "Have faith and be faithful." 833

Curley, Francis X., S.J.
"Preachers Are Shorn Sheep, Dewdrops and Locusts," *Homiletic and Pastoral Review,* May, 1959, pp. 724-34. This article investigates some unusual metaphors used by ecclesiastical writers throughout the church's history to describe the office and work of the preacher. 834

Dunbar, Spence
"Preaching's Basic Problem Is the Preacher," *Religion in Life,* Summer, 1949, pp. 344-51. An interesting and challenging essay on causes for poor preaching. The author suggests that most preachers are not effective because "they don't want to be." 835

Dunwoody, Richard G.
"Don't Preach Above Your Experience," *Christianity Today,*
November 8, 1963, p. 13. The article refutes the statement of its
title on biblical grounds. 836

Farmer, Herbert H.
"The Preacher and Culture," *Review and Expositor,* January,
1947, pp. 34-49. The author strongly urges the preacher to partake
seriously of the better things of the several dimensions of culture.
He suggests that the minister who has no desire or patience to
explore the great things of literature and art is "under some suspi-
cion as to the quality of his religious life." 837

Frost, S. B.
"The Preacher's Worship," *The Preacher's Quarterly,* September, 1956, pp. 195-201. Timely and suggestive thoughts about
what the minister himself brings to the service of worship. He
needs a blessing from it and to make his offering in it. Three
principles are needed: worthiness, fullness, and unity. 838

Fuller, Carlos Greenleaf
"Spiritual Training of the Pastor," *Christianity Today,* July
18, 1960, p. 5. A brief article on the significance of seminary
training in the spiritual life of a preacher. 839

Furgeson, Earl H.
"Preaching and Personality," *Pastoral Psychology,* October,
1959, pp. 9-14. A professor of preaching and pastoral theology who
believes that the sermon is "the lengthened shadow of the
man" suggests some possible correlations between personality
types and the sermons preached by men of the types. He urges that
homiletics take into account the preacher's personality as well as
teaching biblical, oratorical, rhetorical, and other principles. 840

Gaebelein, Frank E.
"The Minister and His Work," *Christianity Today,* January 1,
1965, pp. 8-10. The author deals with aspects that he considers
central to the minister and his work: his identity, burden, preaching, and purpose. These are to be used to contribute to the unity
of the body of Christ. 841

Grey, W. Gregory
"To a Future Preacher," *The Priest,* August, 1959, pp. 658-62.
An eloquent plea for seminarians to prepare sermons and take
advantage of occasions to speak; strong emphasis is placed on
the preaching office of the priest. 842

Haworth, Swan
"The Minister's Personal Religious Life," *Review and Expositor*, April, 1939, pp. 199-203. A minister points out the necessity for a minister to cultivate private, personal religious experiences in order for his life to have genuine value in the Christian work.   843

Henry, H. T.
"Courageous Preaching," *Homiletic and Pastoral Review*, July, 1942, pp. 899-906. Rambling article affirming that it takes courage to preach the whole truth.   844

"The Indignant Preacher," *Homiletic and Pastoral Review*, January, 1938, pp. 346-54. The preacher in his sermons should avoid indignation. He should show displeasure at unworthy acts by some of his parishioners, but he should not scold them with heated denunciations. A self-controlled and calmly reasoned protest on the well-known evil will be more effective.   845

" 'Jocular' Preachers," *Homiletic and Pastoral Review*, July, 1937, pp. 1018-27. Some fine points relevant to the "decorum battle" in preaching.   846

"The Pompous Preacher," *Homiletic and Pastoral Review*, November, 1939, pp. 113-21. An article on a defective manner of preaching.   847

"The 'Unlearned' Preacher," *Homiletic and Pastoral Review*, June, 1941, pp. 879-86. A discussion of the importance of learning for the preacher, with an unfortunate recommendation to use Latin quotations and other devices to indicate that the preacher is learned.   848

Henry, W. Everett
"The Minister's Mental Equipment," *Review and Expositor*, July, 1942, pp. 339-47. A minister discusses "a trained mind" and "a full mind" as necessary qualifications for an effective ministry.   849

Holdsworth, G. Leslie
"The Minister's Life of Prayer," *The Preacher's Quarterly*, June, 1958, pp. 135-39. A discussion of the minister as intercessor and the relationship of this office to life. Practical suggestions.   850

Hough, Lynn Harold
"The Preacher as a Pastor of Men's Minds," *Religion in Life*, Spring, 1951, pp. 236-44. A scholarly study of the preacher's use of his own mind and his ministry to the minds of congregants.   851

James, A. Gordon
"The Preacher's Vocation," *The Preacher's Quarterly,* September, 1958, pp. 223-28. Emphasizes vocational conviction rather than fluency or a flair for books. Views regarding supernatural, sacramental, and social aspects of the preacher's vocation. Serious conception of ministry.   852

John XXIII, Pope
"Documents," *Furrow,* April, 1959, pp. 263-67. An English translation of an address delivered by Pope John XXIII to the Lenten preachers of Rome. The practice of preaching when placed at the service of priestly action may be designated by the threefold note of wisdom, simplicity, and charity.   853

Keck, Herbert H.
"The Credentials of a Cleric," *Religion in Life,"* Summer, 1954, pp. 430-37. A readable analysis of intrinsic qualities which are the preacher's credentials.   854

King, Howard W.
"The Atmosphere of Preaching," *Church Management,* March, 1956, pp. 11, 49-50. Argues that dead and listless sermons may be the result of a neglected devotional life.   855

"What Makes Preaching Effective?" *Church Management,* September, 1962, pp. 17-18. The answer rests on the quality of the preacher's Christian experience.   856

Kirkland, William H.
"Priest and Prophet," *The Pulpit,* November, 1955, pp. 2-5. Relationship of priest to prophet, counselor to preacher, as functions of the ministry.   857

Lauck, Anthony, C.S.C.
"A Novelist Deals with the Preacher," *Homiletic and Pastoral Review,* December, 1955, pp. 205-8. Observations on preaching as seen in the novels of Bruce Marshall.   858

LeCount, R. Dale
"On Preparing the Preacher," *The Pulpit,* March, 1954, p. 20. Pious comments on the preacher's personal preparation.   859

Luchs, Fred E.
"Can Men over Fifty Write Good Sermons?" *Church Management,* December, 1957, pp. 13-14. Indolence, indifference, and

an over-detailed existence often result in a marked decline in creativity for those over fifty, but they can cultivate continuing creativity.   860

Lund, Gene
"At Home with the Clergy: The Protestant Parsonage Today," *Christianity Today,* September 12, 1960, pp. 3-4. The article addresses itself to the kind of person that comes from the Protestant minister's home with emphasis on current problems.   861

Lutz, Robert S.
"Young Man Don't Quit," *Christianity Today,* January 4, 1963, p. 47. The article encourages the preacher.   862

McAllister, F. B.
"The Face of the Ministry: Landscaping the Ministerial Terrain," *Christianity Today,* January 18, 1963, pp. 27-28. A retired pastor indicates that the minister's personality is a key aspect to his effectiveness with people and these valuable qualities can be developed.   863

McLain, Robert Wayne
"Honesty and the Holy Spirit," *The Pulpit,* June, 1948, pp. 140-41. The minister's spiritual development is an important step in being used by the Holy Spirit.   864

MacLennan, David A.
"The Minister as a Prophet," *Church Management,* November, 1948, pp. 13-14, 16. The preacher and his role as a prophet.   865

Munger, Robert
"A Prepared Messenger and His Message," *Christianity Today,* September 2, 1957, pp. 22-23. This is an editorial summary of an address to ministers in New York in which the author emphasizes the need for the preacher being personally prepared as well as having his message prepared.   866

Oates, Wayne
"The Preacher and His Relation to the Unconscious," *Review and Expositor,* October, 1945, pp. 427-43. A professor of psychology of religion points out dangers as the minister projects his own problems in his preaching. Insight into the unconscious, suggests the writer, may be used toward effective preaching as the minister perceives his "role" correctly.   867

Pearson, Roy M.
"Who Is the Preacher?" *Pulpit Digest,* October, 1957, pp. 7-14. The man who can preach the gospel with "converting assurance" should possess the qualities of wholeness and coherence of personality, an educated wisdom, conviction of the centrality of the Christian proclamation, and skillfulness in communication. 868

Pepler, Conrad, O.P.
"The Sanctification of the Apostle Through Preaching," *Life of the Spirit,* October, 1955, pp. 146-52. The apostle, to be a true apostle, must in some way preach the Word of God to others. The purpose of this article is to ascertain what effect this activity of preaching has upon the preacher himself. 869

Rees, Paul S.
"The Minister's Workshop: The Craftsman's Character," *Christianity Today,* September 14, 1962, p. 43. The preacher is not only a craftsman, but he must also be a man of character; otherwise his craftsmanship becomes craftiness. He must be a man of integrity. 870

"The Minister's Workshop: The Preacher as Steward," *Christianity Today,* June 5, 1964, p. 35. The author indicates that the responsibilities of preachers impose certain restrictions and yet give unusual freedom and opportunity. 871

Rest, Karl
"Can a Preacher Also Be Saved?" *The Pulpit,* March, 1952, pp. 2-4, 17. Sins which beset the preacher. 872

Roche, Stephen J.
"Preaching—and the Consumer," *Homiletic and Pastoral Review,* August, 1955, pp. 928-31. The author asserts that the priest must speak from a full mind—a mind filled with the knowledge gleaned from reading. 873

St. Clair, Robert James
"Crucifixion of the Pastor," *Christianity Today,* November 9, 1959, pp. 12-14. The author is concerned about the detours which prevent the pastor from doing his primary task of preaching and ministering the Word of God to people. A twofold solution is suggested: (1) a "Pastor's minister" for every fifty to one hundred ministers, and (2) a more thoroughly trained laity who would aid in preventing detoured preachers. 874

Schuette, Walter E.
"The Minister's Pastoral Relations," *Pulpit Digest,* October, 1953, pp. 17-23. The author points out areas of contact of the minister with his people—in the church, the home, at social gatherings, on the streets—and the importance of how he handles these contacts as it influences his ministry to such persons, including the effectiveness of his preaching.   875

Sessler, J. J.
"The Preacher in His Pulpit," *Church Management,* September, 1939, pp. 632-34. Attempts to answer the question: "Who is the preacher?" The importance of preaching is stressed.   876

Shafer, Floyd Doud
"And Preach As You Go!" *Christianity Today,* March 27, 1961, pp. 8-9. This is an incisive article pressing in graphic language the need for the preacher by diligent study to again become the parson (the person) of the community.   877

"Listen, People, Listen!" *Christianity Today,* July 17, 1961, pp. 3-4. The article is an incisive reminder to congregations of the disturbing sermons their preachers will preach when he is a man of God.   878

Sheerin, John B., C.S.P.
"Conquest by Courtesy," *Homiletic and Pastoral Review,* August, 1944, pp. 801-6. Attitude in a preacher is important; a reminder that duty is accepted more through a sympathetic voice.   879

Shen, Philip
"The Danger of Preaching," *Religion in Life,* Spring, 1955, pp. 249-56. The author contends that only the "prophet" will move people, for he speaks with an inner fire.   880

Sockman, Ralph W.
"The Preacher," *Religion in Life,* Spring, 1949, pp. 190-98. A very significant study of the preacher by a pulpit master.   881

Sperry, Willard L.
"The Minister as a Man of Truth," *Pastoral Psychology,* October, 1959, pp. 15-19. A seminary dean urges upon the work of the minister (including preaching) the double definition of truth: "agreement of my ideas with reality and agreement of my ideas with each other."   882

Steen, Robert S.
"The Minister's Inner Life," *The Pulpit,* March, 1948, pp. 68-69. What the minister does with himself helps determine his ministry.   883

Super, J. J.
"This Business of Preaching," *Homiletic and Pastoral Review,* September, 1944, pp. 916-19. An appeal for more conscientious preaching.   884

Thompson, John
"When Preaching Has Relevance," *Church Management,* September, 1962, pp. 13-14. A call for consistency between the preacher's life and words as the key to relevance.   883

Tonne, Arthur J.
"Relive Your Studies in Preaching," *Pastoral Life,* September, 1963, pp. 15-20. Preaching power and eloquence increase in proportion to learning things well and living intensely what is learned.   886

"Virtues That Make the Preacher," *Pastoral Life,* July–August, 1963, pp. 27-33. Neither natural talents nor gifted eloquence will ever replace the basic virtues of holiness required in every spokesman for Christ.   887

"Want to Preach Well? Pray Well," *Pastoral Life,* June, 1963, pp. 10-14. Pulpit success does not come overnight; prayer and meditation are here considered as an essential part of remote sermon preparation.   888

White, Samuel Pierce
"The Pastor as Preacher or the Pastor in His Pulpit," *Review and Expositor,* October, 1942, pp. 463-69. The writer warns against trends that make for preacher-centered preaching. Additionally, he points up some factors in the occasion that may negate the force of preaching.   889

White, Travis
"The Claims of Preaching," *College of the Bible Quarterly,* October, 1955, pp. 1-14. A college president offers his suggestions concerning the makeup of a "good preacher." He must be a good minister, stand up like a man, be willing to work, and know God other than by hearsay.   890

The Congregation

Adams, Theodore F.; Charles T. Holman
"Preaching Versus Counseling?" *Pastoral Psychology,* January, 1964, pp. 41-44. The authors react to a letter by a pastor who asserts that counseling usurps sermon preparation time and dulls the edge of the pastor's prophetic role.   891

Bartlett, Gene E.
"The Preaching and Pastoral Roles," *Pastoral Psychology,* March, 1952, pp. 21-28. A minister, in answer to the question "How can preaching promote mental health?" suggests several ways in which preaching has failed to heal and may have injured persons. He implies in so doing the ways in which this can be avoided, then briefly states a few practical suggestions on the positive side.   892

Bennett, Willis
"Play and Its Meaning for Preaching," *Review and Expositor,* January, 1950, pp. 165-72. The author defines play and shows historical attitudes toward it. He then explains how play can be used as a motive appeal and a methodology in the sermon.   893

Bowman, Howard L.
"Counseling Can Improve Preaching," *Pastoral Psychology,* February, 1957, pp. 13-15, 65. A minister urges that preaching ought to be done against the background of people's needs and that counseling insights provide awareness and appreciation of those needs.   894

Brigstocke, David, S.J.
"The Assent of the Boy," *Lumen Vitae,* December, 1965, pp. 705-15. Valuable study of the communication of the Christian message to adolescent boys, with particular emphasis on this triple objective: interest or commitment, acceptance of authority in religion, and exercise of liberty.   895

Burkhart, Roy A.
"Preaching with Counseling Insight," *Pastoral Psychology,* May, 1957, pp. 21-26. A minister offers definitions of both preaching and counseling and then urges preaching to utilize the findings of counseling. He illustrates how the process works and evaluates its results and its perils.   896

Burns, James H.
"The Application of Psychology to Preaching," *Pastoral Psychology*, March, 1952, pp. 29-33. A hospital chaplain states nine psychologically derived principles for use in preaching. They suggest respect for and support of persons, acceptance of persons as they are, some expectation of growth in persons, but they carefully skirt judgment. 897

Casteel, John L.
"Homiletical Method for Pastoral Preaching, Part I," *Pastoral Psychology*, November, 1955, pp. 11-15. A seminary speech professor offers principles and methods by which the minister can use preaching as "a complimentary method and resource" in his counseling. Using the insights of late rhetorical theory and psychology, he sets down the principles which characterize preaching in its interpersonal context. 898

"Homiletical Method for Pastoral Preaching, Part II," *Pastoral Psychology*, December, 1955, pp. 27-34. A seminary speech professor describes in detail the five steps in sermon construction and presentation which he believes will make preaching an effective counterpart to the ministry of counseling. The approach is based on psychological principles. 899

Clark, Robert L., Jr.
"The Pulpit and the Pew—a Two-Way Street," *Today's Speech*, April, 1961. A retired preacher discusses a number of attitudes and values he expects from his listeners. 900

Curran, C. A.
"Psychological Reactions to Sermons," *Theology Digest*, Winter, 1962, pp. 40-44. An important article, wherein the author shows that theological truths alone will not make an effective preacher, nor will the tricks of the trade of public speaking. What is needed is a better understanding of how people react to preaching and of how Christ preached in order to accomplish personal change in his hearers. 901

Donnelly, Malachi J., S.J.
"Advertising, Selling and Preaching," *American Ecclesiastical Review*, December, 1955, pp. 381-87. A comparison between the priest and salesman; the components of the complete selling process adjusted and applied to the priest. Modern psychology requires an approach attuned to it. There is an emphasis on the interior qualities of the priest-salesman. While certainly not profound and sometimes guilty of belaboring the obvious, the

article does manage to score some good points, particularly on the necessity of modernizing vocabulary and phraseology.　902

Fairchild, Roy W.
"Is Anybody Listening?" *The Pulpit,* February, 1963, pp. 9-11. An informed plea to involve sermon-listeners more actively in preaching by reevaluation of their role in the total sermon-event.　903

"Removing the Obstacles to Hearing," *The Pulpit,* March, 1963, pp. 7-9. A report of attempts made by some preachers to facilitate good listening by sermon discussion groups.　904

Fosdick, Harry Emerson
"Personal Counseling and Preaching," *Pastoral Psychology,* March, 1952, pp. 11-15. A minister restates his well-known thesis that sermons must deal with personal needs, contrasts this with two other types of preaching, and points out some dangers inherent in his approach.　905

Furgeson, Earl H.
"Psychology and Preaching," *Pastoral Psychology,* October, 1963, pp. 5-7. A seminary professor editorializes briefly concerning the shift from "preaching as a branch of rhetoric" to the newer understanding from the psychological point of view and suggests that psychology deals not only with the "how" of preaching, but with the "what."　906

Gibson, George Miles
"How to Listen to a Sermon," *Religion in Life,* Spring, 1943, pp. 223-30. A practical set of principles for the man in the pew.　907

Grensted, L. W.
"The Psychology of the Pulpit," *The Preacher's Quarterly,* September, 1956, pp. 252-57. A study of the living relationship between preacher and congregation. Some good thoughts on an unexplored field.　908

Hall, James T.
"Measuring the Communication of Feeling During Worship," *Pastoral Psychology,* October, 1963, pp. 50-58. A hospital chaplain reports his use of a questionnaire to assess the response of the congregation to his preaching. He concludes that preaching does communicate, not only what the preacher says, but what he is, in the context of the occasion. His conclusions are accepted by the director of pastoral care and a seminary professor who discuss the experiment in an addenda to the article.　909

Halpin, Joseph P.
"The Psychology of Preaching," *Pastoral Life,* July–August, 1958, pp. 27-31. Preaching is difficult because of the multiple elements involved. It can be made easier by keeping in mind the object, the end, and preparation of the sermon.   910

Hertz, Karl
"Preaching Is for Insiders," *Dialog,* Winter, 1964, pp. 48-54. An extremely keen analysis of the effects of preaching by a Lutheran sociologist.   911

Hiltner, Seward E.
"On Preaching," *Pastoral Psychology,* April, 1961, pp. 7-9. A professor of counseling editorializes briefly concerning his psychology of preaching. This short statement, occasioned by a current book, asserts that psychology must deal not only with the "how" of preaching, but with the "what."   912

"Pastoral Psychology and Preaching," *Pastoral Psychology,* November, 1955, pp. 9-10. A counseling professor editorializes briefly that much can be learned by a study of preaching in its dimension of interpersonal communication from preachers who report subjectively their own understandings of what goes on psychologically in preaching.   913

Hodges, Graham R.
"Counseling from the Pulpit," *Pulpit Digest,* February, 1962, pp. 21-24. The sermon should say something concretely about daily living and the great issues of society. Concerns include alcoholism, mass media, religious instruction in the home, etc. Such prophetic preaching about life as it is can accomplish much in the lives of the people.   914

Homrighausen, E. G.
"Evangelism: Ministry of the Church," *Pastoral Psychology,* December, 1956, pp. 12-16. A seminary dean offers a definition of evangelism which is bigger than "revivalism" and takes into account the insights of pastoral psychology. He also suggests some of the persistent problems of evangelism.   915

Hudson, R. Lofton
"Preaching and Mental Health," *Pastoral Psychology,* October, 1963, pp. 33-39. The director of a counseling center, seeing preaching as a strategy for inclining people in need to the revelation

which fills their needs, suggests that more attention be given to seeing people where and how they are in order to preach effectively. He suggests that some specific sermon-content is "harmful" and some is "helpful" in this strategy.   916

Hulme, William E.
"Effective Preaching Includes Counseling," *The Pulpit,* July, 1952, pp. 2-4. What kind of preaching leads to counseling.   917

Jackson, Edgar N.
"The Therapeutic Function in Preaching," *Pastoral Psychology,* June, 1950, pp. 36-39. A minister suggests how preaching is different when viewed as healing ministry to the illnesses and anxieties of individuals in his congregation. He asserts that every homily should assume the presence of a power able to solve human difficulties.   918

King, Willis J.
"Racial Conditions in the South as They Affect the Preparation of Ministers," *Review and Expositor,* July, 1937, pp. 279-86. The author, President of Gammon Theological Seminary, Atlanta, Georgia, a Negro institution, discusses the limited educational opportunities for both Negro and white in the South, the separation of the races in their church life, the limited library facilities available to Negro theological students, and the appalling lack of opportunity for Negro contact with scholars of other racial groups. He points to the danger of Negroes becoming at odds with "organized Christianity as represented by the white churches."   919

Lacour, Lawrence L.
"Revivalism and Pastoral Care," *Pastoral Psychology,* June, 1956, pp. 17-24. The director of an evangelism commission attempts to show that the current situation is ripe for a new revivalism coupled with a pastoral care approach. The analysis of revivalism is more comprehensive than the understanding of pastoral care, but the article does suggest a few basic principles of cooperation between the two.   920

Luccock, Halford E.
"What Preaching Owes to Pastoral Counseling," *Pastoral Psychology,* March, 1952, pp. 9-10, 66. A homiletics professor states very briefly six ways in which counseling helps the preacher to address people about live realities.   921

McBride, C. R.

"The Village Pulpit," *Church Management,* April, 1944, pp. 23-25. The distinctive nature (unchanging) of the village pulpit; its message is based upon life itself.   **922**

MacLennan, David A.

"Preaching and Pastoral Counseling Are One Task," *Pastoral Psychology,* March, 1952, pp. 16-20. A professor of preaching and pastoral care contends that preaching and counseling are inseparable in the effective minister, although preaching retains primacy and counseling is an indispensable partner in the endeavor.   **923**

Meiburg, Albert L.

"The Preaching Pastor," *Review and Expositor,* October, 1953, pp. 430-33. The author discusses the relationships between the pastoral and preaching duties of the minister. The article suggests that general counseling methods may be used in preaching.   **924**

Middleton, Robert G.

"Preaching to the 'New' American," *Religion in Life,* Winter, 1956, pp. 50-61. A careful analysis of the preacher's modern (new) audience.   **925**

Moeller, Charles

"Jesus Christ in the Minds of Moderns," *Lumen Vitae,* October–December, 1952, pp. 509-27. Analysis of how different groups of people look on Christ. Warnings and guides are proposed to aid in presenting Christ to these groups.   **926**

Morlan, George K.

"Preaching and Psychological Research," *Pulpit Digest,* January, 1952, pp. 15-17. In order to become continually more effective in reaching the minds of people, the church should utilize two techniques of advertising agencies—market analysis and the measurement of the response of people. The experience of the author with open-end interviews to measure sermon response is given with the conclusion that an analysis of sermons recalled revealed that word pictures were best retained; next, those that concerned the problems and interests of the people; third, those that shocked, and least of all, sermons that "stuck to religion."   **927**

Oates, Wayne

"Evangelism and Pastoral Psychology," *Pastoral Psychology,* June, 1956, pp. 7-9. A professor of pastoral care briefly editorializes on the task confronting the pastoral psychologist who would obey the great commission or the preacher-evangelist who would use the insights of pastoral care in his evangelism.   928

Pearson, Roy M.
"Preaching and the Understanding of the Congregation," *Pastoral Psychology*, March, 1959, pp. 37-46. A seminary dean attempts to describe in general terms the congregation which listens to sermons. He finds it ignorant of the faith, appalled by world and community problems, fragmented and separated from each other, rootless, unconfessedly sinful, shallowly "tolerant" of any belief, but containing a group of real Christians.   929

Reid, Clyde H.; Reuel L. Howe; Gene E. Bartlett
"A 'Give and Take' on Psychology and Preaching," *Pastoral Psychology*, February, 1964, pp. 53-59. A stimulating series of answers to a pastor's searching letter by three experts in Christian communication.   930

Robson, C. Lewis
"The Preacher as Pastor," *The Pulpit*, June, 1961, pp. 7-8. Preaching as it relates to the pastoral ministry.   931

Sangster, W. E.
"Sermons Classified According to Psychological Method," *Pastoral Psychology*, March, 1952, pp. 35-41. A minister suggests that sermons can be classified psychologically as "Authoritative, Persuasive, or Cooperative." In each, the preacher takes a different stance in relation to persons in the congregation.   932

Scotford, John R.
"Only Pastors Should Preach," *The Pulpit*, September, 1954, pp. 2-3. Criticizes "random preaching" and relates pastoral ministry to preaching.   933

Shaw, Donald F.
"Preaching to a Parade," *Church Management*, June, 1958, pp. 17-18, 31-34. Preaching in an age of rootlessness and its influence on culture; the influence of culture on preaching.   934

Shuy, Roger W.
"Learning to Listen to a Sermon," *Eternity*, September, 1965, pp. 7-9, 43. The author asserts that "dull preaching" is frequently the fault of an unskilled listener. He draws on listening theory to provide helpful listening technique.   935

Thevollier, Pierre
"God and the Man in the Street," *Lumen Vitae,* July–September, 1952, pp. 379-87. Suggestions on approaches to nonbelievers to introduce doctrines of the faith, especially belief in God.   936

Tonne, Arthur J.
"Listeners in the Pew—How Varied!" *Pastoral Life,* March, 1964, pp. 25-29. Very pertinent remarks with regard to audience analysis.   937

Voss, B. Margaret
"After Delivery, What?" *Church Management,* September, 1962, pp. 18-21. A professional counselor reports on interviews with churchgoers in response to the sermons. Some insightful elements are noted which may determine the hearer's response to the sermon.   938

Wright, Nathan, Jr.
"Touch with Glory! An Approach to an Urban Ministry," *Christianity Today,* June 7, 1963, pp. 26-28. The author sees need for a new approach to our urban population with a preaching and ministry that identifies itself with the people to whom the preacher ministers.   939

The Setting—Liturgical

Best, Ernest
"Two Modes of Encounter," *Interpretation,* January, 1963, pp. 25-38. A study of the relationship between the Eucharist and preaching.   940

Buckley, Senan, O.C.D
"The Sunday Homily," *Clergy Monthly,* October, 1963, pp. 326-34. A competent treatment of the meaning and significance of liturgical preaching, its history and legislation (prior to Vatican II); some observations are added on the selection of Sunday Gospel texts.   941

Carlton, John W.
"Preaching and Worship," *Review and Expositor,* Summer, 1965, pp. 319-34. A Baptist discusses ways in which preaching can participate in the total worship experience—and must participate, if it is biblical preaching.   942

Cass, John

"Sermon Forms," *American Ecclesiastical Review*, April, 1941, pp. 368-75. The nature of the homily, instruction, and formal sermon with emphasis on the first; the distinction of these types and their possible concurrence. A not very useful treatment of the subject. It does, however, present the most fundamental facts clearly. **943**

Crichton, J. D.

"Liturgical Preaching," *Clergy Review*, December, 1960, pp. 725-33. Excellent article on the true nature and purpose of liturgical preaching: first, as the continued proclamation of God's Word as found in the Epistles and Gospels and, secondly, as a preparation for the central liturgical mystery that follows in the Mass. Includes also practical tips on building a liturgical sermon. **944**

Darby, J. H.

"Sunday Sermons," *Clergy Review*, October, 1954, pp. 592-600. A practical and mature consideration of the problems facing the Sunday preacher. Stresses the needs of the complex, worldly, semipelagian congregation; bewails the absence of a Christian humanism which would link their faith to their lives; looks to the preacher to instruct and elevate his people. **945**

Evans, Illtud, O.P.

"The Place of the Sermon," *Clergy Review*, November, 1951, pp. 283-90. An excellent discussion of the place of the sermon within the liturgy. Notable both for the strong historical argument about the sermon in the Mass and for the practical, temperate suggestions on realizing this in the liturgy of today. **946**

Farmer, Herbert H.

"Preaching and Worship," *Review and Expositor*, July, 1946, pp. 243-60. An Englishman, lecturing on preaching, emphasizes the fact that "the intention of worship" should govern preparation for preaching and that the sermon should be part of true worship. **947**

Finlator, W. W.

"A Church with a Chancel," *Review and Expositor*, October, 1955, pp. 460-65. A pastor traces the process of changing from a pulpit-centered church auditorium to a chancel sanctuary for worship in his own pastorate. Several effects are described. **948**

Fischer, Balthasar

"The Homily: Biblical Phrase-Preaching," *Furrow*, September, 1965, pp. 527-36. In this informative and practical article, the author recommends, as an alternative to the time-consuming homily on a whole scriptural passage, a homily on a single sentence or phrase from the text. This, he insists, would not be an arbitrary rebounding from the text into topical, thematic preaching, but a thorough penetration of a single segment of the passage. After substantial explanation of his theory, Father Fischer offers an extended example from an epistle, gospel, and introit psalm. 949

Fournier, Elie

"Morality and Liturgical Preaching," *Lumen Vitae*, March, 1961, pp. 27-40. This excellent article points out that doctrine ultimately has a moral implication. It is not some truth to be merely known, but must be acted upon. The preacher, in the liturgical action, need not fear moral preaching. But he must preach Christian morality as it appears in the Scriptures. The primary feasts of the year present a broad outline for presentation of Christian morality. All phases of morality are to be preached, including hell. How this can be done is shown with apt quotations from *Mediator Dei*, the sermons of the Fathers, and papal allocutions to Lenten preachers. 950

"When the Council Speaks of the Sermon," *Lumen Vitae*, March, 1964, pp. 115-30. In this enlightening commentary on the Constitution on the Liturgy, the author stresses that the sermon must not bring into the celebration a subject extraneous to it— those topical sermons that "creep into the celebration like a foreign body." He demonstrates how it is possible to start from the liturgical texts and adequately explain the mysteries of faith and the rules of Christian life. 951

Gavaler, Campion, O.S.B.

"Theology of the Sermon as Part of the Mass," *Worship*, March, 1964, pp. 201-7. This essay demonstrates that the liturgy of the Word together with the eucharistic liturgy makes up but one celebration and then suggests a practical methodology for preaching an authentic liturgical sermon. A truly significant article, fully in accord with the best theological thought on the subject and the Constitution on the Liturgy. 952

Grabowski, Stanley

"Emphasis on Liturgical Preaching," *Pastoral Life*, February, 1964, pp. 31-34. A fair summary of some of the recent thoughts on the theology of preaching and liturgical preaching.　　　　953

Haig, Frank R., S.J.

"Why Not a Daily Sermon?" *Homiletic and Pastoral Review*, December, 1964, pp. 209-11. A cogent exhortation for a daily homily, a plea fully in accord with the recommendations of the Constitution on the Liturgy.　　　　954

Hellriegel, Martin B.

"Church and Parish," *Orate Fratres*, October–November, 1951, pp. 495-97. An article urging that a good sermon on the "important realities" of our faith, or a well-prepared homily, should be part of *every* Sunday (and even principal daily) Mass to help bring the faithful to the altar. The sermon is an integral part of the Mass and should form an organic unity with the church year.　　　　955

Hofinger, Johannes, S.J.

"Kergyma in the Service of Liturgy in the Missions," *Lumen Vitae*, March, 1959, pp. 92-102. The catechetical function of the liturgy demands preaching to explain the readings to the people. The preaching should not overshadow the aspect of worship, but should give worship a healthy reality. The sermon at Mass should not be an interruption. It should take its proper place in the service of the Word and provide an initiation into the Eucharist.　956

James, Stanley B.

"Altar and Pulpit," *Irish Ecclesiastical Record*, April, 1939, pp. 408-14. Preaching should have the nature of commentary on the worship offered and concretely presented. The author explains why and how preaching of this kind is to be produced.　　957

"Priests and Prophets," *Orate Fratres*, February, 1949, pp. 145-49. The author argues for the interdependence of altar and pulpit as a necessary condition for the effectiveness of both. In the pulpit we can and should "bring the truth embodied in the liturgy to bear on the contemporary mood, and apply it to the individual and social circumstances of the hour." The action of the priest should have a direct bearing on the particular spiritual and moral problems of the congregation, as the prophets of old did.　　　　958

Jarman, W. J.
"The Context of Preaching," *Encounter,* 1963, pp. 135-72.
Preaching considered as integral part of worship with theological
and artistic suggestions for the free worship of the Disciples of
Christ.   959

Kraus, J. E.; Thomas Duffy
"Liturgical Preaching," *Worship,* June–July, 1963, pp. 424-27.
A report of progress made toward understanding the nature and
structure of the homily, as undertaken by the Ohio Regional
Committee of the Liturgical Conference.   960

Lantz, John Edward
"The Setting of the Congregation," *Church Management,*
April, 1948, pp. 54-55, 57-58. Good preaching is most effective in
the proper setting.   961

Leahy, Frederick S.
"Preaching and Worship," *Christianity Today,* September 12,
1960, pp. 5-6. The author makes a discerning reply to the
modern cry for less preaching and more worship.   962

Lechner, Robert, C.PP.S.
"Liturgical Preaching," *Worship,* November, 1963, pp. 639-50.
Very scholarly analysis of the function of the homily within the
liturgy. Lechner claims that the challenge is to invoke a response
to what is preached; a free act of saying "yes" to what is announced. A statement of mere fact or a syllogism cannot elicit this
free act; the Word is better understood in the categories of value
and action rather than truth. Strong defense of the homily as an
integral part of the Mass (preaching within the liturgy *is* liturgy).   963

Long, Edward
"Preaching and the Liturgy," *Furrow,* April, 1953, pp. 201-6.
Arguments are offered for using liturgical sources in preaching
and coordinating sermons with the liturgical year.   964

McBride, Alfred, O.Praem.
"How to Do a Homily," *Bible Today,* October, 1965, pp. 1254-
60. With a sprightly style, McBride exhorts homilists to be men
of the Book, fully attuned to modern scholarship and the demands of adaptation to varying audiences; two examples are also
offered in illustration of how to present a homily that will lead
men to the saving deed of the eucharistic action.   965

Macleod, Donald
"Worship and Evangelism," *Princeton Seminary Bulletin*, May, 1957, pp. 26-32. Deals primarily with worship but indicates the relationship of preaching to worship.   **966**

Marshall, Peter
"The Setting for the Sermon," *Religion in Life*, Spring, 1945, pp. 195-204. An excellent analysis of the elements essential as an effective setting for the sermon which is considered an integral part of worship.   **967**

Noble, Charles C.
"A New Deal in Preaching," *Today's Speech*, January, 1957, pp. 8-11. This article stresses the renewed emphasis on the importance of the sermon in liturgical life and free church worship. It presents a very helpful perspective.   **968**

Norris, Frank B., S.S.
"Preaching the Word of God," *North American Liturgical Week* (Proceedings), 1964, pp. 217-20. A short but excellent treatment of the Mass homily: its definition, nature, relevance to the congregation, and continuity with the sacramental action, with a salutary warning about topical sermons.   **969**

Orchard, W. E.
"The Place of Preaching in the Catholic Church," *Catholic World*, April, 1941, pp. 46-50. For the year in which it was written, a surprisingly enlightened treatment of the sermon as an integral part of the Mass.   **970**

O'Shea, William, S.S.
"The Sermon Is Part of the Mass," *Homiletic and Pastoral Review*, March, 1960, pp. 517-26. This article is one of the most significant contributions in the last decade to the renewal of liturgical preaching in the United States. In demonstrating that the homily is an integral part of the Mass and that it must seek to expound the Mass texts in the context of the sacrifice, the author shared with the American clergy the very best of recent European scholarship, all of which has received the highest endorsement in the Constitution on the Liturgy of Vatican II.   **971**

Parsch, Pius
"Sunday Sermons," *Orate Fratres*, January, 1948, pp. 101-8. The liturgy offers the preacher a vast wealth of matter, but there are misunderstandings about the liturgical sermon. Parsch studies

the entire question from a practical and theoretical point of view. His position follows from the fact that the sermon is organically part of the very structure of the Mass.   972

Peterson, Hugh
   "Come, Let Us Worship," *Review and Expositor,* October, 1945, pp. 413-26. A theological seminary educator points out quite cogently how the preacher and his themes may interfere with congregational worship. He then proposes solutions to the problems.   973

Plastoras, James C., C.M.
   "Ritualist or Minister of the Word?" *Worship,* August–September, 1965, pp. 400-411. An important article, based on sound sacramental theology, demonstrating the crucial significance of the priest's role as an effective preacher of God's Word, with particular attention being paid to liturgical celebration.   974

   "Preaching as an Act of Worship," *Christianity Today,* September 12, 1960, pp. 20-21. Defining preaching as "the divinely appointed means of bringing the listener face to face with God as revealed in Jesus Christ," the author goes on to discuss how this can be done.   975

Rees, Paul S.
   "The Minister's Workshop: The Art of Preaching as an Act of Worship," *Christianity Today,* May 10, 1963, p. 22. The author wrestles with the present situation in which "it is implied—and occasionally declared—that in the liturgy *God* is acting, while in preaching it is *man.*" His thesis is that the sermon cannot be considered apart from the congregational context.   976

Richards, H. J.
   "The Word of God at Mass," *Clergy Review,* September, 1961, pp. 543-47. Forceful discussion of the need to appreciate the first part of the Mass, the instructional part, including the homily. Notes the twofold presence of Christ in the Mass: in the Word and in the Eucharist.   977

Richardson, Cyril Charles
   "Preaching and Worship," *Religion in Life,* Summer, 1942, pp. 396-402. A significant analysis of the relationship of "Word" and "sacrament," and a special plea for effective preparation of liturgy.   978

Sloyan, Gerard S.
"Faith Comes Through Hearing," *North American Liturgical Week* (Proceedings), 1965, pp. 125-31. Exhilarating study of the necessity for the full sign in liturgical celebration, possible only when the homily is truly God himself addressing man in the most personal and direct way, inviting a faithful response.   979

"Preaching at Mass," *North American Liturgical Week* (Proceedings), 1963, pp. 191-94. This short but insightful article points up the necessity for parochial preaching that is subordinate to the Word of God, that is, a preaching that is biblically oriented, free from pious moralism, archeological data, and other similar encroachments.   980

Stowell, Jerome, C.P.
"Only Half a Priest," *The Priest*, October, 1964, pp. 864-68. A short but excellent article offering practical suggestions for composing authentic homilies for the celebration of the Eucharist.   981

Tonne, Arthur J.
"What Is a Homily?" *Pastoral Life*, November, 1964, pp. 33-38. Some good points are brought out in this short article, but further supplementary reading will have to be done before an adequate answer to the question posed in the title is found.   982

Toohey, William, C.S.C. et al.
"Let's Look at the Homily," *Homiletic and Pastoral Review*, July, 1965, pp. 832-36. Segments from a panel discussion on the Mass homily, recorded at the 1965 Catholic Homiletic Society convention, St. Louis, Mo.   983

Toohey, William, C.S.C.
"Preaching and the Constitution on the Liturgy," *Yearbook of Liturgical Studies*, 1964, pp. 15-28. An extensive commentary on the aspects of the Constitution pertinent for preaching; combines a consideration of the theory and principles involved with practical suggestions for actual structuring of preaching within the context of the liturgy.   984

The Setting—Special Occasions

Armstrong, April Oursler
"A Hard Look at the Parish Mission," *The Priest*, June, 1959, pp. 472-76. In this honest, candid, provocative article, a laywoman

gives her reactions to a typical parish mission. She adds indications for what positive means could be used to improve the mission.   985

Auw, Andre, C.P.
"Community Retreats, Same Song, New Lyrics," *Review for Religious,* September, 1965, pp. 797-802. Informative discussion of community-centered retreats, where the effort is to create an atmosphere of real community, in which participants experience the love of Christ flowing amongst them.   986

Bassett, R. J.
"Want to Preach a Retreat?" *The Priest,* October, 1962, pp. 867-70. Some hints on preparing for retreats and other preaching opportunities; aimed especially at the diocesan priest.   987

Biskupek, A., S.V.D.
"The Mass as Subject of the Retreat," *American Ecclesiastical Review,* May, 1938, pp. 445-58; June, 1938, pp. 116-27. Demonstration of how the topic of the Mass might be used as a means of treating the elements necessary for a thorough renewal of the spiritual life.   988

Browne, Patrick W.
"Outdoor Preaching," *American Ecclesiastical Review,* September, 1936, pp. 284-91. This type of preaching is not new or foreign to the church: an effort to share with others the treasure of the goodness God has given. Seminarians could do it during the summer to concretize their theology; the field is vast in the U. S.   989

Byrne, W.
"The Priest on the Mission and Catholic Action," *Irish Ecclesiastical Record,* January, 1947, pp. 1-10. A lecture given to senior ecclesiastical students suggesting the preaching of the great crusade; the awakening of the response to the great call for action, enlisting the masses in the service of the apostolate; the mystical body of Christ as a means of Catholic action.   990

Cavanaugh, Paul W., S.J.
"Twilight Retreats," *The Priest,* December, 1965, pp. 1042-47. Helpful suggestions for conducting four-hour retreats for public-school Catholics, as to the organizational demands; but of questionable value on the topic of retreat theme and conference material.   991

Daves, Michael
"The Funeral Sermon," *The Pulpit,* September, 1964, pp. 26-27.
A criticism of some contemporary funeral sermons and some
guidelines for preaching that will meet the needs of mourners.   **992**

"The Preacher on Television," *The Pulpit,* August, 1961,
pp. 27-29. Advice on religious speaking on television.   **993**

Delcuve, George, S.J.
"Should We Still Proclaim the Gospel?" *Lumen Vitae,* December, 1965, pp. 651-63. Important study on evangelization, in the
light of Vatican II's Constitution on the Church, which demonstrates the continuing need for careful concern for the church's
missionary preaching.   **994**

Donovan, Victor J., C.P.
"Apostolate to the Jews in the Pulpit," *Homiletic and Pastoral
Review,* December, 1952, pp. 234-44. The author speaks of the
usefulness of preaching about the Jews in sermons to correct
the ignorant impressions of many Catholics about them and
perhaps to lead some Jews to an appreciation of the church.   **995**

Ebner, James D. R.
"The Junior Pews Talk Back," *Homiletic and Pastoral Review,*
November, 1949, pp. 144-52. Fine study of what boys want in a
retreat master—mainly kindness and interest in their souls. Many
other qualifications are brought out, plus the attitudes needed.   **996**

Farmer, Hugh
"St. Augustine on Catechizing," *Life of the Spirit,* October,
1958, pp. 172-81. A summary of Augustine's work on subject
matter and the methods of catechetics, preaching, and teaching.   **997**

Finley, James Fenlon, C.S.P.
"The Dialogue Mission Presents Christ," *Lumen Vitae,* October–December, 1952, pp. 543-48. The dialogue mission technique is illustrated with the divinity of Christ as the subject
matter. The article states the purposes and planning for such a
dialogue.   **998**

"The Sunday Mass Mission," *Homiletic and Pastoral Review,*
February, 1955, pp. 392-98. Ideas for those who do not make the
mission. A plan via a series of five Sundays. Of possible historical
interest, but generally outdated by the Constitution on the
Liturgy and the demands of proper liturgical preaching.   **999**

Fischer, Balthasar

"New Problems in Preaching Occasioned by the Restoration of Holy Week," *Lumen Vitae,* March, 1959, pp. 103-12. Father Fischer comments on preaching during each of the major celebrations of Holy Week. He notes times and subjects to be considered. One section is devoted to preparation of the laity during lent. A third section is devoted to the consequences for preaching during the rest of the year.   1000

Geaney, Dennis J., O.S.A.

"Is the Parish Mission Outdated?" *Worship,* January, 1964, pp. 95-100. Illuminating article describing an experiment with a Bible-centered mission, an approach much in line with the contemporary call of the church for more preaching based on sacred Scripture, and the recent Liturgical Constitution endorsement of Bible services.   1001

"A Priest on Stage," *Today,* March, 1963, pp. 11-13. Excellent tips from a veteran retreat master on preaching to adolescents.   1002

Gille, A.

"The Teaching of Religion," *Homiletic and Pastoral Review,* October, 1942, pp. 59-63; November, 1942, pp. 147-51; December, 1942, pp. 260-63; January, 1943, pp. 335-38. Indications of a revised approach to catechesis based on child psychology.   1003

Henry, H. T.

"Preaching to Children," *Homiletic and Pastoral Review,* March, 1942, pp. 510-18. A fair article on particular audience approach.   1004

"The Priest at Public Assemblies," *Homiletic and Pastoral Review,* June, 1936, pp. 906-15. Some good ideas are offered on this type of special preaching.   1005

Hofinger, Johannes, S.J.

"Adaptation in Missionary Catechesis," *Lumen Vitae,* July–September, 1952, pp. 425-31. A general outline of broad areas of study needed to allow the missionary to adapt to a people.   1006

Ignatius, F., C.P.

"School Missions," *Clergy Review,* December, 1959, pp. 720-33. A highly practical article outlining the reasons for conducting school missions, together with detailed instructions on technique.   1007

Kay, Hugh
"A Layman's Point of View," *The Way*, July, 1961, pp. 214-23.
Candid suggestions from a layman to help correct the misconceptions of modern retreatants, to whom "God the Father is an austere, overshadowing law-giver, His Son the alchemist of the grace we so frequently confuse with magic, the Holy Ghost the one who waves the wand." 1008

Kennedy, Gerald
"Preaching Effectively to College Students," *Religion in Life*, Summer, 1946, pp. 391-402. Some very practical suggestions are made for preachers in college centers. 1009

Kevin, Neil
"Apologetics for Undergraduates," *Irish Ecclesiastical Record*, June, 1942, pp. 530-34. Some observations on apologetical sermons in general and on Ronald Knox's *In Soft Garments* in particular. 1010

Klee, Robert A.
"A Survey on Street Preaching," *The Priest*, July, 1945, pp. 34-37; August, 1945, pp. 22-25. Review of a survey on street-preaching methods, personnel, and results in 1944 and the years immediately preceding. 1011

Lechner, Robert, C.PP.S.
"Rethinking the Annual Retreat," *Review for Religious*, March, 1963, pp. 211-17. Very general discussion of some preliminary points prerequisite to any revision of the format for the yearly retreat; lays a good groundwork in the spirit of the modern renewal in theology. 1012

Lee, W. Howard
"A Sermon at Funerals," *Church Management*, February, 1954, p. 16. Argues for the preaching of a sermon at funerals. 1013

LeFrois, Bernard J., S.V.D.
"A Marian Retreat for Men," *American Ecclesiastical Review*, November, 1956, pp. 300-308. Outlines of conferences given during a retreat based on Marian topics; of some value. 1014

Leven, Stephen A.
"Can Street Preaching Help?" *Homiletic and Pastoral Review*, April, 1937, pp. 691-97. The effectiveness, fittingness, and some practical conclusions of street preaching. 1015

McBriarty, Anthony, C.SS.R.
"Parish Missions," *American Ecclesiastical Review,* March, 1940, pp. 193-207. An article on general mission-giving techniques and norms.   1016

McCarthy, Dennis F., O.M.I.
"Revitalizing the Parish Mission," *Homiletic and Pastoral Review,* November, 1965, pp. 137-42. A rather standard appraisal of the total programing necessary for a successful mission, with specific attention placed on the steps of planning and preparation.   1017

McDermott, Eric, S.J.
"A Scriptural Retreat Plan," *Worship,* November, 1965, pp. 493-97. An interesting proposal on a retreat format based on Bible themes, combining in each session a short conference, prayerful reading of Scripture, group-sharing of the nourishment received, and private prayer.   1018

McLoughlin, Seamus
"Confraternity Preaching," *Furrow,* April, 1951, pp. 237-45. Rather discursive treatment of preaching at evening devotions.   1019

Malloy, Richard A., C.S.P.
"A Kerygmatic Parish Mission," *The Priest,* October, 1964, pp. 859-63; December, 1964, pp. 1046-52. A refreshingly positive approach to the parish mission, advocating topics incorporating contemporary advances in the appreciation of the gospel message (the *good* news, not the bad news) —God's wonderful deeds in the history of salvation; the author also suggests many practical points to help make this event a true parish renewal.   1020

Marie, Sister Vera, O.C.D.
"Thoughts on Retreats for Nuns," *Review for Religious,* July, 1964, pp. 473-80. A very perceptive and candid treatment by a sister on the question of giving nuns' retreats; suggestions are given to retreat masters for content and general approach to different facets of this important work.   1021

Mead, Jude, C.P.
"The High School Retreat," *Homiletic and Pastoral Review,* May, 1956, pp. 640-53. In an interesting essay, the author speaks of a retreat in Catholic high schools and academies, for Catholics in public high school, and the closed retreat.   1022

Mereto, Joseph J.
"Missions or Retreats for High and Grade School Pupils," *Homiletic and Pastoral Review,* October, 1951, pp. 36-43. This article adequately treats of the value and need of these missions and retreats and touches various problems met in such a task, as well as conference topics and time schedules.
1023

Mullins, Sister Patrick Jerome, O.P.
"Retreats for Sisters: A New Look," *American Ecclesiastical Review,* December, 1965, pp. 411-20. Of interest to all who conduct retreats for sisters, this article offers suggestions and observations on the question of silence, possibilities for retreatant dialogue, schedule variations, and conference topics; an urgent appeal for a retreat of sound theological content and dynamic personal prayer.
1024

Nebreda, Alphonso M., S.J.
"Conversion: Key-Stone of the Missionary Process," *Lumen Vitae,* December, 1963, pp. 661-78. The author discusses the precise nature of conversion, as the human answer to the divine proclamation of good tidings (kerygma), against the background of the three processes of pre-evangelization, evangelization, and catechesis. Extremely important study for missionary and catechetical preaching.
1025

"East Asian Study Week on Mission Catechetics," *Lumen Vitae,* December, 1962, pp. 717-30. Pages 723-25 present a schema and commentary for the kerygmatic approach to the missions. The stages of pre-evangelization, evangelization, and catechesis grew from Fr. Hofinger's system and were much discussed at this Bangkok Study Week in 1962.
1026

"The Preparation of the Message," *Lumen Vitae,* September, 1961, pp. 399-416. The necessity of pre-evangelization in mission areas (pagan and dechristianized) is presented with reference to kerygma preaching. The basic purpose is to compare modern mission facts with the situation of the apostolic preaching reported in Acts. "How can anyone who has no idea of sin understand the doctrine of salvation? . . . what liberation does the pagan of today sigh after?"
1027

O'Riordan, Sean
"Round the Reviews," *Furrow,* August, 1951, pp. 465-72. A report on the proceedings and papers read at the Belgian Missionary Bodies at Namur—a meeting devoted to the special subject of missionary preaching.
1028

Overman, Conleth, C.P.
"The American Street-Preaching Movement," *Homiletic and Pastoral Review*, March, 1946, pp. 432-37. An interesting and helpful treatment of this type of special preaching.　　1029

Pargiter, J., C.SS.R.
"Parochial Missions," *Clergy Review*, November, 1957, pp. 641-50. A prudent yet progressive discussion of the function and utility of the parish mission stressing both the continual need for the mission and the necessity of adaptation to modern conditions.　　1030

Quinlivan, Thomas, O.M.I.
"Retreats for Priests: An Approach Positive," *Homiletic and Pastoral Review*, December, 1956, pp. 240-41. An effective plea for a retreat that inspires, lifts up, and encourages.　　1031

Ronan, Edwin J., C.P.
"In Defense of the Old Parish Mission," *Homiletic and Pastoral Review*, March, 1961, pp. 562-70. The author believes there is a need for many of the "hard sayings." He points out that the old style parish mission lends itself to this and offers ideas on "operation doorbells," leakage, concept of mission, sermon content. A traditional viewpoint.　　1032

"Missions and Sermons," *American Ecclesiastical Review*, October, 1936, pp. 396-400. A defense of the old style mission sermons.　　1033

Schmiedeler, Edgar, O.S.B.
"Motor Missions," *American Ecclesiastical Review*, February, 1939, pp. 132-42. This article is a general report on the rapid development of the motor missions in the rural sections of the South, Midwest and Far West, up until the year 1939. General results and examples of techniques used by motor-mission priests are cited. The reader will find historical interest in the early development of missions. The effectiveness of street preaching in "breaking the ice" for many people who have never come in direct contact with the Catholic religion is clearly brought out.　　1034

Scriven, G. F.
"Retreats for Small Children," *Clergy Review*, February, 1944, pp. 67-69. A brief description, from the experience of the author, on how to give a school retreat to children. Includes practical

suggestions on the style of preaching to be used, on the need for hymns, processions, and spiritual exercises.   1035

Sheerin, John B., C.S.P.
"Opening a Retreat," *Homiletic and Pastoral Review,* February, 1946, pp. 333-37. This article stresses how to give incentives to recollection and offers some very good leading questions.   1036

"Pulpit Dialogues," *Homiletic and Pastoral Review,* March, 1945, pp. 410-16. A very interesting article; the idea of pulpit dialogue is worth looking into as a means to use in contemporary preaching.   1037

"Retreat for Children," *Homiletic and Pastoral Review,* March, 1946, pp. 401-6. Speaks of the difficulties and gives some good hints and insights.   1038

Siekmann, T. C.
"The Spiritual Direction of Teen-Age Boys," *Homiletic and Pastoral Review,* June, 1946, pp. 651-62. A helpful article on this form of special preaching.   1039

Siqueira, J., S.J.
"Retreats for the Clergy," *Homiletic and Pastoral Review,* October, 1943, pp. 37-40. This article treats of the lack of a truly sacerdotal retreat for the clergy—one based upon the Sacrament of Holy Orders. The author makes worthwhile suggestions as to the content of such a retreat and includes a select bibliography on the priesthood.   1040

Smith, Gregory M., O.Carm.
"The Parish Mission," *North American Liturgical Week* (Proceedings) , 1963, pp. 140-46. This excellent study examines a crucial area of preaching with profound perception; it is an urgent appeal for a renewal of missionary preaching, with scriptural, Christocentric, eschatological, ecclesial, and existential dimensions.   1041

Smith, William C.
"The Priest in Radio," *American Ecclesiastical Review,* October, 1948, pp. 285-92; November, 1948, pp. 367-74; December, 1948, pp. 424-35; February, 1949, pp. 113-22. A four-part treatment of the various phases of the topic: the power of radio for religious purpose; audience analysis; formulation of content; technique of presentation; practical matters of program arrangement (publicity, music, finances) .   1042

Stone, Theodore G.
"The Bangkok Study Week," *Worship*, February, 1963, pp. 184-90. Report of an important gathering of catechetical experts, of special import for missionary and catechetical preaching.   **1043**

Sullivan, Walter, C.S.P.
"Doctrinal Missions," *American Ecclesiastical Review*, August, 1948, pp. 115-17. A plea not to dismiss methods that have been found excellent in the past and are still feasible and successful today.   **1044**

Turner, A.
"More About Sermons," *Clergy Review*, November, 1962, pp. 675-79. A special-interest report by a retired factory owner who established a religious atmosphere in his factory, with factory chapel, evening Mass, and preaching by visiting bishops and priests. Practicality of the sermons is noted; in that authentic setting they related the life of the faith to the life of the factory.   **1045**

Walsh, Nicolas E.
"Missions and Retreats: Do They Differ?" *American Ecclesiastical Review*, September, 1949, pp. 192-202. The individual natures of these two types of preaching are contrasted, through consideration of their respective purposes; there is also an examination of the differences of the varying topics of each format.   **1046**

Weitzel, Eugene J., C.S.V.
"The Seminar—A New Approach to High School Retreats," *American Ecclesiastical Review*, November, 1965, pp. 316-24. Valuable discussion of recent experiments attempting to make Christianity relevant for teens. Various retreat formats are considered, through which there runs a pattern of talks, discussions, and recreation.   **1047**

The Sermon

Allen, Marion C.
"The Minister's Use of Literature," *Religion in Life*, Winter, 1958, pp. 86-97. Some very practical suggestions for using literature in sermons.   **1048**

Bair, Charles R.
"A Sermonic Filing System," *Church Management*, October, 1936, p. 18. Contains helpful suggestions which are well illustrated.   **1049**

Bell, James E.
"Illustrating the Sermon," *Pulpit Digest,* April, 1937, pp. 18-22. A wide-ranging discussion, citing contemporary and earlier preachers.　　　　1050

Blackwood, Andrew W.
"Expository Preaching: Preparing for a Year of Pulpit Joy," *Christianity Today,* June 8, 1962, pp. 16-17. The author suggests a pattern for planning a church year of expository sermons.　1051

"The Mastery of the Sermon," *Pulpit Digest,* May, 1947, pp. 34-38. The minister should prepare his sermons by budgeting sufficient time for study, outlining, writing out his sermon in full, and then delivering the sermon without notes.　　1052

"The Minister's Workshop: Finding Materials for a Sermon," *Christianity Today,* February 1, 1963, p. 50. A sharing of ideas on finding two types of materials for a sermon—biblical and contemporary.　　　　1053

"The Minister's Workshop: How to Plan a Teaching Sermon," *Christianity Today,* August 2, 1963, p. 43. The title suggests the contents of the article. The procedures given are quite traditional.　　　　1054

Blakey, Joseph
"Style and the Preacher," *Church Management,* February, 1962, pp. 18, 21. An appeal for more attention to the use of style in preaching.　　　　1055

Bodgener, J. H.
"Poets of Today and the Preacher," *The Preacher's Quarterly,* June, 1956, pp. 175-78. A short article with one or two useful insights for the preacher who wonders what to do with modern poetry.　　　　1056

Bolton, Robert H.
"Where's That Illustration?" *Church Management,* April, 1964, pp. 18-21. Five filing systems and some great preachers who use them.　　　　1057

Buchanan, Henry D.
"The Language of Preaching," *American Ecclesiastical Review,* December, 1949, pp. 475-77. "Unless we preach the application of the gospel in current terms, we are not reaching the people's minds." A point well made.　　　　1058

Burns, John
"Need of Sound, Terse, Practical Preaching," *American Ecclesiastical Review,* April, 1939, pp. 153-59.　　1059

Callaghan, J. Calvin
"How Long Should a Sermon Be?" *Today's Speech,* February, 1964, pp. 10-11, 35. The author asserts that sermon length should vary, depending on the subject and the situation.　　1060

Carroll, William, S.J.
"Notes on Medieval Preaching," *Homiletic and Pastoral Review,* November, 1944, pp. 108-16. This article deals with a characteristic feature of medieval preaching: love for symbolism.　　1061

Carter, Manfred A.
"Poetry Using Ministers," *Religion in Life,* Spring, 1953, pp. 243-50. A minister and poet, the author suggests how poetry can be used to homiletic advantage.　　1062

Cass, John
"How to Declare the Word of God," *American Ecclesiastical Review,* July, 1940, pp. 81-89. The question of the article is how to arrive at the appropriate style for preaching. Should one use rhetoric and persuasion in sermons or simply declare the message of God in straightforward statements? Authorities for both sides are brought forth, and it is left to the reader to choose his style.　　1063

"Sermon Interest or Weariness," *American Ecclesiastical Review,* September, 1940, pp. 230-40. The preacher should try to shed new light on an old subject. His sermon should include appeals to reason and the emotions, plus a story or illustration.　　1064

Chrisman, Lewis H.
"Confessions of a Sermon-Taster," *Church Management,* January, 1955, pp. 16, 18-19. The value of reading sermons and how to improve your style; in addition, sermons used as a means of gaining an insight into a particular historical age.　　1065

"The Preacher's English," *Church Management,* January, 1936, pp. 181-84. A "how-to" article on the development of preaching style.　　1066

"Pulpit English—Living or Dead?" *Church Management,* December, 1947, pp. 8-10. The use of careless English is a sin which approaches the deceitful use of the Word of God.　　1067

"What Is Good English?" *Church Management,* December, 1946, pp. 8-10. The effectiveness of a public speaker depends to a large degree upon his mastery of English.   1068

Christians, Wilbur Carl
"Twenty-Five Ministers on Sermon Filing," *Church Management,* February, 1938, pp. 253-54. The results of a survey of twenty-five ministers concerning their filing system.   1069

Connors, Charles, C.S.SP.
"The Sermon Hatched on Saturday Night," *Homiletic and Pastoral Review,* September, 1957, pp. 1094-99. Worthwhile suggestions on proper remote preparation.   1070

Cotter, John A., S.J.
"Preaching and the Young Priest," *American Ecclesiastical Review,* January, 1944, pp. 43-47. This article presents excellent ideas on how to organize a sermon. The author also proposes a good classical sermon plan.   1071

Cox, James W.
"Forming the Pattern of the Sermon," *Princeton Seminary Bulletin,* June, 1965, pp. 31-38. An insightful discussion on arranging sermonic ideas.   1072

Coyle, Edward, S.S.
"Toward an Effective Oral Style," *American Ecclesiastical Review,* February, 1940, pp. 97-107. Describes oral style, or that special manner of expressing thought by such a choice and combination of words as will be made in view of direct address to a body of hearers. Oral style borrows its tone, its vocabulary, its turns of thought, expression, and frankly communicative spirit from conversation.   1073

Crocker, Lionel
"Poetry in the Pulpit," *Central States Speech Journal,* Fall, 1956, pp. 33-35. Since poetry is a helpful ornament in sermon preparation, it should be used well. This article presents suggestions about the incorporation of poetry, as well as some principles of oral interpretation of poems.   1074

Daly, John K.
"The Word for Preaching," *The Priest,* May, 1956, pp. 410-11. Every sermon should have an issue. It should begin somewhere and go somewhere. The priest must attack a problem and handle it as a personal involvement and as a specific concern.   1075

Davidson, J. A.

"Beginning a File-System for Sermon Materials," *Church Management,* June, 1965, pp. 8, 22, 29. Brief description of a simple filing system for sermon materials. In addition, some helpful suggestions and pointers.   1076

"Humor and Homiletics," *The Pulpit,* July, 1952, p. 20. Principles and importance of the use of humor in preaching.   1077

"Some Cautions on Sermon Illustrations," *The Pulpit,* July, 1960, p. 26. Dangers to avoid in the use of illustrations.   1078

Delaney, S. P.

"The Preparation of Sermons," *Clergy Review,* August, 1935, pp. 109-14. Practical discussion of four types of sermon preparation: (1) the casual armchair type, (2) the peripatetic, (3) the formal written sermon, (4) the meditative type which begins and ends in prayer. Also, the suggestion that the sermon be divided into three parts appealing respectively to the imagination, to the mind informed by faith, and, finally, to the emotions.   1079

Doherty, Martin W.

"Fine Language in Catholic Press and Pulpit," *American Ecclesiastical Review,* April, 1936, pp. 391-99. The author speaks of the absolute necessity of speaking in the simple language of the people both for the Catholic press and pulpit. Simplicity must be substituted for erudition since the message of God is for the people, and the ability of most to understand complicated and theologically phrased sermons is severely limited.   1080

Drinkwater, F. H.

"The Sacrament of the Word," *Furrow,* April, 1953, pp. 187-92. The writer suggests that we can never do any harm and may do some extra good by concentrating simply on choosing the best words for what we have to say.   1081

"We Have to Use Words," *Furrow,* April, 1951, pp. 213-22. Convincing argument for the use of "poetic-simple" language in sermons, i.e., words that are both understandable and image-arousing.   1082

Dunkle, William F., Jr.

"Planning a Year's Work," *The Pulpit,* September, 1963, pp. 7-9. The values of planned preaching, along with some suggestions.   1083

Fortune, Alonzo W.
"How the Sermon Grows," *College of the Bible Quarterly*, October, 1945, pp. 17-31. A former professor of pastoral theology suggests that sermons are not made or found or put together— they grow "out of our lives." In an abstract of a course on preaching, he discusses the way in which this growth takes place and some of the constituent elements, as well as some of the forms the sermon takes.   1084

Foster, John
"When We Preach Church History," *Christian Advocate*, February 16, 1961, pp. 9-10. A professor of ecclesiastical history champions church history as a valuable source of sermonic materials.   1085

Francis, David N.
"The Use of Illustrations," *The Preacher's Quarterly*, June, 1963, pp. 111-16. Defines what illustrations are for, rather than discussing their types. Some good tests of illustrations.   1086

Frost, S. B.
"The Preacher's Beginnings," *The Preacher's Quarterly*, March, 1956, pp. 4-10. A useful discussion of sermon introductions and endings. Familiar observations, but all will be well taken.   1087

"The Preacher's Illustrations," *The Preacher's Quarterly*, September, 1955, pp. 292-97. Illustrations in the service of relevance are a "must" for preaching. Types of illustrations are discussed. Value of biblical illustrations emphasized.   1088

"The Preacher's Sermon Construction," *The Preacher's Quarterly*, December, 1955, pp. 388-95. A discussion of four structures of sermons: formless, classic, straight line, and the point. Orderly and thoughtful.   1089

"The Preacher's Text," *The Preacher's Quarterly*, June, 1955, pp. 195-200. A discussion of a rationale for use of texts, pitfalls to be avoided, and three main ways rightly to handle biblical passages for preaching. Elementary observations, but altogether commendable.   1090

Furgeson, Earl H.
"Abstractions in Preaching," *Pastoral Psychology*, October, 1963, pp. 8-16. A professor of preaching and pastoral theology finds that abstractions, although necessary and useful tools of

conceptualization, are in too many sermons "theological drift-words." They are detached from any experience which gives them meaning. Using the insights of depth psychology, he investigates why and how preaching uses abstractions as "the language we use when we do not know precisely what we are talking about." 1091

Garrison, Webb B.

"Plagiarism and the Development of Originality," *Religion in Life,* Autumn, 1952, pp. 573-84; and *Church Management,* January, 1956, pp. 7, 20 ff. A brief history of plagiarism and a method for developing originality in preaching. 1092

Glover, George

"Sermon Titles Are Important," *Church Management,* March, 1951, p. 54. The selection of sermon titles. 1093

Grieser, Ralph

"Toward a Briefer Sermon," *Church Management,* September, 1962, pp. 15-16. A rationale for the short sermon. 1094

Gumbinger, Cuthbert, O.F.M.Cap.

"The Art of Persuasion," *The Priest,* August, 1959, pp. 650-53. A plea for well-prepared sermons with some general hints on preparation and notation of some model preachers. 1095

Henry, H. T.

"The Comforting Panegyric," *Homiletic and Pastoral Review,* February, 1935, pp. 458-64. An attempt to appeal to everybody's own experience of life with its various trials and sufferings via love, sympathy, and helpfulness; illustrated by some ideas on preaching the lives of the saints. 1096

"The Compliment in Sermons," *Homiletic and Pastoral Review,* May, 1942, pp. 705-13. A discussion of the possibilities for compliments as a part of preaching. 1097

"The Eloquent Preacher," *Homiletic and Pastoral Review,* February, 1938, pp. 458-65. A study of the true ingredients of eloquence—a simple and plain style. 1098

"Homiletic Misquotation," *Homiletic and Pastoral Review,* May, 1939, pp. 795-803. 1099

"The Learned Preacher," *Homiletic and Pastoral Review,* May, 1941, pp. 777-85. The article is a plea for preaching that communicates ideas in simple language. 1100

"Making Distinctions in Sermons," *Homiletic and Pastoral Review,* July, 1936, pp. 1018-25.

1101

"Most Profane Buffoonery," *Homiletic and Pastoral Review,* April, 1943, pp. 584-89. Interesting examples of a unique style of wit in the sixteenth century.

1102

"Oft-Repeated Texts," *Homiletic and Pastoral Review,* September, 1940, pp. 1290-99. Imaginative and competent style provides an improved setting for familiar pericopes.

1103

"The Pathetic Preacher," *Homiletic and Pastoral Review,* March, 1938, pp. 570-77. A defense of pathos in sermons—its proper use and its various limitations.

1104

"The 'Plain' Preacher," *Homiletic and Pastoral Review,* April, 1939, pp. 682-89. With the small amount of time allotted to sermons, they must be plain and to the point.

1105

"Plans for Preachments," *Homiletic and Pastoral Review,* May, 1937, pp. 794-802. Methods used in planning sermons; practicable ways for organizing or correlating thoughts on the theme of a sermon.

1106

"The Psalter in Sermons," *Homiletic and Pastoral Review,* February, 1942, pp. 422-30. A general treatment of minimum import on carefulness in quoting the Bible and particularly the psalter.

1107

"The Scriptures in Preaching," *Homiletic and Pastoral Review,* December, 1938, pp. 225-32. Henry urges an exact use and "impressive" quoting of scripture, tolerance for difficult wordings, concern for context, and avoidance of fanciful interpretation.

1108

"Sermon Composition," *Homiletic and Pastoral Review,* April, 1940, pp. 717-25. Random thoughts on this crucial topic.

1109

"Style in Sermon Composition," *Homiletic and Pastoral Review,* June, 1937, pp. 906-14. A routine appraisal advocating a sermon style that is simple, effective, and obtained through study.

1110

"Variety in the Exordium," *Homiletic and Pastoral Review,* December, 1937, pp. 234-40. An appeal for variety in the introduction, something unexpected and interesting in its own right.

1111

Holland, DeWitte T.
"Humor in the Pulpit," *Today's Speech*, November, 1964, pp. 17-18. An exposition of the functions of humor in preaching and some guidelines for using it.   1112

Hunt, Robert A.
"A File of Recorded Sermons," *Church Management*, December, 1953, p. 20. Three uses of tape-recorded sermons. Author advocates a planned file of recorded sermons; the advantageous use of such.   1113

Ingles, James Wesley
"The Place of Poetry in Preaching," *Review and Expositor*, April, 1957, pp. 264-79. After paying proper respects to various aspects of revered facets of preaching, the author presents with illustrations several worthy uses of poetry in pulpit speaking.   1114

Jenkins, Leonard R.
"The Art of Sermon Illustration," *Church Management*, March, 1947, pp. 17-18, 20-21. How to select and use stories effectively.   1115

Jewett, Paul King
"The Wit and Humor of Life," *Christianity Today*, June 8, 1959, pp. 7-9. The subject of humor for Christians in general is the main thrust of the article, but the author includes a section on humor as used by the minister in preaching. If used with propriety, humor can help people digest solid theology.   1116

Jordan, G. Ray
"Imagination in Preaching," *Church Management*, December, 1959, pp. 13-16. Argues for the necessity of imagination in contemporary Christian preaching.   1117

Kay, J. Alan
"Imagination in Preaching," *The Preacher's Quarterly*, December, 1961, pp. 265-70. Genuine imagination is the preacher's necessity because vividness and conviction strengthen his pulpit presentations. Good observations by a competent preacher.   1118

Keller, Wayne H.
"Discussion Sermon Technique," *Church Management*, September, 1965, pp. 12-13. A methodology for an interesting sermon technique to increase pastor-congregation communication.   1119

Kepler, Thomas S.
"Lenten Preaching and Devotional Literature," *The Pulpit*, March, 1962, pp. 23-24. A suggested preaching pattern for Lent.　**1120**

Killgallon, James J.
"Our Inept Religious Vocabulary," *Pastoral Life*, July–August, 1962, pp. 24-27. Notwithstanding traditional terminology, nothing hinders the priest from using simple, understandable terms in the pulpit.　**1121**

Koller, Charles W.
"The Minister's Workshop: Memorization and Note-Free Preaching," *Christianity Today*, December 4, 1964, p. 41. The author gives rules to help in memorization for preaching without notes.　**1122**

"The Minister's Workshop: The Way to Note-Free Preaching," *Christianity Today*, October 9, 1964, p. 40. The author suggests that note-free preaching depends on three factors in preparation: saturation, organization, and memorization.　**1123**

Lantz, John Edward
"The Minister's Use of Words," *Religion in Life*, Winter, 1947, pp. 94-103. An appealing essay on style and pronunciation.　**1124**

"Putting Words Together," *Church Management*, March, 1952, pp. 30, 34. A study of oral composition for more effective preaching.　**1125**

"The Style of the Spoken Word," *Church Management*, April, 1952, pp. 28-30. The essentials of a good pulpit style.　**1126**

"Using Figures of Speech," *Church Management*, February, 1952, pp. 13-15. An excellent analysis of figures of speech and their place in preaching; illustrative examples given.　**1127**

Large, Dwight S.
"Putting the Sermon to Work," *The Pulpit*, January, 1954, pp. 2-3. A suggestive plan for helping the hearer with his response to the sermon and for helping the preacher make sermons more concrete.　**1128**

Leech, Cyril V.
"A Few Practical Tips on Preaching," *The Priest*, March, 1957, pp. 191-94. The "Ten Commandments" and "Six Precepts" of good preaching are presented as an aid to better sermons.　**1129**

Leedy, Paul D.
"The Minister's Scrap Book," *Church Management,* December, 1936, p. 137. Helpful suggestions on the use of the scrapbook for filing sermon materials.   1130

Lewis, Greville P.
"Dialogue Preaching," *The Preacher's Quarterly,* June, 1956, pp. 153-57. Commends dialogue format in preaching. A sample outline is provided. Rather brief, but does indicate possibilities in discreet use of a contemporary trend.   1131

Lightbourn, Francis C.
"The Minister's Use of Bible Commentaries," *The Pulpit,* February, 1960, pp. 26-27. Value of commentaries in sermon construction.   1132

Lofthouse, W. F.
"The Application in the Sermon," *The Preacher's Quarterly,* September, 1958, pp. 229-31. Application of the sermon is always a concern for the preacher. Eight succinct suggestions are given from exegetical and theological orientations.   1133

Loizeaux, Marie D.
"The Minister and the Public Library," *Christianity Today,* June 5, 1964, pp. 10-11. A librarian discusses how a public library may aid ministers but also how the preachers can aid the libraries in becoming useful instruments in their work of sermonizing.   1134

Lowe, James Lewis
"Preacher, What's Your Style," *Christianity Today,* January 17, 1964, p. 15. The style of a sermon is important because it is the means by which the author can "project his thoughts and emotions to his listeners." The author pleads for each preacher to find his own style, develop it, and use it rigorously.   1135

Lowrie, Hamish
"The Preacher's Barrel," *Church Management,* May, 1961, pp. 38-39, 62. A defense of repeating old sermons.   1136

Luccock, Halford E.
"What Literature Can Do for a Preacher," *Review and Expositor,* July, 1945, pp. 255-65. Warnings and counsel on the preacher's use of literature are clearly and wisely delineated by this well-known author. An excellent overview is presented.   1137

Luchs, Fred E.
"Sermon Writing—Tough Task," *Church Management,* May, 1961, pp. 12-13, 16. A string of quotations about preaching, largely unrelated to the article's title.   1138

Luff, S. G. A.
"Our Faith as It Is Spoken," *Furrow,* October, 1962, pp. 584-88. A criticism of a previous article (cf. Mould, July, 1962) with further observations and suggestions on Christian semantics pointing out the need for a living Word within and without the church.   1139

Lutz, Robert S.
"Swinging the Sword of the Spirit," *Christianity Today,* December 3, 1965, p. 33. A first-person account of a pastor's preaching methods.   1140

Maccallum, Donald J.
"Put Your Sermon in Writing," *Church Management,* September, 1961, pp. 34-35. A discussion of the advantages of preparing a full sermon manuscript.   1141

McGlon, Charles A.
"How I Prepare My Sermons: A Symposium," *Quarterly Journal of Speech,* February, 1954, pp. 49-62. Six men share their preparation techniques: Harry Emerson Fosdick, Joseph M. Dawson, Ralph Sockman, Edgar DeWitt Jones, Vincent J. Flynn, Joseph Rauch. The group includes four Protestants, one Catholic, and one Jew. The fame of these six men indicates the high quality and value of this article.   1142

MacLennan, David A.
"The Preacher as an Interpreter," *Church Management,* October, 1948, pp. 9-10, 16, 33. The interpretative function of the preacher and his preaching.   1143

"Resources for Preaching," *Review and Expositor,* January, 1954, pp. 48-61. Even though Sundays come with daunting regularity, the Christian minister has adequate reserves to assist him in his weekly task of sermon preparation affirms the article. Specific sources are listed, described, and procedures for use are illustrated.   1144

MacLoughlin, James
"What About the Reception?" *Furrow,* June, 1950, pp. 282-89. This article concerns itself with the importance and need of simplicity of language or speech in sermons.   1145

Mallett, Frank J.
"Humor in Pulpit and Pew," *Review and Expositor,* July, 1937, pp. 294-301. The author concerns himself principally with humor and good nature as personality characteristics of an effective minister. These are not necessarily evidenced in pulpit delivery. **1146**

Marsh, Thomas H.
"The Bible as Source Material for Public Speaking and Oral Reading," *Quarterly Journal of Speech,* April, 1938, pp. 199-204. This article is tangential to homiletics, but contains good examples of the use of biblical passages as illustrative materials in the minister's nonpulpit speaking situations. **1147**

Maynard, Arthur H.
"The Use of Humor in the Sermon," *Church Management,* March, 1958, p. 13. Argues that humor should be employed with the greatest of care—in most cases it should be completely avoided. **1148**

Mead, Frank S.
"Are Good Sermons Made in Heaven?" *Pulpit Digest,* December, 1952, pp. 11-13. Good sermons come from hard work. Ministers who preach good sermons consistently prepare far ahead and read widely. Some outline their sermons, while others write them out in full. Whatever the method, a good sermon requires hours of hard work! **1149**

Meadley, Thomas D.
"How Sermons Come," *The Preacher's Quarterly,* September, 1965, pp. 164-170; December, 1965, pp. 261-67. This article, in two parts, outlines the genesis of the sermonic idea. Conventional in structure but fresh in examples. **1150**

Meister, John W.
"Planning a Year's Sermons," *The Pulpit,* December, 1952, p. 20. Practical advice on sermon planning. **1151**

Missett, Luke, C. P.
"The Audience Factor in Preaching," *American Ecclesiastical Review,* November, 1944, pp. 358-66. This article aims at making the priest conscious of his audience when he prepares his sermon, in such a way that he adapts himself to the educational and emotional level of his people. **1152**

Montgomery, W. Gracey
"Extempore Preaching," *Pulpit Digest,* January, 1962, pp. 17-20. Extempore preaching is the climax of an involved preparation. The material must be well organized and not too long. A good beginning and ending are essential, with an illustration from actual life tying the theme to the people. Extempore preaching can be creative and spiritually uplifting to both minister and people.   1153

Mould, Daphne D.
"Preach the Word," *Doctrine and Life,* July, 1963, pp. 367-74. Considers the importance of understandable, comprehensible language in sermons.   1154

"Speaking of God," *Furrow,* July, 1962, pp. 371-77. The author's thesis is that language in Catholic sermons has become jargon and is therefore incomprehensible because the primary meaning conveyed by these words is commonly derived from a very different use in everyday language.   1155

Ockenga, Harold J.
"How to Prepare a Sermon," *Christianity Today,* October 13, 1958, pp. 10-12. The author gives seven steps in preparing to preach a sermon without notes with emphasis on its biblical content.   1156

Oman, John B.
"Using Other Men's Sermons," *Church Management,* March, 1952, pp. 76, 79. The art of gracefully giving credit for borrowed material.   1157

O'Neil, David P.
"Sermons in the Vernacular," *Worship,* January, 1964, pp. 104-7. A short but eloquent castigation of ecclesiastical jargon—the rolling verbiage that says nothing—and an appeal for the communication of God's Word in the direct and simple language of real people.   1158

Patrick, Johnstone G.
"Sermon Starts and Stops," *The Pulpit,* February, 1958, pp. 22-24. How to begin and end a sermon, with examples.   1159

Quinn, Edward
"Preaching to Adults," *Life of the Spirit,* August–September, 1963, pp. 79-86. The manner and the matter of our sermons to

adults will be directed according to their needs, conditions, education, and other circumstances of life. 1160

Rees, Paul S.
"The Minister's Workshop: Arrested by Anecdote," *Christianity Today*, March 12, 1965, p. 42. Definition and instruction in the use of anecdotes. 1161

"The Minister's Workshop: Captured by the Concrete," *Christianity Today*, November 8, 1963, pp. 51-52. Concerned with the problem of abstract sermons, the author gives some ways to become concrete. 1162

"The Minister's Workshop: The Lure of Lucidity," *Christianity Today*, July 5, 1963, pp. 44-45. The author outlines the necessary procedures in order to preach lucidly. 1163

"The Minister's Workshop: The Pictorial Pool, Part I," *Christianity Today*, September 11, 1964, pp. 41-42. This is a discussion on ways to help the listener *see* what the preacher is saying. 1164

"The Minister's Workshop: The Pictorial Pool, Part II," *Christianity Today*, November 6, 1964, p. 43. The author encourages ministers to prepare sermons which have eye appeal. The reading of great literary works can help the minister develop his ability in this area. 1165

"The Minister's Workshop: Put a Levy on Literature," *Christianity Today*. January 1, 1965, p. 36. The author urges ministers to read the sermons of men who used pictorial language as a means of developing such an art. 1166

"The Minister's Workshop: The Texture of Preaching," *Christianity Today*, September 13, 1963, pp. 44-45. The texture is the indefinable but unmistakable "feel" of a sermon at the moment of delivery and determined by the preacher. 1167

"The Minister's Workshop: Those First Two Minutes," *Christianity Today*, November 9, 1962, p. 51. The author deals with types of effective introductions. 1168

"The Minister's Workshop: Toward a Strong Finish," *Christianity Today*, January 4, 1963, p. 43. This article deals with an effective conclusion which, along with the introduction, is one of the most important parts of the sermon. 1169

Robbins, Howard Chandler
"Preaching and the Christian Calendar," *Religion in Life*, Spring, 1937, pp. 235-43. A professor of pastoral theology presents

a convincing case for basing a preaching schedule on the Christian calendar. 1170

Roquet, A. M.
"Popularizing Mystery," *Orate Fratres*, November, 1947, pp. 546-55. Sermons today often consist of theological inaccuracies or near-misses. Clichés that are often theologically incorrect are considered, and the author lists and analyzes various clichés used in reference to the Eucharist. 1171

Rossel, John
"The Minister as Artist," *Christianity Today*, February 16, 1962, pp. 17-19. The preacher is an artist in both sermon preparation and delivery. He is viewed in relation to the varied art forms. 1172

Saul, Stuart C.
"Preaching Without Notes," *Church Management*, April, 1961, pp. 18, 38-39. A helpful methodology consisting of six steps. 1173

Schwegler, Edward S.
"That Sunday Sermon," *The Priest*, April, 1951, pp. 284-87. Suggestions on writing and filing sermon notes for the liturgical year and special occasions with some ideas on how they can be used several times. 1174

Scotford, John R.
"How to Be Original," *Church Management*, December, 1962, pp. 12-13. The mechanics of new ideas: resources for originality. 1175

"How to Get New Ideas," *Church Management*, December, 1960, pp. 14-15. Several interesting sources of inspiration discussed. 1176

"Should Sermons Have 'Happy Endings'?" *Minister's Quarterly*, Autumn, 1960, pp. 15-17. Too many sermons end happily and fail to present a prophetic challenge for people to accept and act upon. Thus there is a need for more "open end" preaching that calls for personal decision. A worthwhile reminder of a dimension of preaching easily overlooked. 1177

Shaw, Arthur W.
"Toward More Effective Preaching," *Church Management*, December, 1963, pp. 20, 21-35. Helpful hints on the choice of words for the sermon. 1178

Sheerin, John B., C.S.P.

"Church History in Sermons," *Homiletic and Pastoral Review,* October, 1944, pp. 1-5. Church history can be a method of teaching and also a literary device. 1179

"The New Sermon Technique," *Homiletic and Pastoral Review,* July, 1944, pp. 721-25. This new sermon technique addresses itself to life situations: catch attention, present problem or need, offer solution, picture the result, urge to action. 1180

"Pictorial Preaching," *Homiletic and Pastoral Review,* June, 1945, pp. 641-46. A plea for concrete terms and visual images as Christ used. 1181

"Sincerity Is Not Enough," *Homiletic and Pastoral Review,* January, 1948, pp. 241-46. A fine treatment of the requisites for effective sermons—accurate knowledge, plain language, simplicity, seriousness. 1182

"Speaking of People," *Homiletic and Pastoral Review,* October, 1947, pp. 1-4. A sermon is different from other forms of literary composition: it should be a conversation with living people; it must contact flesh and blood to be successful. A very good analysis. 1183

"Theology: Dead Letter or Living Teacher?" *Catholic World,* April, 1963, pp. 4-7. This article contains some pertinent remarks on the proper style and language for communicating the Word of God. 1184

Shenefelt, O. P.

"Where Is That Sermon?" *Church Management,* November, 1936, p. 72. A triple-indexed filing system presented. 1185

Siekmann, T. C.

"Pastoral Reflections: Sermons That Work," *Pastoral Life,* July–August, 1955, p. 42. The use of the story in the sermon is one way of gaining the interest and attention of the audience. 1186

Smith, C. Ralston

"One Man's Way of Working," *Christianity Today,* November 5, 1965, pp. 26-27. A first-person account of a pastor's sermonizing method. 1187

Smith, Horace G.

"The Best That Money Could Buy," *Church Management,* March, 1960, pp. 40-41, 43-44, 58. Argues for self-dependency on the part of preachers in the preparation of sermons. Also, discusses the increasing tendency of preachers to depend on others for sermonic materials.

1188

Smith, Neil Gregor *et al.*
"The Minister's Reading," *Religion in Life,* Autumn, 1954, pp. 483-515. An excellent discussion of reading materials and methods for preachers.

1189

Snow, Arthur J.
"The Modern Novel in Preaching," *Minister's Quarterly,* Summer, 1960, pp. 7-10. A defense of the proper use of contemporary fiction as a source for preaching and for use while preaching a sermon. The writer briefly and succinctly sets forth cogent reasons for his plea.

1190

Sperry, Willard L.
"The Preacher as Artist," *Minister's Quarterly,* May, 1951, pp. 3-6. While the minister's sermon pattern may vary and need not adhere to a strictly classical form, he must be certain that its order does not do violence to its integral relation to the order of worship. The article sets forth a concern that preaching and worship be considered as essentially related. The theme is timely.

1191

Sprunger, Meredith J.
"Are Methods Important in Preaching?" *Pulpit Digest,* May, 1948, pp. 41-46. The Purdue Research Foundation financed the study of the preaching of outstanding and of average pastors. This survey found that the outstanding pastor does not differ from the average in ideas, evaluations, and goals. The difference is in working habits, working methods, and educational background. More effective preaching comes from employing more effective study habits.

1192

Stang, Joseph
"Father Joe's Sermon on Fire and Brimstone," *Homiletic and Pastoral Review,* October, 1941, pp. 46-56. A fair effort at describing the genesis and working out the process of a sermon in story form.

1193

Stidger, William L.
"Preaching Through Stories," *Pulpit Digest,* November, 1947, pp. 33-36. Using stories is a good technique for both preaching and teaching. Examples are Christ's use of stories, Aesop's Fables,

Mother Goose rhymes, and the McGuffey Readers. Human interest stories from everyday life can give power, meaning, and spirit to preaching.　　1194

Strait, C. Neil
"Plan Your Preaching," *Christianity Today,* June 7, 1963, pp. 10-11. The author makes a plea for series preaching, by which he means "any program that includes preaching on either a book of the Bible or a biblical doctrine, theme, or character over a period of several Sundays or even several months."　　1195

Thomas, Percy E.
"The Parish Preacher and the Tyranny of Words," *Minister's Quarterly,* March, 1958, pp. 4-9. Rigid adherence to theological terms may produce an orthodoxy which creates bitter differences between people of good faith. At the same time, the preacher must understand the words of theology, realizing their inadequacy to express life's deepest experiences. The problem is stated, but the conclusion is not entirely satisfactory.　　1196

Thompson, John
"Imagination in Preaching," *Church Management,* September, 1965, pp. 10-12. The nature and function of imagination in preaching and arguments for its importance.　　1197

Tonne, Arthur J.
"Are You Filing Sermon Material?" *Pastoral Life,* March, 1963, pp. 21-25. An experienced speaker offers tips on how to find, file, and use material for more effective preaching.　　1198

"Effective Sentences in Our Sermons," *Pastoral Life,* January, 1964, pp. 43-48. A short treatise suggesting methods to communicate with listeners with clearness, coherence, emphasis, and variety.　　1199

"Getting Material for Your Sermon," *Pastoral Life,* June, 1964, pp. 25-29. The author suggests steps for structuring the sermon.　　1200

"Liven Those Sermon Conclusions," *Pastoral Life,* October, 1964, pp. 27-32.　　1201

"Outline Your Sermon Ideas," *Pastoral Life,* May, 1964, pp. 37-42. Helpful hints on outlining sermons.　　1202

"Putting Your Sermon Together," *Pastoral Life,* December, 1964, pp. 23-26. A few remarks on sermon craftsmanship.　　1203

"Sacred Eloquence vs. Good English," *Pastoral Life,* December, 1963, pp. 26-30. With the growing number of educated people in our congregations, a priest must use correct English. Here are pointed out some glaring mistakes often made by priests, which could be avoided by reviewing some of the basic rules of grammar.　1204

"Vary Those Sermon Introductions," *Pastoral Life,* September, 1964, pp. 27-31. Following the principles of general public speaking, the author suggests methods for securing audience attention right from the start of the sermon.　1205

"What Shall I Preach About?" *Pastoral Life,* April, 1963, pp. 23-27. The first rule of every successful preacher: decide on a single subject and put it in words people will understand.　1206

"Where Do You Get Those Stories?" *Pastoral Life,* January, 1963, pp. 16-20. The author offers hints for finding apt anecdotes to illustrate the various types of sermons preachers must deliver.　1207

"Words Are a Preacher's Tools," *Pastoral Life,* November, 1963, pp. 25-30. A preacher's success depends largely on the size of his vocabulary. Time spent in cultivating apt words is a pastoral must.　1208

Toohey, William, C.S.C.
"Bafflegab: Sermon Suicide," *Homiletic and Pastoral Review,* April, 1960, pp. 642-46. This article hits at a very old and well-known problem: the priest's tendency to use a vocabulary that fails to move his audience. Short and to-the-point.　1209

Tralle, Millicent
"Stop That Man!" *Church Management,* June, 1958, p. 22. Too-long sermons are usually the result of inadequate preparation.　1210

Trever, John C.
"The Revised Standard Version in the Pulpit," *The Pulpit,* November, 1952, p. 2-4. How the RSV can lead to better expository preaching.　1211

Vann, Gerald, O.P.
"On Teaching in Parables," *Clergy Review,* December, 1959, pp. 734-44. An instruction for teachers and preachers on the need in Christian instruction for the use of symbol, metaphor, and parable. The preacher need not himself be poet and parable-maker but as a pedagogue of Christ he should draw his hearers to penetrate the biblical parable and the mystery of the Divine Poet.　1212

"Symbolism in Preaching," *Thomist,* January, 1965, pp. 46-59. Eloquent plea for understanding, appreciation, and employment of the language of Revelation—imagery.   **1213**

Voigt, Robert J.
"Your Sermon: A 'Many Splendored Thing,'" *Homiletic and Pastoral Review,* June, 1964, pp. 762-66. A sermon is both form and thought, sprinkled with condiments. Write it out, simple and brief; always be prepared.   **1214**

Voss, Charles H.
"The Minister's Use of Poetry," *Church Management,* June, 1946, pp. 38-39. Discussion on the use of poetry in sermons.   **1215**

Wachter, Peter, O.S.B.
"Simplicity and Plainness in the Pulpit," *Homiletic and Pastoral Review,* September, 1938, pp. 1263-76. Every priest who desires to be a good preacher must be sure his preaching is clear and well-defined, unified in plan, and interestingly presented.   **1216**

Walker, E. DeVer
"Planning a Year's Preaching Program," *Church Management,* December, 1962, pp. 21-23. An apologetic and some principles.   **1217**

Walsh, James J., M.D.
"Magnalia Dei: Sermons and Nature Study," *Homiletic and Pastoral Review,* January, 1935, pp. 362-67; February, 1935, pp. 494-501. This article examines the suggestion that comparisons from the study of nature along with a technicality-free explanation of principles of real science as used in sermons, may be of aid to priests. This was the style of Christ, St. Francis de Sales, St. Thomas, etc.   **1218**

"What Good Are Old Sermons?" *Church Management,* April, 1958, p. 13. An editorial concerning the repetition of sermons previously used.   **1219**

Winder, J. M.
"Originality in Preaching," *Homiletic and Pastoral Review,* August, 1939, pp. 1185-89. Every writer and orator has to seek originality in his own "mode of experience." The preacher ought to have learned of human life and its relation to Christ in the church.   **1220**

"Ten-Minute Sermons," *Homiletic and Pastoral Review,* May, 1939, pp. 828-32. Ten-minute sermons are short; hence the subject matter must be narrowed down to an immediate purpose and/or particular act. 1221

Delivery

Adams, Henry Babcock
"The Speaker's Problem of Audibility," *Church Management*, December, 1965, pp. 19-22. The problem of audibility: correct and incorrect solutions. 1222

Blackwood, Andrew W.
"The Minister's Workshop: Making Ready to Deliver a Sermon," *Christianity Today*, February 14, 1964, p. 34. Varied suggestions, including writing a manuscript and voice development, are made by the author to lead to effective delivery. 1223

Bussis, Dale
"Preaching the Sermon," *Princeton Seminary Bulletin*, March, 1964, pp. 41-52. An intensive look at the moment of delivery, based upon a clearly defined "subjective approach"—an approach which invites the participation of the audience. 1224

Carroll, Charles, S.S.J.
"The Cure for Voice and Speech Troubles of Priests," *American Ecclesiastical Review*, October, 1936, pp. 371-79. The author gives some very good suggestions. 1225

Harper, Ralph M.
"Control of the Breath," *Church Management*, November, 1946, pp. 32-33. The relation between posture and voice production. 1226

"G-Suiting the Body," *Church Management*, October, 1946, pp. 17-18. A practical exercise for improving one's speaking voice. 1227

"Suspensory Ligament of the Diaphragm," *Church Management*, December, 1952, pp. 11-12. Proper breathing mechanics as an aid to better speaking. 1228

Henry, H. T.
"Homiletic Mnemonics," *Homiletic and Pastoral Review*, March, 1941, pp. 592-600. Some standard thoughts on the art of memorization. 1229

"Preaching from Manuscript," *American Ecclesiastical Review,* January, 1935, pp. 34-36. This article presents the pros and cons of preaching from a written text and the types of sermons which are suitable to this type of delivery.　　　　**1230**

"Sermon Delivery," *Homiletic and Pastoral Review,* March, 1940, pp. 609-18. Much depends upon the way a sermon is delivered: good and bad composure; use of the whole body.　　　**1231**

Herring, A. G.
"Public Speaking," *Clergy Review,* August, 1951, pp. 96-99. A brief article on certain psychological aspects of effective preaching: the notion of leadership, the power of the human voice, identification with one's audience, the notion of focus and definition.　　　**1232**

Hill, Prudence
"Notes on Voice Production," *Clergy Review,* July, 1952, pp. 411-15. A short but helpful article on certain problems in voice production for the priest-preacher. Stresses proper breathing, resonance, articulation of consonants, and appropriate style.　**1233**

Hudson, R. Lofton
"A Note on Reading Sermons," *Review and Expositor,* July, 1944, pp. 278-80. Giving supporting evidence, the writer advises against reading sermons from the pulpit.　　**1234**

Jordan, A. Homer
"As Others See Us," *Church Management,* March, 1943, pp. 56-57. The importance of proper pulpit decorum: the elimination of offensive mannerisms.　　　**1235**

Lantz, John Edward
"Preparing the Body for Preaching," *Church Management,* February, 1948, pp. 11-12, 16. A healthy body is one prerequisite for effective preaching.　　　**1236**

"Speaking into Microphones," *Church Management,* May, 1952, pp. 42-44. Speaking on radio, over public-address systems, and on television is discussed.　　　**1237**

"The Use of the Body in Preaching," *Church Management,* March, 1948, pp. 52-55, 57-58. The effective use of bodily gestures in preaching.　　　**1238**

Marsh, Thomas H.
"Some Problems of Oral Bible Reading," *Quarterly Journal of Speech,* October, 1937, pp. 396-402. A professor of oral

interpretation presents three common faults of liturgical reading and makes helpful suggestions about the choice of translations, interpretation of the language, and sentence structure of biblical literature.

1239

Marshman, John T.
"Design for Delivery of the Sermon," *Central States Speech Journal,* Winter, 1961, pp. 118-25. The author describes three faulty voice patterns frequently heard in preaching and suggests ways to achieve "communicative vitality."

1240

Missett, Luke, C. P.
"Don't Blame Your Voice," *The Priest,* February, 1946, pp. 30-33. This article suggests three requirements of good voice use: relaxation of body, especially neck and throat; adequate breathing; energetic use of tongue, lips, and jaw.

1241

"There Is a Speed Law," *American Ecclesiastical Review,* October, 1948, pp. 281-84. The most common fault of the American pulpit is too rapid speech. Missett gives a speed law of 150 words per minute on the average. Two ways of slowing down: increase the number and length of pauses and increase the quantity of the words, i.e., by taking more time to enunciate them.

1242

Mulligan, Arthur G.
"Outwitting the Monotone," *Homiletic and Pastoral Review,* February, 1950, pp. 424-29. A very good article on speech production. The author gives some good insights and drills.

1243

Overman, Conleth, C.P.
"What to Do About Your Voice," *Homiletic and Pastoral Review,* August, 1946, pp. 860-63. A discussion of the fundamentals of speech production plus some good suggestions.

1244

Pepler, H. D. C., O.P.
"The Gestures of Our Lord," *Clergy Review,* July, 1936, pp. 44-50. Not addressed directly to preachers but of possible use for them. The author uses Scripture to reconstruct looks, posture, walk, gestures, movements, etc., of our Lord, indicating their power, their significance, their perfect deliberation, swiftness, and spontaneity.

1245

"Sermons and Gesture," *Clergy Review,* December, 1935, pp. 453-57. Practical discussion of the use of gestures in preaching, including nine rules for the making of formal gestures and a

detailed imaginative reconstruction of the gestures that might
have been used in Peter's sermon on Pentecost. 1246

Pierce, Harry Raymond
"Reflex Actions to Preaching," *Church Management,* November, 1940, pp. 85-87. Argues that preachers must develop a
conversational style of speaking. 1247

Rees, Paul S.
"The Minister's Workshop: Beware the Vices of Preaching,"
Christianity Today, March 1, 1963, p. 52. The author outlines
noticeable faults observable in sermon delivery. 1248

Ripley, Francis J., C.M.S.
"Pastoral Preaching," *Pastoral Life,* September–October, 1957,
pp. 5-11. Practical ways for the preacher to deliver his sermons
more effectively to his audience. 1249

Roberts, Edward H.
"Imitating the Sons of This World," *The Pulpit,* March, 1954,
pp. 2-4. Application of modern speech principles to preaching. 1250

Sallaway, F. X.
"Summary of a Course to Seminarians on Microphonic Technique," *The Priest,* February, 1947, pp. 98-101. To relieve
monotony in the speaking voice, the standard elements of variety
must be used. Volume, pitch, tempo, and pause within the conversational range of the individual help give lively presentation
that reaches the hearers. 1251

Sheerin, John B., C.S.P.
"Action in the Pulpit," *Homiletic and Pastoral Review,*
June, 1944, pp. 647-51. The correct use of natural gestures,
position, facial expression, etc., are considered, all of which will
aid the conveyance of a message. 1252

"Conversational Preaching," *Homiletic and Pastoral Review,*
March, 1944, pp. 418-22. A good treatment on the need for
direct, familiar, and natural speech today. 1253

"Monotonous Preaching," *Homiletic and Pastoral Review,*
April, 1944, pp. 481-86. This study contains practical suggestions
and helps for remedying a monotonous voice. 1254

"Some Speech Defects and Inhibitions," *Homiletic and Pastoral
Review,* May, 1944, pp. 574-78. The article gives some good hints
on how to correct problems of speech production. 1255

Stanfield, V. L.
"Sermon Delivery at Its Best," *Review and Expositor,* October, 1952, pp. 445-53. A homiletics professor urges free delivery of the sermon without notes as the most effective form of delivery. He discusses advantages and objections to this form of delivery. **1256**

Stidger, William L.
"How to Sleep on Saturday Night," *Church Management,* December, 1944, pp. 11-12. Sound, restful sleep on Saturday night is essential to good preaching on Sunday morning. Author gives sound advice on how to achieve that rest. **1257**

Traver, Amos John
"Preacherisms," *Church Management,* February, 1948, pp. 8-10, 17-18. Pulpit mannerisms and their influence on preaching effectiveness. **1258**

Warner, Thomas H.
"Habits in the Pulpit and in the House of God," *Church Management,* December, 1939, pp. 140-41. Twenty-four items listed. Some are repetitious and outdated (originally formulated in 1827). **1259**

Williams, John H., S.J.
"The Mike and Father's Sermon," *Homiletic and Pastoral Review,* August, 1947, pp. 916-17. Very brief article on the value and use of the microphone, with an outline of the types, trade names, and uses of the microphone. **1260**

Yarbrough, Robert Clyde
"The Preacher and His Vocal Equipment," *Today's Speech,* September, 1961, pp. 22-24, 29. A helpful discussion of the preacher's speech goals and the ways to achieve them. **1261**

History—Individual Preachers

Ahlstrom, Sidney E.
"The Levels of Religious Revival," *Confluence,* 1955, pp. 32-43. A critique of the "revival of religion" in the fifties, with special reference to Norman Vincent Peale. **1262**

Arendzen, J. P.
"St. Leo the Great," *Clergy Review,* June, 1935, pp. 481-94. Historical article on St. Leo, which also contains excellent comments on Leo's sermons on content and rhetorical values. **1263**

Ballard, Frank H.
"Puritanism and Richard Baxter," *Church Management,* November, 1954, pp. 14-15. Puritanism: the role and importance of Richard Baxter then and now.   1264

Banowsky, William; Wayne C. Eubank
"The Preaching of H. Leo Boles," *Southern Speech Journal,* Summer, 1963, pp. 318-29. The authors, both with graduate training in speech, analyze briefly in standard rhetorical criteria the preaching ministry of a well-known minister of the Church of Christ. Delivery, invention, arrangement, and style are covered, together with a brief rhetorical biography.   1265

Barbour, William R.
"Charles Ray Goff," *Church Management,* March, 1952, p. 50. A biographical sketch and tribute.   1266

Barmann, Lawrence F., S.J.
"The Spiritual Teachings of Newman's Early Sermons," *Downside Review,* April, 1962, pp. 226-43. A worthwhile treatise of the framework within which Newman's version of the true Christian life in this world is developed.   1267

Barnhart, Elbert; Wayne C. Eubank
"N. B. Hardeman, Southern Evangelist," *Southern Speech Journal,* December, 1953, pp. 98-107. A minister and a speech professor team to analyze the preaching of a prominent Church of Christ preacher. After a brief rhetorical biography, Hardeman's audiences, general occasions, delivery, and general effectiveness are characterized.   1268

Belden, Albert David
"What America Owes to George Whitefield," *Religion in Life,* Summer, 1951, pp. 445-49. A brief analysis of the significance of George Whitefield's preaching in America.   1269

Bishop, John
"John Wesley as a Preacher," *Religion in Life,* Spring, 1957, pp. 264-73. A scholarly study of Wesley's preaching, his ethos, his message, and his methods.   1270

Blackwood, James R.
"Frederick W. Robertson as a Pulpit Expositor," *Interpretation,* October, 1951, pp. 436-49. A short study under three heads: (1) his theory of inspiration, (2) his main teachings, and (3) how he went about his preaching.   1271

Blench, J. W.
"John Longland and Roger Edgeworth, Two Forgotten Preachers of the Early Sixteenth Century," *Review of English Studies,* 1954, pp. 123-43. A discussion of the style and the themes used by these two which points out the similarity between Longland and John Fisher in their use of rhetorical schemes and between Edgeworth and Latimer in their use of the popular speech idiom.

1272

Breen, Quirinus
"John Calvin and the Rhetorical Tradition," *Church History,* 1957, pp. 3-21.

1273

Burns, George, S.J.
"Father De Ravignan's Power and Secret as a Preacher," *Clergy Review,* August, 1938, pp. 112-23. Informative and inspiring article on Father De Ravignan, the Jesuit preacher who followed Lacordaire in the pulpit of Notre Dame. In addition to a résumé of his preaching career and an account of his fervent prayer-life, the author quotes verbatim an extended statement of Father De Ravignan himself of his own principles and practice in preaching the Word of God.

1274

"A Priest and His People," *Clergy Review,* May, 1943, pp. 209-16. This is an account of the pastoral methods of St. Francis Xavier, including several notable excerpts on preaching from St. Francis' own instruction on pastoral duties. The instruction stresses the special dignity of the act of preaching, the need to know the people to whom you preach, the choice of apt motives for virtue, the qualities (in the preacher) of prudence and humility.

1275

Cairns, David S.
"Sir George Adam Smith," *Religion in Life,* Autumn, 1942, pp. 529-38. An excellent biographic sketch of a renowned Scottish scholar and preacher.

1276

Camp, Leon R.
"Roger Williams: Rhetoric or Ranting?" *Today's Speech,* September, 1964, pp. 21-22, 30. A rhetorical analysis of Williams' debates in Rhode Island with the Quakers.

1277

Carroll, William, S.J.
"St. Augustine's Christmas Sermons," *Homiletic and Pastoral Review,* December, 1948, pp. 161-67. A brief analysis of the leading features in these sermons.

1278

"St. Augustine's Preaching on Miracles," *Homiletic and Pastoral Review,* July, 1948, pp. 755-62.

1279

"Sermons of Pope St. Leo the Great," *Homiletic and Pastoral Review,* March, 1944, pp. 401-12. Analysis of Leo's sermons on Passiontide.

1280

"Sermons of St. Leo the Great," *Homiletic and Pastoral Review,* February, 1944, pp. 321-29. Analysis of St. Leo's Lenten sermons.

1281

Cass, John
"St. Paul and the 'Ratio' of Preaching," *American Ecclesiastical Review,* June, 1940, pp. 519-24. The key to St. Paul's success was his grasp of the dignity and importance of his mission, and a realization of the supreme necessity of properly fulfilling it.

1282

Clark, Robert D.
"The Oratorical Career of Bishop Matthew Simpson," *Speech Monographs,* August, 1949, pp. 1-20. Based on a doctoral dissertation, this biographical study describes both the preaching and political oratory of a Methodist bishop during the Civil War.

1283

Connors, Joseph, S.V.D.
"Saint Charles Borromeo in Homiletic Tradition," *American Ecclesiastical Review,* January, 1958, pp. 9-23. This is an article concerning the "Instructions" St. Charles Borromeo wrote on preaching the Word of God. The article gives a brief summary of each of the chapters contained in the "Instructions." A very informative article and well worth reading.

1284

Conrad, Leslie, Jr.
"Jonathan Edwards' Pattern for Preaching," *Church Management,* September, 1957, pp. 45-47. A significant and scholarly study of this great preacher.

1285

Cowie, L. David
"Apostolic Preaching in Los Angeles," *Christianity Today,* October 25, 1963, pp. 11-13. The article relates to the preaching of Billy Graham and an evaluation of its mysterious impact in spite of imperfections in homiletical principles.

1286

Cox, J. Powhatan
"Robert Hall," *Review and Expositor,* October, 1951, pp. 424-41. The article presents in well-documented form a survey biography of Robert Hall, together with some description of his delivery and sermon craftsmanship.

1287

Crocker, Lionel
"Henry Ward Beecher and the English Press of 1863," *Speech Monographs*, March, 1939, pp. 20-43. A scholarly analysis of a significant relationship in the life of a great American preacher by an outstanding Beecher student.   1288

Delany, B., O.P.
"Father Vincent McNabb in the Field," *Blackfriars*, July–August, 1954, pp. 295-305. Written as a loving tribute to Father McNabb, the article contains an excellent estimate of the work of the Catholic Evidence Guild, of the need for outdoor preaching, and of the singular work of Father McNabb in this unique apostolate. Includes also McNabb's own *Credo* on the qualities of a controversialist.   1289

DesChamps, Margaret Burr
"Benjamin Morgan Palmer, Orator-Preacher of the Confederacy," *Southern Speech Journal*, September, 1953, pp. 14-22. A biographical study of a New Orleans Presbyterian minister. This study presents an interesting insight into the problems of a preacher involved in social concerns.   1290

Dibelius, Otto
"My Life in Preaching," *Christianity Today*, December 20, 1963, pp. 6-10. It is an autobiographical article in which the author sketches the place of the sermon in Germany during and previous to World War I. Instead of placing a premium upon great orators, he places great importance upon the "power of the average sermons."   1291

Dieterich, H. R.
"Revivalist as Reformer—Implications of George D. Herron's Speaking," *Quarterly Journal of Speech*, December, 1960, pp. 391-99. Herron stands squarely in the tradition of moral and religious leadership in the social reform in America. This article analyzes Herron's unity of speaker, address, and audience in two of his sermons. Through the textual analysis presented, one may observe many helpful techniques.   1292

Driver, George Hibbert
"Moody—God's Man," *Church Management*, March, 1937, pp. 303-7. Moody—the man and his attitudes toward God and mankind as exhibited in his life and preaching.   1293

Ellis, Carroll B.
"Alexander Campbell as a Preacher," *Southern Speech Journal*, November, 1948, pp. 99-107. Campbell was both a

preacher and a debater. This article analyzes the preaching style and shows the polemical influence on his homiletical work. 1294

Emerson, Everett
"John Udall and the Puritan Sermon," *Quarterly Journal of Speech,* October, 1958, pp. 282-84. 1295

Flynn, Clarence Edwin
"The Valedictory of Washington Gladden," *Church Management,* October, 1958, p. 42. A brief study of Gladden and his last sermon. 1296

Fortkamp, Frank E.
"St. Robert Bellarmine on the Composition of Sermons," *Homiletic and Pastoral Review,* July, 1962, pp. 868-72. The twofold obligation of the Christian preacher: faithfully instruct the people in those divine teachings which they can and must know and, at the same time, move them to acquire virtue and avoid sin. 1297

Fritsch, Charles T.
"Bengel, the Student of Scripture," *Interpretation,* April, 1951, pp. 203-15. A well-written, scholarly article on the German Pietist Johann Albrecht Bengel. 1298

Gartenhaus, Jacob
"Julius Kobner—His Life and Labors," *Review and Expositor,* July, 1948, pp. 326-34. A brief biographical sketch of a nineteenth-century Jewish Christian who was a pioneer of the German Baptist movement. An interesting piece on an unfortunately little-known minister. 1299

Gehring, Mary Louise
"Russell H. Conwell: American Orator," *Southern Speech Journal,* Winter, 1954, pp. 117-24. A speech professor shows reasons for the effectiveness of a famous preacher as an occasional lecturer. 1300

Golden, James L.
"John Wesley on Rhetoric and Belles Lettres," *Speech Monographs,* November, 1961, pp. 250-64. An excellent and scholarly study of John Wesley's rhetorical theory. It covers Wesley's precepts on taste, genius, style, the speaker's content and organization, delivery, poetry, and historical and philosophical writing. 1301

"Hugh Blair: Minister of St. Giles," *Quarterly Journal of Speech,* April, 1952, pp. 155-60. The article analyzes the rhetoric of Blair, the man James Boswell said "would stop hounds by his eloquence." The analysis includes his choice of subject matter, the practicality of his sermons, and the attractiveness of his expression.   1302

Goldhawk, Norman P.
"Bernard Manning" (Notable Preacher Series), *The Preacher's Quarterly,* June, 1958, pp. 101-7. One of England's most influential Christian laymen in the twentieth century whose published sermons and ideas about preaching were quite unusual.   1303

"Donald M. Baillie" (Notable Preacher Series), *The Preacher's Quarterly,* June, 1959, pp. 93-100. A fitting reflection upon the theology and preaching of a great Scotsman whose thought influenced the outlook of a generation of ministers. Overloaded with quotes, but useful.   1304

"Emil Brunner" (Notable Preacher Series), *The Preacher's Quarterly,* September, 1959, pp. 190-98. A discussion of the biblical and theological character of the sermons of the great Swiss "crisis theologian." His sermons are his theological beliefs popularized. A good estimate.   1305

"Paul Tillich" (Notable Preacher Series), *The Preacher's Quarterly,* December, 1958, pp. 284-90. A helpful article to read after a perusal of Tillich's three volumes of sermons. Describes his homiletical method and explains background of his pulpit offerings. Very worthwhile.   1306

"Phillips Brooks" (Notable Preacher Series), *The Preacher's Quarterly,* March, 1959, pp. 4-11. Focuses upon Brooks's emphasis upon the personal factor in preaching and the communal nature of Christianity. A good essay.   1307

Goodbar, Octavia W.
"Dr. Sockman at Christ Church," *Church Management,* June, 1942, p. 16. A biographical sketch.   1308

Goodrich, Laurence B.
"Chrysostom, 'King of Preachers,'" *Quarterly Journal of Speech,* February, 1938, pp. 27-35. Chrysostom is presented as a model for preachers in large towns today. The article points to the universality, practicality, and immediacy which marked his homilies. This article is very challenging to the contemporary reader.   1309

Grayston, Kenneth
"The Great Sermon," *The Preacher's Quarterly*, December, 1955, pp. 395-401. An introductory study of the Sermon on the Mount. Its preaching values are dealt with *seriatim* in both vols. one and two. **1310**

Hance, Kenneth G.
"The Elements of the Rhetorical Theory of Phillips Brooks," *Speech Monographs*, March, 1938, pp. 16-39. A valuable study of the rhetorical theory of one of America's great preachers by a very competent speech scholar. **1311**

Hardon, John A., S.J.
"St. Robert Bellarmine—Preacher," *Homiletic and Pastoral Review*, December, 1946, pp. 186-92. An article on St. Robert's expression of doctrine in preaching. **1312**

Harper, Ralph M.
"Phillips Brooks's Voice Lessons," *Church Management*, January, 1947, pp. 22-24. The importance of voice lessons to the effectiveness of this great preacher. **1313**

Henry, H. T.
"The Humor of Gabriele Barletta," *Homiletic and Pastoral Review*, July, 1941, pp. 976-84. Humor and anecdote were frequently used by medieval and postmedieval preachers. Gabriele Barletta was a famous exponent. **1314**

"The Humor of Michel Menot," *Homiletic and Pastoral Review*, February, 1943, pp. 385-90. A defense of Michel Menot's sixteenth-century style of preaching; he adapted the message to the vocabulary and mentality of his audience. **1315**

"The 'Jocular' Olivier Maillard," *Homiletic and Pastoral Review*, August, 1939, pp. 1156-63. A novel article about Olivier Maillard. **1316**

"Jocular Père André," *Homiletic and Pastoral Review*, May, 1943, pp. 680-88. An exploration of the style of the seventeenth-century preacher, Père André. **1317**

"A Prescription for Preaching," *Homiletic and Pastoral Review*, April, 1937, pp. 682-90. Mediocre commentary on R. H. Benson's system for learning how to preach. **1318**

Hickey, Robert L.
"Donne's Art of Preaching," *Tennessee Studies in Literature*, 1956, pp. 65-74. **1319**

Hill, Edmund, O.P.

"St. Augustine as a Preacher," *Blackfriars*, November, 1954, pp. 463-71. Informative and stimulating article on St. Augustine as a preacher, explaining elements of his theory of preaching and giving examples of his preaching style as found in his sermons. The writer stresses the liveliness and directness of Augustine's style, the sure mark of the apostle.   1320

"St. Augustine's Theory and Practice of Preaching," *Clergy Review*, October, 1960, pp. 589-97. Interesting and instructive article on Augustine's preaching, stressing the directness and vigor of his style against the elegant rhetoric he could have cultivated if he chose. Powerful argument for directness and simplicity in preaching.   1321

Hochmuth, Marie

"Phillips Brooks," *Quarterly Journal of Speech*, April, 1941, pp. 227-36. The author, a respected voice in the field of rhetorical theory, analyzes the sermon as "the inevitable expression of what the man is and what he thinks." She develops this article by answering three questions: What was Brooks's message? Why did he say it the way he did? What was the nature of his audience? Excellent insight into Brooks and his times. The article demonstrates a method of audience analysis which is still useful.   1322

Honan, William Holmes

"John Jaspar and the Sermon That Moved the Sun," *Speech Monographs*, November, 1956, pp. 255-61. An interesting description of a sermon and its delivery which gained considerable fame in 1878. This study is of interest primarily because of its sociological relationships.   1323

Hope, Norman V.

"Arthur John Gossip," *Church Management*, March, 1941, pp. 368-71. A summary of Dr. Gossip's ideas on preaching and sermon preparation.   1324

"Frederick Townley Lord," *Church Management*, April, 1943, pp. 13-14. A biographical sketch of Dr. Lord. In addition, a summary of contemporary English Baptists.   1325

"Herbert Henry Farmer," *Church Management*, September, 1942, pp. 19-20. Farmer—the man and his thoughts.   1326

"James Stuart Stewart," *Church Management*, November, 1941, pp. 48-51. A biographical sketch.   1327

"John Seldon Whale," *Church Management,* June, 1944, pp. 26-28. A biographical sketch of Whale and a summary of contemporary English Congregationalism.   1328

"Leslie Dixon Weatherhead," *Church Management,* September, 1941, pp. 724-25, 728-30. A biographical sketch.   1329

"The Preaching Technique of James Reid," *Church Management,* June, 1941, pp. 562-64. A study of James Reid—the preacher and his method.   1330

Houser, Emerson O.
"Vignette of John Henry Jowett," *Church Management,* June, 1959, pp. 41, 53. A short sketch.   1331

Howell, A. C.
"John Donne's Message for the Contemporary Preacher," *Religion in Life,* Spring, 1947, pp. 216-33. The author points out the relevance of Donne's preaching to the modern scene. A scholarly and valuable study.   1332

Huber, Robert
"Dwight L. Moody: Master of Audience Psychology," *Southern Speech Journal,* May, 1952, pp. 252-71. A careful analysis of the audience and the psychological approaches to its members is an important consideration of every preacher. Huber shows how Moody studied these characteristics and used his findings. One may learn much from the observation of Moody's technique.   1333

Hudson, Robert B.
"Richard Sibbes's Theory and Practice of Persuasion," *Quarterly Journal of Speech,* April, 1958, pp. 137-48. About an English clergyman, 1577-1635.   1334

Huntsinger, Jerald
"Sermons Designed for Listening," *Christian Advocate,* May 10, 1962, pp. 14-15. A significant analysis of Harry Emerson Fosdick's methodology for keeping interest level of sermons high.   1335

Ingram, H.
"James Reid of Eastbourne," *Church Management,* March, 1948, pp. 25-26. A tribute.   1336

Jackson, C. E.
"I Saw This Happen," *Church Management,* October, 1950,
pp. 60, 62. A first-hand observation of the preaching of Billy
Graham.   **1337**

Jackson, George D.
"P. T. Forsyth's Use of the Bible," *Interpretation,* July, 1953,
pp. 323-37. A well-organized study of the Congregationalist
Peter Taylor Forsyth, as a preacher.   **1338**

Johnson, C. Oscar
"Edgar Young Mullins," *Review and Expositor,* April, 1942,
pp. 141-50. A memorial address reciting some details of the
life of the famous Southern Baptist minister and educator.   **1339**

Kedlec, Valerie M.
"Dwight L. Moody in the British Isles," *Church Management,*
February, 1953, pp. 78-81, 86. The impact of Moody on the people
of the British Isles.   **1340**

King, C. Harold
"George Whitefield: God's Commoner," *Quarterly Journal of
Speech,* February, 1943, pp. 32-36. This article is a rhetorical
analysis of the man described in Lecky's *History of England*
"as a popular preacher indeed . . . appears never to have been
equalled in England." The article contains an excellent audience
analysis as well as analysis of the message and its form of
presentation.   **1341**

Kuist, Howard Tillman
"Brooke Foss Westcott (1825-1901) ," *Interpretation,* October,
1953, pp. 442-52. Deals with Westcott as an interpreter of
Scripture.   **1342**

"Liberal Preacher with an Orthodox Heart," *Church Management,* July, 1957, pp. 9-10. An editorial: a tribute to Joseph
Fort Newton.   **1343**

Lievsay, John L.
"Silver-tongued Smith, Paragon of Elizabethan Preachers,"
Huntington Library Quarterly, 1947, pp. 13-36. A rhetorical
study of Henry Smith, reader or lecturer at St. Clement Danes.   **1344**

Ludlow, William Linnaeus
"Charles G. Finney," *Church Management,* January, 1943,
pp. 34-37. A biographical sketch and tribute.   **1345**

McConnell, Francis J.
"Francis Asbury," *Religion in Life,* Winter, 1945, pp. 23-36. An inspiring biographical sketch of Methodism's pioneer "circuit rider." **1346**

McDowell, John
"Dwight L. Moody," *Church Management,* May, 1936, pp. 411-12, 422-23, 426-29. An address of eulogy given at East Northfield, ninety-nine years after Moody's birth. **1347**

McKenna, Stephen, C.SS.R.
"An Ancient Bishop and Preacher," *Homiletic and Pastoral Review,* February, 1941, pp. 475-81. The author discusses the history of pastoral theology and homiletics as seen in the sermons of St. Caesarius of Arles. **1348**

McKirachan, J. Frederick
"The Preaching of Paul Tillich," *Princeton Seminary Bulletin,* January, 1960, pp. 33-42. A rather thorough discussion of Tillich's sermons, published in *The Shaking of the Foundations* and *The New Being.* **1349**

MacLennan, David A.
"S. Parkes Cadman: Adventurer for Happiness," *Church Management,* October, 1936, pp. 15-16. A tribute. **1350**

McLeod, N. Bruce
"The Preaching of Phillips Brooks: A Study of Relevance Versus Eternal Truth," *Religion in Life,* Winter, 1964–65, pp. 50-67. Brooks's preaching took the human situation into account, but his loose hold upon the Bible sometimes made him confuse biblical truth with cultural assumptions. **1351**

Manierre, William Reid
"Verbal Patterns in Cotton Mather's *Magnalia,*" *Quarterly Journal of Speech,* December, 1961, pp. 402-13. When Mather wrote the *Magnalia,* he used the techniques of his preaching experience. The analysis of his writing throws more light on his methodology and style of speaking than on written communication. **1352**

Maxwell, William W.
"George Herbert Morrison," *Church Management,* July, 1937, pp. 511-12, 514. A tribute. **1353**

May, J. L.
"Newman, the Preacher," *Clergy Review,* December, 1938, pp. 497-508. An eloquent review of Newman's preaching life

in its various phases: the University sermons, the simple addresses at St. Mary's, the fuller discourses, such as the "Apologia" and the "Idea of a University." Includes stirring accounts of his farewell sermon in leaving the Anglican Church and the joyful "Second Spring," celebrating the reestablishment of the Catholic hierarchy in England.   1354

Mueller, William R.
"The Sermons of John Donne," *Christianity Today,* September 28, 1962, pp. 7-10. The article is a biographical review which touches upon many significant dimensions of preaching.   1355

Oates, Wayne
"The Billy Graham Crusade: An Evaluation," *Pastoral Psychology,* December, 1956, pp. 17-26. A professor of pastoral care evaluates a Graham crusade in his home city. He makes some sociological observations, then gives rather close attention to a psychological evaluation. He finds some psychological naïveté in the approach and apparent presuppositions of the crusade.   1356

Padrow, Ben
"Norman Vincent Peale: The Power of Positive Speaking," *Today's Speech,* February, 1962, pp. 8-10. A critical analysis of a famous clergyman.   1357

Parkander, Dorothy J.
"Puritan Eloquence: The Sermons of Samuel Ward of Ipswich," *Anglican Theological Review,* 1959, pp. 13-22.   1358

Parsons, Edward Smith
"Lyman Abbott," *Religion in Life,* Summer, 1939, pp. 449-55. A vivid portrayal of a great American preacher by one who knew him well.   1359

Paton, William
"William Temple," *Religion in Life,* Autumn, 1942, pp. 483-95. A sketch of William Temple by an intimate, on the occasion of his appointment as Archbishop of Canterbury.   1360

Pitts, John
"Alexander Maclaren: Monarch of the Pulpit." *Christianity Today,* June 5, 1964, pp. 7-9. This is a brief study of Maclaren's method of sermonizing.   1361

"Charles Haddon Spurgeon: An Appreciation," *Religion in Life,* Spring, 1950, pp. 273-80. A brief sketch of the famous Baptist evangelist with a brief review of several sermons.   1362

"G. Campbell Morgan: The Prince of Expositors," *Christianity Today*, June 7, 1963, pp. 13-14. An article about G. Campbell Morgan, his background, call to the ministry, and his preaching.   1363

"John Henry Jowett: Prince of Preachers," *Christianity Today*, December 6, 1963, pp. 11-13. This article is a tribute to Jowett on the one-hundredth anniversary of his birth.   1364

Politzer, Jerome F.
"The Doctrine of Man in Phillips Brooks's Sermons," *The Pulpit*, September, 1963, pp. 23-24. An analysis of Brooks's sermons which portrayed man as "the giant with the wounded heel."   1365

Quimby, Rollin W.
"Charles Grandison Finney: Herald of Modern Revivalism," *Speech Monographs*, November, 1953, pp. 293-99. A brief biographical sketch of the evangelist who originated new revivalist techniques in the middle of the nineteenth century.   1366

"How D. L. Moody Held Attention," *Quarterly Journal of Speech*, October, 1957, pp. 278-83. The author does not attempt to analyze the entire rhetorical style of Moody, but rather only his methods of controlling his audience. This analysis of the mixture of rhetorical and extra-rhetorical devices is very helpful to the practical rhetorician.   1367

"The Western Campaigns of Dwight L. Moody," *Western Speech Journal*, March, 1954, pp. 83-90. This is a helpful presentation of the style and work of Moody in the western area of the country. It adds to the overall appreciation of the man and his ministry.   1368

Quinn, Dennis
"Donne's Christian Eloquence," *Journal of English Literary History*, 1960, pp. 276-97.   1369

Reid, Emily J.
"Preacher Under Asbury," *Church Management*, April, 1948, pp. 75-76. The life of a typical Methodist itinerant preacher: James Jenkins (1764-1842).   1370

Richards, Paul H.
"J. B. Lightfoot as a Biblical Interpreter," *Interpretation*, January, 1954, pp. 50-62. A short, accurate paper on Joseph Barker Lightfoot.   1371

Rose, Ben L.
"Joseph Parker," *Interpretation,* April, 1954, pp. 172-87. An
excellent article on Parker as an expository preacher.   1372

Rosser, J. L.
"George W. Truett, Preacher," *Review and Expositor,* January,
1938, pp. 3-23. A frank appraisal of some of the qualities contributing to the effectiveness of this able Southern Baptist
minister, including physical, intellectual, and spiritual proper-
ties.   1373

"James Boardman Hawthorne: Pulpit Orator," *Review and
Expositor,* October, 1939, pp. 415-33. Dr. Rosser writes from personal knowledge about a well-known Southern Baptist minister-
orator. The brief study talks of the man himself, his oratorical
ability, delivery, style, and personal proof.   1374

Schmidt, Ralph N.
"The Message of Olympia Brown, Preacher," *Today's
Speech,* April, 1964, pp. 2-5, 35. A critique of a woman Uni-
versalist preacher, followed by brief reactions given by two
homileticians.   1375

Sheerin, John B., C.S.P.
"The More Excellent Way," *Homiletic and Pastoral Review,*
November, 1947, pp. 81-85. St. Augustine's ideas on instruction.   1376

Smith, C. Ralston
"Billy Graham's Evangelistic Thrust: The Crusaders and
Changing Times," *Christianity Today,* November 10, 1961, pp.
3-7. The article describes the evangelistic ministry of Billy
Graham with a section devoted to the message that centers in
the Bible so much that Graham considers himself a mere
messenger boy.   1377

Spivey, Ronald
"Alexander Whyte: 1836-1921" (Notable Preachers Series),
The Preacher's Quarterly, March, 1958, pp. 4-9. An interesting
sketch of Scotland's most famous nineteenth-century preacher.
Insights into facets of his pulpit power.   1378

"Hugh Latimer: 1485-1555" (Notable Preachers Series), *The
Preacher's Quarterly,* June, 1957, pp. 104-9. Latimer's preaching
heralded the Reformation in England. He inveighed against
religious abuses and was martyred under Mary. One of Protestantism's greatest sons.   1379

"John Donne: 1573-1630" (Notable Preachers Series), *The Preacher's Quarterly*, December, 1957, pp. 287-94. A brief study of England's outstanding pulpit personality of the seventeenth century. Emphasis upon his wit, imagination, prose style, and pulpit relevance.   1380

"Lancelot Andrewes: 1555-1626" (Notable Preachers Series), *The Preacher's Quarterly*, September, 1957, pp. 189-95. A study of a sixteenth-century churchman who was preacher, administrator, and theologian. Known chiefly for his devotional books; yet his sermons are classics.   1381

Stanfield, V. L.
"Elements of Strength in the Preaching of John Albert Broadus," *Review and Expositor*, October, 1951, pp. 379-404. A seminary teacher of homiletics appraises the preaching of a famous teacher of preaching. Specific traits and practices are singled out and carefully documented.   1382

Staples, Edward D.
"S. Parkes Cadman: The Man and His Methods," *Church Management*, November, 1938, pp. 68-70, 72, 74. A revealing study of this great preacher: a tribute.   1383

Stefun, Bonaventure, O.F.M.Cap.
"St. Augustine, Preacher," *Homiletic and Pastoral Review*, April, 1964, pp. 591-96. Good commentary on St. Augustine's preaching.   1384

Stransky, Thomas, C.S.P.
"The Pastoral Sermons of St. Augustine," *American Ecclesiastical Review*, May, 1960, pp. 311-20. Enumerates and describes several sermon techniques of St. Augustine.   1385

"Saint Augustine's Use of Scripture," *American Ecclesiastical Review*, December, 1960, pp. 376-83. St. Augustine's use of the Bible as his primary source book in his technique of planning and delivering a sermon.   1386

Trimble, James C.
"Jowett and His Bible," *Interpretation*, January, 1951, pp. 62-79. An excellent study of the questions, "How did Jowett study the Bible?" and "How did he use the Bible in preaching?"   1387

Turnbull, Ralph G.
"Jonathan Edwards—Bible Interpreter," *Interpretation*, October, 1952, pp. 422-35. An excellent study of Edwards as a preacher.   1388

Turnbull, Roland E.
"Was Jowett Unethical?" *Church Management,* February, 1953, pp. 88-89. A defense of Jowett's ethical character as a man and preacher.   1389

Wakefield, Gordon S.
"Arthur John Gossip," *The Preacher's Quarterly,* March, 1962, pp. 95-101. A worthy discussion of and tribute to Scotland's Christocentric preacher of the twentieth century. A master of the good illustration.   1390

Wall, Ernest
"Vignette of S. D. Gordan," *Church Management,* January, 1959, p. 18. A short sketch.   1391

Wallace, Ronald S.
"Calvin, the Expositor," *Christianity Today,* May 22, 1964, pp. 8-10. The article discusses the place in the Reformation of the revival of true biblical interpretation through preaching. The principles on which Calvin based his approach and method are outlined.   1392

White, Eugene E.
"Cotton Mather's *Manuductio ad Ministerium,*" *Quarterly Journal of Speech,* October, 1963, pp. 308-19. This historical and analytical paper throws light on the content of Cotton Mather's preaching and helps the reader understand Mather's rhetoric more thoroughly.   1393

"George Whitefield's Preaching in Massachusetts and Georgia: A Case Study in Persuasion," *Southern Speech Journal,* May, 1950, pp. 249-62. The article is an extensive study of the persuasive techniques used in the sermons of Whitefield. It compares the techniques in the sermons preached in the north and the south with a discussion of why Whitefield was less effective in Georgia than elsewhere. Aside from its historical values, the article is an excellent primer for the preacher who needs an understanding of persuasive theory.   1394

"The Great Awakener: George Whitefield," *Southern Speech Journal,* September, 1945, pp. 6-15. A speech teacher analyzes the personal qualities of George Whitefield as they contribute to his effectiveness as a revivalist.   1395

"The Preaching of George Whitefield During the Great Awakening in America," *Speech Monographs,* March, 1948, pp. 33-43. A scholarly analysis based on a doctoral dissertation of the effectiveness, methodology, and content of Whitefield's preaching during a significant religious movement in colonial America.   1396

"The Protasis of the Great Awakening in New England," *Speech Monographs,* March, 1954, pp. 10-20. An interesting description of Whitefield's forty-six day tour of New England in 1740.   1397

"Whitefield's Use of Proofs During the Great Awakening in America," *Western Speech Journal,* January, 1950, pp. 3-6. The use of supporting materials and proofs is an important part of sermon craftsmanship. Whitefield's use of these tools is outlined and illustrated in this paper. From the historical observation, the modern preacher may gain new insights.   1398

White, Eugene E.; Clair R. Henderlider
"What Norman Vincent Peale Told Us About His Speaking," *Quarterly Journal of Speech,* December, 1954, pp. 407-16. The authors report on an interview with Dr. Peale. The article rambles through the preparation techniques, rhetorical philosophy, and formal training of this popular pulpiteer.   1399

Wicke, Myron Forrest
"Mystic's Way: A Study of Ralph Waldo Emerson," *Religion in Life,* Autumn, 1946, pp. 556-69. A penetrating analysis of Emerson's personality and preaching.   1400

History—Groups

Baskerville, Barnet
"The Cross and the Flag: Evangelists of the Far Right," *Western Speech,* Fall, 1963, pp. 197-206. An analysis of several Protestant clergymen who link their preaching to right-wing political theory.   1401

Blocker, Hyacinth, O.F.M.
"Effective Preaching," *The Priest,* January, 1949, pp. 21-25. A review of well-known saint-preachers and their method: practice before preaching.   1402

Caemmerer, Richard R.
"Preaching in St. Louis," *The Pulpit,* February, 1965, pp. 8-9. One of a series of descriptions and critiques of preaching in various regions.   1403

Cass, John
"Traditions in Preaching," *American Ecclesiastical Review,* October, 1940, pp. 339-48. This is a survey of the traditions of leading preachers (Chrysostom, Augustine, Bernard, Bossuet, etc.), as representing their age, along with the trends and characteristics of these traditions.   **1404**

Clausen, Bernard C.
"They Have Shaped My Life," *Church Management,* April, 1939, pp. 380-81, 388. The author discusses the lives and influences on his life of Emerson, Beecher, and Rauschenbusch.   **1405**

Crocker, Lionel
"Beecher and Fosdick," *Central States Speech Journal,* Winter, 1961, pp. 100-105. A comparative study of two preachers, each the best known of his generation.   **1406**

Edwards, K. Morgan
"Preaching in Greater Los Angeles," *The Pulpit,* May, 1965, pp. 7-9. One of a series of descriptions and critiques of preaching in various regions.   **1407**

Ellis, Carroll B.
"Background of the Campbell-Purcell Religious Debate of 1837," *Southern Speech Journal,* November, 1945, pp. 32-41. A speech teacher/minister examines the climate of opinion of the period during which Alexander Campbell and Bishop Purcell engaged in public debates on religious topics.   **1408**

Gibson, George Miles
"Chicago Voices," *The Pulpit,* November, 1964, pp. 7-9. A description and evaluation of contemporary preaching.   **1409**

Gorden, William
"An Antiphonal Negro Sermon," *Today's Speech,* February, 1964, pp. 17-19. A description of the overt responses by Negro congregations during preaching.   **1410**

Halvorson, Arndt L.
"Preaching in the Twin Cities," *The Pulpit,* February, 1965, p. 12. One of a series of descriptions and critiques of preaching in various regions.   **1411**

Hardin, H. Grady
"Preaching in the Southwest," *The Pulpit,* March, 1965, pp. 8-10. One of a series of descriptions and critiques of preaching in various regions.   **1412**

Harris, Erdman
"Harry Emerson Fosdick and Reinhold Niebuhr: A Contrast in the Methods of the Teaching Preacher," *Religion in Life,* Summer, 1943, pp. 389-400. An interesting comparison of a noted theologian-teacher and a famous preacher-teacher.   **1413**

Heston, Edward L., C.S.C.
"The Dogmatic Preaching of the Fathers," *American Ecclesiastical Review,* November, 1940, pp. 408-17; December, 1940. pp. 497-512; January, 1941, pp. 26-42; February, 1941, pp. 129-43; March, 1941, pp. 210-19. This is a five-part article on the doctrine of the fathers of the church on the divine life of the Christian living in grace. The extensive treatment considers the divine life in God, the divine life transmitted men through Christ, the Christian life in general with respect to particular virtues.   **1414**

Hogue, Harland E.
"Preaching in the Bay Area," *The Pulpit,* July–August, 1965, pp. 12-14. One of a series of descriptions and critiques of preaching in various regions.   **1415**

Ivey, James Houston
"A Study of Preaching in Southern Churches," *Review and Expositor,* October, 1943, pp. 449-57. The author reports on a study of how well the average pastor is meeting the great objectives of the worship service in his preaching. Data for the study came from announced sermon subjects of three denominational groups in a large southern city over a three-month period and were evaluated in terms of specific mental hygiene measurements.   **1416**

Lantz, John Edward
"The Christian Ministry and Industrial Conflict," *Religion in Life,* Summer, 1946, pp. 349-59. Drawing on the experience of two great American preachers of the past, Washington Gladden and Henry Ward Beecher, the author suggests strategy for present labor tensions.   **1417**

"A Survey of Modern Preaching," *Quarterly Journal of Speech,* April, 1943, pp. 167-72. The article has two main thrusts: first, to present some principles of effective preaching—drawn mainly from Fosdick's article in *Harper's* magazine of July, 1928 (q.v.); second, to apply the principles to specimen sermons of twenty-five outstanding American preachers. The first section is practical; the second is interesting for the homiletical historian.   **1418**

Lewis, W. Davis
"Three Religious Orators and the Chartist Movement," *Quarterly Journal of Speech*, February, 1957, pp. 62-68. The role of Christian ministers—Joseph Raynor Stephens, Charles Kingsley, and Frederick W. Robertson—in the pursuit of social justice is presented. The article is very helpful for contemporary churchmen interested in applying the Christian gospel to social structures.   1419

Macleod, Donald
"The Middle Atlantic Pulpit," *The Pulpit*, September, 1964, pp. 11-13. A description and evaluation of contemporary preaching.   1420

Martin, Howard
"Ramus, Ames, Perkins, and Colonial Rhetoric," *Western Speech*, 1959, pp. 74-82. The influence of Peter Ramus, William Ames, and William Perkins, Renaissance practitioners, on colonial rhetoric.   1421

Miller, William L.
"The 'Religious Revival' and American Politics," *Confluence*, 1955, pp. 44-56. A discussion of the preaching of Peale, Graham, and Sheen and their relationship to the culture through the mass media.   1422

"The New York City Pulpit," *The Pulpit*, May, 1964, p. 10. An anonymous description and evaluation of contemporary preaching.   1423

Newman, Henry
"German Pastors Speak Out to Hitler," *Pulpit Digest*, January, 1937, pp. 13-18. Timely praise for brave and articulate preaching.   1424

Northcott, Cecil
"Preaching and Preachers in London," *The Pulpit*, July–August, 1964, pp. 9-11. A description and evaluation of contemporary preaching.   1425

Pierce, Richard D.
"The Boston Pulpit," *The Pulpit*, April, 1964, pp. 12-13. A description and evaluation of contemporary preaching.   1426

Pipes, William H.
"Old-Time Negro Preaching: An Interpretative Study," *Quarterly Journal of Speech*, February, 1945, pp. 15-21. This article

attempts to analyze the heritage of Negro preaching by studying eight modern Negro sermons. It is a very helpful study and presents conclusions on sources of effectiveness. 1427

Potthoff, Harvey H.
"The Denver Heritage," *The Pulpit,* April, 1965, pp. 10-12. One of a series of descriptions and critiques of preaching in various regions. 1428

Reissig, Frederick E.
"Preachers and Preaching in the National Capital Community," *The Pulpit,* October, 1964, pp. 7-10. A description and evaluation of contemporary preaching. 1429

Scotford, John R.
"New York's New Preachers," *Church Management,* October, 1936, pp. 13-14. Short biographical sketches of Chalmers, Peale, Bonnell, and Sizoo. 1430

Skoglund, John E.
"The Rochester Heritage," *The Pulpit,* June, 1964, pp. 10-13. A description and evaluation of contemporary preaching. 1431

Southard, Samuel
"The Pulpit Heritage of Louisville and Nashville," *The Pulpit,* January, 1965, pp. 8-10. One of a series of descriptions and critiques of preaching in various regions. 1432

Stevenson, Dwight E.
"Current Trends in Disciple Preaching," *The Pulpit,* August, 1952, pp. 2-4. An analysis of preaching in the Disciple Churches. 1433

Weir, Samuel C.
"East North Central Preaching Metropolitan Detroit," *The Pulpit,* December, 1964, pp. 6-8. A description and evaluation of contemporary preaching. 1434

History—Periods

Bader, Jesse M.
"We Preach," *Church Management,* September, 1936, pp. 626-27. A description of the National Preaching Missions of various lengths. 1435

Batchelder, Robert C.
"The Rumination of a Map Reader," *The Pulpit*, September, 1965, pp. 26-28. A discussion of some of the reasons for the changing influence of the contemporary pulpit. 1436

Blackwood, Andrew W.
"The Evangelical Pulpit Today," *Christianity Today*, December 22, 1961, pp. 8-10. The material grows out of an evaluation of the monthly sermons in *Christianity Today* during 1961. Blackwood then makes several pertinent suggestions for sermonizing. 1437

Boase, Paul H.
"The Education of a Circuit Rider," *Quarterly Journal of Speech*, April, 1954, pp. 130-36. Using the life of James A. Finley, the author presents the training of a Methodist circuit rider. Special attention is given to the rhetorical training of these men who are often mistakenly stereotyped as uneducated ranters. 1438

Braybrooke, Neville
"The London Pulpit: The 1660's and the 1960's," *The Pulpit*, February, 1964, pp. 26-29. Some rambling, personal reflections from a book in preparation on how Londoners spend their Sundays. 1439

Bristol, Lyle Osborne
"Preaching: Apostolic and Modern," *The Pulpit*, January, 1952, pp. 2-4. What a study of apostolic preaching can suggest to modern preaching. 1440

Brown, H. C.
"Power in the Pulpit," *Christianity Today*, January 2, 1961, pp. 7-8. Though preaching has been in the doldrums, the author finds signs of encouragement for increased effectiveness in the pulpit. 1441

Butler, G. Paul
"Trends in Contemporary Preaching," *Christianity Today*, April 13, 1962, pp. 5-7. The distinguished author shares the patterns of preaching which he has discovered in reading over 55,000 sermons during the past twenty years. An excellent evaluation is given. 1442

Dana, Ellis H.
"What's the Matter with Protestant Preaching?" *Church Management*, September, 1957, pp. 21-22. A layman speaks frankly to the clergy. 1443

Daves, Michael

"Is Modern Preaching So Bad?" *Pulpit Digest,* July, 1959, pp. 12-14. This article refutes the charge that present-day preaching is mediocre by giving three signs of good health: the presence of prophetic preaching in an age of pretense; the presence of personal-problem preaching in an age of perplexity; and the presence of people in the pews. 1444

Froelicher, Helene E.

"A Preaching Crusade," *Lumen Vitae,* April–June, 1946, pp. 260-64. A review of statements on the poor condition of Sunday preaching. A history of the "Crusade for a More Fruitful Preaching and Hearing of the Word of God," with an outline of its objectives and methods. 1445

Gilpin, P.

"New Light from the Pulpit," *The Priest,* January, 1964, pp. 45-49. A history of the Catholic Homiletic Society and a review of two local workshops. 1446

"Great Preachers and Great Churches," *Church Management,* June, 1955, p. 6. An editorial: great preachers and great churches do not coincide. 1447

Hagspiel, Bruno

"An American Preaching Crusade," *Furrow,* December, 1952, pp. 295-97. A short account of the need for, the founding of, the aims and methods of "The Crusade for a More Fruitful Preaching and Hearing of the Word of God." 1448

Henry, H. T.

"Preaching in the 'Dark Age,'" *Homiletic and Pastoral Review,* September, 1941, pp. 1161-68. Illustrating his article with examples of sermons preached in those times, the author concludes that there was more light in the Dark Ages than we sometimes believe. 1449

"Some Queer Preachments," *Homiletic and Pastoral Review,* July, 1943, pp. 878-87. Examples of the strange style of preaching in the fifteenth, sixteenth, and seventeenth centuries. 1450

"History of Preaching in the Church," *Life of the Spirit,* October, 1958, pp. 146-51. The entire issue is devoted to preaching. The editorial gives the development of preaching in the history of the church. 1451

Kerr, Harry P.
"The Election Sermon: Primer for Revolutionaries," *Speech Monographs*, March, 1962, pp. 13-22. A rhetorical analysis of a specialized type of preaching that was popular in America from 1763 to 1783. This study will be of some interest to students of preaching and politics.   1452

"Politics and Religion in Colonial Fast and Thanksgiving Sermons, 1763-1783," *Quarterly Journal of Speech*, December, 1960, pp. 372-82. This article has a dual value: first, it presents an interesting stage in the history of American preaching; second, it indicates some helpful ideas on the relationship of the pulpit to politics.   1453

Liddle, Ernest V.
"Revival Through the Bible," *Christianity Today*, January 6, 1958, pp. 12-16. The author's main thrust is that revival comes through heavy emphasis on the Bible, but he repeatedly shows the place of preaching in this emphasis in the history of the church.   1454

Martin, Howard
"Puritan Preachers on Preaching: Notes on American Colonial Rhetoric," *Quarterly Journal of Speech*, October, 1964, pp. 285-92. An insightful, descriptive study.   1455

Mercer, Robert H.
"The Decline of American Preaching," *Church Management*, April, 1942, pp. 11-12. The author suggests several probable causes for this decline.   1456

O'Neill, Joseph H.
"New Approach to Better Preaching," *Pastoral Life*, January, 1963, pp. 24-29. A report of the work, aims, and efforts of the Catholic Homiletic Society in providing encouragement and practical techniques for preachers and preachers-to-be.   1457

Quimby, Rollin W.; Robert H. Billigmeier
"The Varying Role of Revivalistic Preaching in American Protestant Evangelism," *Speech Monographs*, August, 1959, pp. 217-28. An analysis and evaluation of revivalistic preaching in American Protestantism. This article will be of some interest to the student of evangelism.   1458

Robertson, D. W., Jr.
"The Frequency of Preaching in Thirteenth-Century England,"
Speculum, 1949, pp. 376-88. Historical notes with some conclusions drawn for modern preachers.   **1459**

Sedgwick, W. B.
"The Origins of the Sermon," *Hibbert Journal,* 1947, pp. 158-64. The source of the modern sermon is the "golden age" of Augustine and Chrysostom. It is indebted to many writers, including Horace, Persius, and Seneca.   **1460**

Shippey, Frederick A.
"Preaching for a New Age," *Church Management,* December, 1940, pp. 144-46, 163-64. Author points out reasons why he feels that in 1940 America stood upon the "threshold of an age of great preaching." This new age is characterized.   **1461**

Smith, Charles Daniel
"Why Is So Much Preaching So Bad?" *The Pulpit,* August, 1957, pp. 27-28. A professor of speech comments on contemporary preaching.   **1462**

Stevenson, Dwight E.
"Trends in Contemporary Preaching," *College of the Bible Quarterly,* July, 1950, pp. 11-19. A professor of homiletics, discounting the importance of differences in homiletical method which characterize the history of preaching, asserts that the trend of importance in modern preaching relates to the content of preaching. He sets the message of sermons against the historical backdrop and sees that preaching has "turned a new corner" in the second quarter of the twentieth century. He discusses the new direction.   **1463**

Stewart, Charles J.
"The Pulpit and the Assassination of Lincoln," *Quarterly Journal of Speech,* October, 1964, pp. 299-307. An analysis of printed sermons, of special interest following the assassination of President Kennedy.   **1464**

Tarver, Jerry L.
"Baptist Preaching from Virginia Jails—1768-1778," *Southern Speech Journal,* May, 1964, pp. 139-48. A rhetorical analysis which concludes that "Preaching from prison cells left a heritage which has a respectable place in the annals of American protest."   **1465**

Winchell, Wallace
"The Teaching Sermon," *Minister's Quarterly,* February, 1954, pp. 18-23. Through a study of "Didactic Preaching in England of the Middle Ages," the author traces some of the teaching themes it presents. He believes that the "teacher-preacher" is an office and function that preaching must include. The thoughtful reader will want to read the author's sources and become acquainted with an era of preaching largely unknown today.   1466

History—Theory

Abernathy, Elton
"Trends in American Homiletic Theory Since 1860," *Speech Monographs,* August, 1943, pp. 68-74. A valuable, general study by a competent scholar.   1467

Anderson, Raymond E.
"Kierkegaard's Theory of Communication," *Speech Monographs,* March, 1963, pp. 1-14. An analysis of rhetorical theory from the existential point of view. This is a provocative study based on a doctoral dissertation.   1468

Barnds, William Joseph
"Jonathan Swift, Preacher," *The Pulpit,* April, 1961, pp. 6-8. Swift's philosophy and advice on preaching.   1469

Connors, Joseph, S.V.D.
"Homiletic Theory in the Sixteenth Century," *American Ecclesiastical Review,* May, 1958, pp. 316-32. Part of the true spiritual revival of the church of the sixteenth century was the art of good preaching. Augustinus Valerius, Bishop of Verona, and Luis of Grandola were probably the most important contributors and creators of this good preaching revival. For not only by their own preaching was their influence felt, but much more so by the homiletic textbooks they wrote. In these books both men agreed that preaching should be based upon classical rhetoric. Valerius relied upon Aristotle; whereas Grandola leaned upon Quintillian and Cicero. This was definitely a change in the history of homiletics.   1470

"The Vincentian Homiletic Tradition," *American Ecclesiastical Review,* October, 1958, pp. 217-27; November, 1958, pp. 338-50; December, 1958, pp. 391-406. Valuable three-part article, considering the strong influence of St. Francis de Sales and the full

details of the Vincentian "little method," analyzed here according
to the principles of classical oratory and evaluated in the light of
the homiletic renewal of seventeenth-century France.   1471

Crocker, Lionel
"Charles Haddon Spurgeon's Theory of Preaching," *Quarterly
Journal of Speech*, April, 1939, pp. 214-24. This analysis of the
elements of Spurgeon's rhetoric contains ample illustrations of
each element. The article is rich in suggestions which the reader
may develop in his own way. There is also a list of important
books on and about Spurgeon.   1472

"The Rhetorical Theory of Harry Emerson Fosdick," *Quarterly
Journal of Speech*, April, 1936, pp. 207-13. An analysis of
Fosdick's techniques for making a sermon attractive begins with
the principle of contrast and continues through the areas of
psychological arrangement and persuasiveness. Chief attention is
given to contrast.   1473

Davidson, J. A.
"Dean Swift Advises Preachers," *Church Management*, October,
1948, pp. 38, 40-41, Jonathan Swift's views concerning pulpit
techniques.   1474

Dieter, Otto A.
"Arbor Picta: The Medieval Tree of Preaching," *Quarterly
Journal of Speech*, April, 1965, pp. 123-44. A description of the
finding and authenticating of the earliest visual aid to the study
of preaching—a "tree of preaching" published in the fifteenth
century, probably inspired by Jacobus de Fusignano's *Libellus
Artis Creadicationis* (early 1300's).   1475

Edney, Clarence W.
"Campbell's Lectures on Pulpit Eloquence," *Speech Monographs*, March, 1952, pp. 1-10. An analysis of Campbell's rhetorical theory in his "Lectures on Pulpit Eloquence." This study
provides an interesting explanation of the adaptation of rhetorical principles to preaching.   1476

Ehninger, Douglas W.
"George Campbell and the Revolution in Inventional Theory,"
Southern Speech Journal, May, 1950, pp. 270-76. A university
rhetorician analyzes how George Campbell, an Anglican cleric,
revolutionized the basis of sermon/speech construction theory
by approaching the nature of knowing rather than the categories
of a subject.   1477

Hudson, Roy F.
"Notes on Thomas Brinton's Views on Preaching," *Western Speech*, Fall, 1962, pp. 211-16. The homiletical theory of a fourteenth-century Roman Catholic bishop, derived from his 103 known sermons.

1478

Mudd, Charles S.
"The Rhetorica Ecclesiastica of Agostino Valiero," *Southern Speech Journal*, Summer, 1956, pp. 255-61. The article summarizes the doctoral thesis of the writer on a sixteenth-century Italian church rhetorician. It presents an area in the history of preacher training that is often neglected.

1479

Murphy, James J.
"St. Augustine and the Christianization of Rhetoric," *Western Speech Journal*, Winter, 1958, pp. 24-29. This article outlines the significant contribution to the history of speech theory made by St. Augustine. It will help the reader appreciate and understand the truly revolutionary place of Augustine in the literature and theory of speech.

1480

"Saint Augustine and the Debate About a Christian Rhetoric," *Quarterly Journal of Speech*, December, 1960, pp. 400-410. Saint Augustine's *De Doctrina Christiana* provided a foundation for medieval preaching theory. This article presents an analysis of its historical significance as well as its modern usefulness.

1481

Nelson, Theodore F.
"Charles Haddon Spurgeon's Theory and Practice of Preaching," *Quarterly Journal of Speech*, April, 1946, pp. 173-81. This article is a thorough study of the rhetorical and homiletical theory of Spurgeon. It draws on his recorded precepts of preaching, *Lectures to My Students*, as well as the author's analysis of eighty-four of Spurgeon's sermons.

1482

Riley, Floyd K.
"St. Augustine, Public Speaker and Rhetorician," *Quarterly Journal of Speech*, December, 1936, pp. 572-78. St. Augustine is less known as a rhetorician than as a theologian. Yet, he was educated in a school of rhetoric and taught rhetoric at Rome and conducted his own school of rhetoric in Carthage. This article discusses his "conversion" from a student of the sophistic school to a crusader for the reestablishment of the Ciceronian concepts. In presenting this change, the author presents a helpful interpretation of these two schools and their influence on pulpit oratory.

1483

Tade, George T.

"The *Spiritual Exercises:* A Method of Self-Persuasion," *Quarterly Journal of Speech*, December, 1957, pp. 383-89. Though the article is only obliquely related to homiletics, it bears on one of the preacher's most pressing motivational problems—"How do I get my congregation to think their way through to formulate convictions on a subject?" The self-persuasion method of St. Ignatius Loyola seems to suggest an approach. This article is well worth the reading time.   **1484**

Teaching

Bowman, Clarice M.

"The Minister's Training—One Pew View," *Religion in Life*, Winter, 1952–53, pp. 58-71. A plea by a laywoman for more careful training of the clergyman in the leadership of worship and in preaching.   **1485**

Bowman, Rufus D.

"Personality and Preaching," *Pastoral Psychology*, November, 1954, pp. 8-12. A seminary president describes how preaching is taught by his seminary. The underlying principle is "the development of a healthy personality as a necessary factor in increasing the effectiveness of preaching." The method utilizes a group-dynamics approach and aims at personal growth (as well as increased competence) on the part of each class member.   **1486**

Casteel, John L.

"College Speech Training and the Ministry," *Quarterly Journal of Speech*, February, 1945, pp. 73-77. The article outlines areas of development of techniques for preaching. The man who is already in the pulpit will find this a helpful checklist for self-evaluation.   **1487**

Clark, William K.

"The Fusion Approach to Preaching," *The Pulpit*, June, 1962, p. 24. A brief article which attempts a synthesis of various theories of preaching, especially as applied to the teaching of preaching.   **1488**

Connolly, James M.

"Meaningful Preaching Within the Present Framework of Homiletics," *Apostolic Renewal in the Seminary*, ed. James Keller and Richard Armstrong. New York: The Christophers, 1965, pp. 266-76. A talk delivered at the second Christopher

Study Week (July, 1964), detailing the arrangement for the course in preaching in the modern seminary. There may be some disagreement about individual points of sequence in the author's outline, but he has competently structured the whole with full attention to the theology of preaching and the study of the various types of preaching: missionary, catechetical, liturgical, and special.   **1489**

Daves, Michael
"I Learned Humility from a Tape Recorder," *The Pulpit*, September, 1959, p. 26. How to use a tape recorder to improve sermons: construction and delivery.   **1490**

Davis, H. Grady
"The Teaching of Homiletics—the Present Situation in American Seminaries," *Encounter*, Spring, 1961, pp. 3-13. Reflections on the author's visits to regional meetings of homiletics professors to conduct seminars.   **1491**

Doherty, Martin W.
"Another Plea for Simplicity," *American Ecclesiastical Review*, March, 1937, pp. 290-99. Speaking from personal experience, the author underscores the importance of the seminarian's ability to paraphrase the formal classroom knowledge into the everyday language of the people. In this way the seminarian will preserve the "common touch" in his sermons later on. Practical suggestions are given on how this can be brought about during the seminarian's training years and after ordination. The author's plea for the need of simplicity in sermons is given in the context of a moderately educated congregation.   **1492**

Fosdick, Harry Emerson
"Learning to Preach," *Pulpit Digest*, October, 1956, pp. 19-22. An extract from Dr. Fosdick's autobiography, *The Living of These Days*. Dr. Fosdick describes his homiletical adventures at his first pastorate in Montclair, revealing his inner thoughts and struggles.   **1493**

Fuller, Carlos Greenleaf
"A Better Trained Protestant Ministry," *The Pulpit*, February, 1938, pp. 44-45. A plea for more thorough training.   **1494**

Hollatz, Edwin A.
"Speech Programs of Illinois Graduate Theological Schools," *Illinois Speech Association News*, Fall, 1964, pp. 14-15. A listing of speech courses offered and required in a selected list of schools. **1495**

Lawton, John H.
"A Speech Program for the Major Seminary," *Homiletic and Pastoral Review,* December, 1963, pp. 242-48. A plea for a more uniform training in homiletics. 1496

McBride, Alfred, O.Praem.
"The Living Room Pulpit," *Ave Maria,* July 17, 1965, pp. 8-9. An interesting report of an experiment for teaching future preachers, whereby they go into homes to give sermons for audiences of chosen laymen, who, in turn, offer critical evaluations. 1497

McGlon, Charles A.
"Early Speech Education in Baptist Seminaries," *Speech Teacher,* March, 1961, pp. 125-32. An insightful article growing out of the author's doctoral dissertation. 1498

"Preface for a Text on the Minister's Speech," *Review and Expositor,* January, 1946, pp. 3-21. A seminary professor of speech sets down his philosophy of speech/preaching/homiletics after tracing the classical foundations of rhetoric and something of the history of American Protestant theological education. 1499

"Preparing Men to Speak for God—Forward to a Study in Educational Research," *Southern Speech Journal,* May, 1954, pp. 261-76. This study speaks to the question of the nature of preparation of ministers. It presents some helpful considerations for those who are preparing curricula in theological institutions. 1500

Meany, William
"A German Conference on Preaching," *Furrow,* May, 1958, pp. 323-26. A report on a conference of clergy engaged in teaching sacred eloquence, held in Wuerzburg, Bavaria, January 3, 1957. 1501

O'Brien, John
"The Young Priest Preaches," *American Ecclesiastical Review,* January, 1937, pp. 76-77. A short but provocative article, offering a program to aid young priests in their preaching. 1502

Pausback, Gabriel N., O.Carm.
"Street Preaching for Seminarians," *American Ecclesiastical Review,* November, 1942, pp. 387-93. This gives excellent ideas on how street preaching increases the apostolic zeal of the seminarian, prompting him to more serious study, as well as aiding his own maturity. 1503

Powers, William T., C.M.
"A Symposium for Preachers," *Homiletic and Pastoral Review,*
November, 1954, pp. 129-33. An offering of practical suggestions
for the giving of a symposium for preachers and some of the ideas
garnered from one such gathering.   **1504**

"Preachers and Their Making," *Christianity Today,* June 5,
1964, pp. 24-25. The article is written in reaction to the publishing of a recent book of essays, *The Making of Ministers.* It
pleads for preachers to work at theological and biblical studies in
order to make their sermons meaningful and authoritative.   **1505**

Quillian, Crystal
"New Techniques in Preacher Pedagogy," *Church Management,* September, 1958, pp. 23-24. Emory University's use of
recordings and movies in preacher training.   **1506**

Regnier, Celestine, O.F.M.Conv.
"Dramatics in the Seminary," *Homiletic and Pastoral Review,*
April, 1961, pp. 671-77. A very good article showing how dramatics can develop the personality of the student, something
vitally necessary for future good preaching.   **1507**

"To Be a Preacher," *The Priest,* December, 1965, pp. 1051-61.
In this article concerning seminary training for preaching, the
author makes an eloquent plea for thorough, competent preparation for those responsible for training seminarians; the essay is
more fragmentary and uneven with regard to the discussion of
actual course content in the seminary curriculum.   **1508**

Sharp, John K.
"The Making of a Good Preacher," *American Ecclesiastical
Review,* September, 1936, pp. 237-57. General plans, suggestions,
and thoughts on an integrated course of homiletics in the
seminary.   **1509**

Sleeth, Ronald E.
"The Teaching of Preaching," *The Pulpit,* October, 1953, pp.
21-22. Some personal observations and suggestions by a teacher of
homiletics.   **1510**

Stevenson, Dwight E.
"Practice Preaching: An Avenue to Personal Growth," *College
of the Bible Quarterly,* October, 1951, pp. 39-47. A professor of
homiletics describes in detail the aim, the method, and the results
of his course entitled "Practice Preaching," and indicates that

the course operates on a group-dynamics basis toward the end of enhancing the personal maturity in faith of each class member, as well as improving his skill in the "sermon arts."

1511

"Pulpit, Mike, and Camera," *Christian Century,* April, 1957, pp. 517-18. The account of a homiletics professor's use of audio-visual devices to teach preaching.

1512

Stewart, Charles W.
"Preaching Before the Sound Camera," *Pulpit Digest,* January, 1958, pp. 16-18. The author tells of the use of the sound movie camera in homiletic classes at the Iliff School of Theology in 1956. This technique enables the student to confront himself, criticize himself, and correct himself.

1513

Stuart, George C.
"Whither Homiletics?" *The Pulpit,* July, 1960, p. 25. A brief and rather pessimistic inquiry.

1514

Taylor, Vernon L.
"The Classical Approach to Homiletics," *The Pulpit,* September, 1961, p. 24. A reminder of the value of Aristotle and the classical rhetoricians in learning to preach.

1515

Townsend, Howard William
"Speech Course for Theological Students," *Western Speech Journal,* May, 1952, pp. 185-92. This paper considers the objectives of a speech course in the theological curriculum. It is a helpful guide to the teachers of such courses. It is also a good checklist for men already in the pulpit and it is helpful in self-analysis and evaluation.

1516

Bibliography

Caplan, Harry; Henry H. King
"Dutch Treatises on Preaching: A List of Books and Articles," *Speech Monographs,* November, 1954, pp. 235-47.

1517

"French Tractates on Preaching: A Booklist," *Quarterly Journal of Speech,* October, 1950, pp. 296-325.

1518

"Italian Treatises on Preaching: A Booklist," *Speech Monographs,* September, 1949, pp. 243-52.

1519

"Latin Tractates on Preaching: A Booklist," *Harvard Theological Review,* July, 1949, pp. 185-206. A bibliography of works on preaching in Latin from 1500 to the present.

1520

"Pulpit Eloquence: A List of Doctrinal and Historical Studies in English," *Speech Monographs,* Special Issue, 1955, pp. 1-159. A monumental bibliographic study, this list should be useful to every serious student of the rhetoric of preaching. It encompasses the theory and practice of preaching as well as critical and historical studies.   1521

"Pulpit Eloquence: A List of Doctrinal and Historical Studies in German," *Speech Monographs,* Special Issue, 1956, pp. 5-106.   1522

"Scandinavian Treatises on Preaching: A Booklist," *Speech Monographs,* March, 1954, pp. 1-9.   1523

"Spanish Treatises on Preaching: A Booklist," *Speech Monographs,* June, 1950, pp. 161-70.   1524

Key, Ralph W.
"Works on Biblical Preaching," *Interpretation,* July, 1949, pp. 314-30. Key gives his list of the classics in homiletics, the general use of the Bible, textual exposition, biographical preaching, and contextual exposition.   1525

Knower, Franklin H.
"Bibliography of Communications Dissertations in American Schools of Theology," *Speech Monographs,* June, 1963, pp. 108-36. A landmark contribution to the study of preaching and other forms of religious address.   1526

Thompson, William D.
"Teaching Speech to the Clergy: A Bibliography," *Speech Monographs,* August, 1964, pp. 350-54. The first comprehensive listing of theses, articles, books, and monographs on the process of teaching preaching.   1527

THESES AND DISSERTATIONS

General Works

Ball, Chester
"The Importance of Public Speaking in the Life of a Priest,"
M.A., Catholic University, 1949.   1528

Bateman, James LaVar
"The Use of Public Speaking in Conducting the Mormon
Church Welfare Plan." M.S., University of Wisconsin, 1947.   1529

Bell, James E.
"The Problem of Preaching." A.M., University of Chicago,
The Divinity School, 1923.   1530

Bresse, Floyd
"A Rhetorical Analysis of Twenty-Five Modern Sermons."
M.A., Sacramento State College, 1964.   1531

Burkholder, Melvin Isaac
"Persuasion in Preaching." Th.D., Northern Baptist Theological Seminary, 1958.   1532

Chamberlain, David B.
"Communication Problems in the Parish Ministry." Ph.D.,
Boston University School of Theology, 1958.   1533

Creighton, Henry R.
"The Value of the Spoken Word in the Priesthood." M.A.
Staley University, 1953.   1534

Dorris, William Glenn
"The Secrets of Pulpit Power." Th.M., Union Theological
Seminary in Virginia, 1956. 1535

Fisher, H. A.
"Communicating the Christian Message." S.T.M., San Francisco Theological Seminary, 1959. 1536

Foote, Gaston
"The Pulpit and the Program of the Non-Liturgical Protestant
Church." Th.D., Iliff Theological Seminary, 1935. 1537

Haas, Frederick W., Jr.
"A Case Study of the Speech Situation Factors Involved in
the Radio Preaching on The Hour of Decision Broadcast."
Ph.D., University of Wisconsin, 1964. 1538

Haberman, Oswald
"Dr. S. Maybaum: Jewish Homiletics (A Translation)."
M.H.L., Hebrew Union College—Jewish Institute of Religion,
1960. 1539

Jones, E. Winston
"Influencing Character Through Preaching Fashioned by
Techniques Derived from the Dramatic Arts." Th.D., Iliff
Theological Seminary, 1947. 1540

Karwehl, Hans Martin
"Preacher, Text, and Situation." S.T.M., Union Theological
Seminary, 1952. 1541

Keach, Stanley Jordan
"Preaching the Christian Faith." S.T.M., Andover-Newton
Theological School, 1946. 1542

Lachlan, Jesse
"Pulpit Eloquence." M.A., Ohio Wesleyan University, 1908. 1543

Malloy, William Charles, Jr.
"Essential Elements of Effective Preaching." Th.M., Union
Theological Seminary in Virginia, 1947. 1544

Osmunsen, Robert L.
"Relationship Between Theory and Practice of Pulpit Speaking." M.A., University of Nebraska, 1950. 1545

Perry, Gordon Lowell
"The Description and Analysis of a Process of Religious Persuasion." Ph.D., Northwestern University, 1956.   1546

Perry, Thomas Benton
"Preaching for Our Age." S.T.D., Temple University School of Theology, 1956.   1547

Platt, Charles A.
"Preaching as a Fine Art and Its Relation to Other Fine Arts." S.T.D., Temple University School of Theology, 1943.   1548

Potts, Donald R.
"Communication Principles Applied to Contemporary Preaching." Th.D., Southwestern Baptist Theological Seminary, 1959.   1549

Powell, Richard Vernon
"Preaching Power from the Living Lord." Th.M., Union Theological Seminary in Virginia, 1953.   1550

Sease, Gene E.
"The Role of the Pulpit in a Comprehensive Program of Bible Instruction." Th.M., Pittsburgh Theological Seminary, 1959.   1551

Shermer, Robert Charles
"The Minister's Extra Preaching." Th.M., Northern Baptist Theological Seminary, 1958.   1552

Shotwell, Willard L.
"A Study of the Sermon in Theory and Practice." M.A., Wayne University, 1947.   1553

Smith, James Clapsaddle
"A Christian Concept of Communication." M.S., Christian Theological Seminary, 1958.   1554

Stiner, Fred C.
"The Value of the Original Languages of the Bible for Exegetical Preaching." S.T.M., Lutheran Theological Seminary, Gettysburg, 1961.   1555

Walter, Marvin R.
"Parables for Modern Ministers." A.M., Seventh-Day Adventist Theological Seminary, 1959.   1556

Watkins, Burgin
"The Implications of Basic Communications Theory for the
Sermon." Th.D., Iliff School of Theology, 1957.   1557

Williams, John Daniel
"Implications of General Semantics for Christian Preaching."
Th.D., Southern Baptist Theological Seminary, 1954.   1558

Wright, Donald Kenneth
"An Analysis of Communicative Breakdown in Religious
Speaking." M.A., Baylor University, 1961.   1559

Preaching and Theology

Backus, William
"An Analysis of Missouri Synod Sermons Based on the Content of the New Testament Kerygma." S.T.M., Concordia Seminary, 1952.   1560

Bishop, John
"The Doctrine of the Word of God in the Scottish Pulpit as
Illustrated in the Warrack Lectures." Ph.D., Drew University,
1958.   1561

Carrell, Gene M.
"A Survey of Some Recent Writing on the Problem of the
New Testament Kerygma." M.S., Christian Theological Sem-
inary, 1959.   1562

Eggold, Henry J.
"The Word of God and Preaching." S.T.M., Concordia Seminary, 1957.   1563

Garrison, Silas Harry
"Theology and Positive Preaching." Th.M., Southern Baptist
Theological Seminary, 1956.   1564

Graves, B. C.
"The Proclamation of the Word of God in the Theology
of Karl Barth." Ph.D., Harvard Divinity School, 1947.   1565

Hardy, Richard B.
"Kerygmatic Preaching." Th.M., Union Theological Seminary
in Virginia, 1958.   1566

Hoitenga, Dewey J., Jr.
"The Symbolic Theory of Religious Language." Ph.D., Harvard Divinity School, 1959.   **1567**

Jaberg, E. C.
"Martin Buber's I-Thou Concept and Radio Preaching." M.A., University of Wisconsin, 1959.   **1568**

Kahn, Robert I.
"Liberalism as Reflected in Jewish Preaching in the English Language in the Mid-Nineteenth Century." D.H.L., Hebrew Union College—Jewish Institute of Religion, 1951.   **1569**

Kaitschuk, Walter Edwin
"The Place of the Holy Spirit in Preaching." S.T.D., Chicago Lutheran Theological Seminary, 1942.   **1570**

Kirk, J. A.
"An Analysis of Four Patterns of Meaning in Religious Language." Th.D., Iliff Theological Seminary, 1959.   **1571**

Kurzweg, Bernhard
"New Testament Preaching: An Analysis of Its Character and Purpose on the Basis of Word Studies." S.T.M., Concordia Seminary, 1952.   **1572**

Liggitt, Eugene
"The Sermon and Barthian Theology." Th.M., Pittsburgh Theological Seminary, 1934.   **1573**

Pancake, Laural Wilford
"Liberal Theology in the Yale Lectures. An Inquiry into the Extent and Influence of Liberal Theology upon Christian Preaching as Set Forth in the Lyman Beecher Lectures on Preaching, 1872-1948." Ph.D., Drew University, 1951.   **1574**

Pickell, Charles N.
"The Meaning of Acts for Preaching Today." Th.M., Pittsburgh Theological Seminary, 1957.   **1575**

Smith, Harold L.
"Reinhold Niebuhr's Doctrine of Man as Evidenced by His Speaking." M.A., Southern Illinois University, 1962.   **1576**

Stapleton, John Mason
"Kierkegaard and the Preacher: An Inquiry into His Interpretation of Christianity as It Relates to Certain Examples of Contemporary Preaching in America." S.T.M., Union Theological Seminary, 1959. 1577

Sukosky, Donald G.
"The Doctrine of the Word of God as the Basis for the Preaching of the Church." Th.M., Harvard Divinity School, 1958. 1578

Wismar, D. R.
"A Sacramental View of Preaching." Th.D., Pacific School of Religion, 1963. 1579

Topics of Preaching

Albright, Edwin W.
"Pastoral Preaching." Th.M., Louisville Presbyterian Seminary, 1954. 1580

Baird, John Stockton
"Preaching on the Holy Spirit in the Light of the New Testament Witness and the Preaching-Example of Selected Men." S.T.D., Temple University School of Theology, 1960. 1581

Brauer, Martin W.
"An Investigation of the Effectiveness of Preaching for the Purpose of Teaching Christian Doctrine." S.T.M., Concordia Seminary, 1947. 1582

Butler, Jerry
"An Analysis of the Ideas and Support in Selected Speeches of Southern, White, Protestant Ministers on Racial Issues Since 1955." M.S., Southern Illinois University, 1964. 1583

Cabbage, Leroy
"The Doctrine of Sin and Salvation in Present-Day Preaching." S.T.M., Oberlin College Graduate School of Theology, 1940. 1584

Clinard, H. Gordon
"An Evangelical Critique of the Use of the Classic Biblical Solutions to the Problem of Suffering by Representative Con-

temporary Preachers." Th.D., Southwestern Baptist Theological
Seminary, 1958.   1585

Freeman, Samuel F.
"Trends of Disciple Preaching on Christian Unity." A.M.,
University of Chicago, The Divinity School, 1936.   1586

Johnson, Clifford Ross
"Problem Preaching." Th.M., Union Theological Seminary
in Virginia, 1942.   1587

Ricks, George Hariss
"A Study of Expository Preaching with Sermons from the
Epistle to the Philippians." Th.M., Union Theological Sem-
inary in Virginia, 1954.   1588

Snipes, Kenneth Franklin
"Biographical Preaching." Th.M., Louisville Presbyterian
Seminary, 1939.   1589

Stephens, James Harris
"The Principle and Practice of Expository Preaching and
Their Application to the Galatian Epistle." Th.M., Union
Theological Seminary in Virginia, 1957.   1590

Summerell, Jouett Vernon Cosby
"Expository Preaching. Its Principles and Practices as Dem-
onstrated in a Study of the Ephesian Epistle." Th.M., Union
Theological Seminary in Virginia, 1956.   1591

Womack, James Thomas
"The Nature and Method of Expository Preaching, with
Illustrations Through Studies of the Corinthian Epistles."
Th.M., Union Theological Seminary in Virginia, 1952.   1592

The Preacher

Baird, John Edward
"A Study of the Relationship of Speech Ability and Success
as a Minister in Northern California." M.A., College of the
Pacific, 1948.   1593

Bingham, James
"The Preacher and His Message." S.T.M., Temple University
School of Theology, 1935.   1594

Crawford, Allen P.
"The Minister's Function in Preaching and Counseling." M.A.,
Union Theological Seminary, 1947. 1595

Kaye, Philip
"An Analysis of the Relationships Between Community Status
and Participation in the Processes of Religious Communication." Ph.D., University of Denver, 1955. 1596

The Congregation

Clay, Thomas Carolin
"Preaching That Meets the Needs of Men." Th.M., Union
Theological Seminary in Virginia, 1945. 1597

Dixon, James Inman
"Major Psychological Factors in Preaching." M.S., Christian
Theological Seminary, 1954. 1598

Dunagin, Martha R.
"The Effect of Study in General Semantics upon the Re-
actions to Religious Problems Presented at a Verbal Level."
M.A., University of Denver, 1945. 1599

Dye, Leslie Eugene
"A Study of the Relationships Between Preaching and Pastoral Counseling." M.S., Christian Theological Seminary, 1952. 1600

Ellis, James Welborn
"Communicating the Gospel to the Secular Mind." Th.M.,
Southern Baptist Theological Seminary, 1956. 1601

Folson, B. W.
"Psychology of Church Audiences." M.A., University of Wisconsin, 1930. 1602

Gettys, Albert C.
"The Psychology of the Revival." Th.D., Southwestern Baptist Theological Seminary, 1923. 1603

Hoyt, Harold Baldwin
"The Psychological Aspects of the Religious Platform."
D.R.E., Southwestern Baptist Theological Seminary, 1956. 1604

Hult, Dertil E.
"The Relationship of Counseling and Preaching." Th.M.,
Harvard Divinity School, 1958.   **1605**

Johnson, R. V.
"Biblical Preaching and Its Relationship to Counselling.
M.Th., Northern Baptist Theological Seminary, 1962.   **1606**

Mandrell, Nelson Eugene
"The Relevance of Dynamic Psychology for Christian Preaching." Th.D., Southern Baptist Theological Seminary, 1956.   **1607**

May, Eugene
"Relating Preaching to the Problems of the Industrial Workers." A.M., University of Chicago, The Divinity School, 1944.   **1608**

Pullen, Milton William
"Preaching and Human Needs." S.T.M., Andover-Newton
Theological School, 1944.   **1609**

Reid, Clyde H.
"Two-Way Communication Through Small Groups in Relation to Preaching." Th.D., Boston University School of Theology,
1960.   **1610**

Samples, Eual Emery
"An Experimental Study of the Effectiveness of Scripture
in Persuasive Speeches upon Attitudes of the Audience."
M.A., Mississippi Southern College, 1956.   **1611**

Seiders, Marlin David
"Survey of the Elements of Counseling and Psychotherapy
Which Apply in Preaching and Corporate Worship." Th.M.,
Harvard Divinity School, 1957.   **1612**

Simpson, James A.
"Preaching to the 'Scientific Mind' (Using the Apologetical
Work of Karl Heim as a Basis)." S.T.M., Union Theological
Seminary, 1959.   **1613**

Thompson, William D.
"A Study in Church Audience Analysis." Ph.D., Northwestern
University, 1960.   **1614**

Walrafen, Donald E.
"An Investigation of Certain Physiological Reactions to Religious Symbols." Ph.D., University of Denver, 1960.　　**1615**

Wilbur, John Milnor, Jr.
"The Relationship of Pastoral Counseling to Preaching." S.T.M., Andover-Newton Theological School, 1952.　　**1616**

Williams, R. J. W.
"The Application of the Principles of Analytic Psychology to Preaching." S.T.M., Andover-Newton Theological Seminary, 1959.　　**1617**

The Setting—Liturgical

Nebiolo, Emilio
"The Theology of the Homily in the Light of the Biblical-Liturgical Renewal." M.A., Catholic University of America, 1964.　　**1618**

The Setting—Special Occasions

Adams, Henry Babcock
"Broadcasting and the Protestant Pulpit." Th.D., San Francisco Theological Seminary, 1957.　　**1619**

Collins, Edward McDaniel
"A Survey of the Non-Pulpit Speech-making of Ministers in Iowa City and Cedar Rapids." M.S., State University of Iowa, 1958.　　**1620**

Cross, Joseph Russell
"Preaching to Children." Th.M., Louisville Presbyterian Seminary, 1938.　　**1621**

Gurganus, George
"A Case Study of a Religious Speaking Campaign." M.A., Syracuse University, 1948.　　**1622**

Youngs, Paul Austin
"A Study of Preaching to Institutionalized Juveniles." Th.M., Southern Baptist Theological Seminary, 1954.　　**1623**

The Sermon

Bogdanovich, John V.
"An Inquiry into Selected Elements of Interest and Attention Embodied in the Sermon on the Mount." M.A., Washington Theological Seminary, 1950. 1624

Brockhaus, Herman Henry
"Suggestion as a Means of Persuasion, with Special Application to the Religious Revival." M.A., University of Wisconsin, 1937. 1625

Calcagno, J. S.
"The Nature of the Oratorical Illustration and Its Use in the Sermon." M.A., Catholic University of America, 1956. 1626

Carmack, William Ross
"Invention in the Lyman Beecher Lectures on Preaching: The Lecturer's Advice on Gathering and Selecting Sermon Material." Ph.D., University of Illinois, 1958. 1627

Dunkle, William F.
"Preaching Values in the Church Year for Evangelical Protestantism." Th.M., Union Theological Seminary in Virginia, 1950. 1628

Eason, Henry Fincher
"Semantic Models Supporting the Sermon Themes of Five Contemporary Preachers." Ph.D., University of Denver, 1961. 1629

Elder, Marjorie Jeanne
"Present-Day American Pulpit Humor." M.A., University of Wisconsin, 1950. 1630

Erb, John David
"Is There a Positive Correlation Between Successful Preaching and the Use of Vivid Imagery Word-Concepts?" M.A., Ohio State University, 1938. 1631

Ewbank, Henry L.
"Objective Studies in Speech Style with Special Reference to 100 English Sermons." Ph.D., University of Wisconsin, 1932. 1632

Fenner, Allan H.
"The Preacher as a Composer." S.T.M., Lutheran Theological Seminary (Gettysburg), 1949. 1633

Foster, Arvilla M.
"An Objective Analysis of the Oral Style of Representative Sermons of Four Protestant Ministers of Fort Worth." M.A., Texas Christian University, 1955.   1634

Hotchkiss, Robert V.
"Metaphor in the Communication of Spiritual Truth." Th.M., Pittsburgh Theological Seminary, 1959.   1635

Klose, Paul Charles
"The Use of Imagination in Preaching." Th.M., Northern Baptist Theological Seminary, 1950.   1636

Liddle, N. I.
"Fundamental Principles of Homiletics Inherent in Literary Expression." Th.D., Northern Baptist Theological Seminary, 1959.   1637

Manes, Everett E.
"The Use of Illustration in Contemporary Preaching." A.M., University of Chicago, The Divinity School, 1935.   1638

Mayfield, James L.
"An Analysis of Expectations for the Responsibility Concerning Topic Selection of Protestant Ministers as Preachers." Ph.D., Michigan State University, 1964.   1639

Miller, Harold Allen
"A Comparison of the Forms of Support Used in Contemporary American Protestant Pulpit Address with the Forms of Support Used in Other Contemporary American Public Address: A Content Analysis." Ph.D., University of Minnesota, 1962.   1640

Olbricht, Thomas Henry
"Methods of Sermon Preparation and Delivery Employed by Clergymen in Iowa City and Cedar Rapids." M.A., State University of Iowa, 1953.   1641

Saylor, Donald Ray
"Literary Devices of Attention in Contemporary Preaching." Th.M., Southern Baptist Theological Seminary, 1956.   1642

Scherich, Millard
"Method in the Homiletic Use of the Dramas of Shakespeare." Th.D., Iliff Theological Seminary, 1937.   1643

Smith, Donald George
"Sermon Illustrations." Th.M., Northern Baptist Theological Seminary, 1951.   **1644**

Smith, E. Debs
"A Relating of Several Formulations from General Semantics to Certain Teachings and Communication Methods of Jesus as Reported in the Synoptic Gospels of Matthew, Mark and Luke." Ph.D., Denver University, 1952.   **1645**

Toohey, William, C.S.C.
"An Investigation of Implicative Inference as a Possible Aid to Preaching the Word of God." M.A., Holy Cross College, 1961.   **1646**

Turnbull, Roland E.
"Principles for Planning a Baptist Preaching Program." Th.D., Northern Baptist Theological Seminary, 1947.   **1647**

Weiss, Daniel E.
"Conceptions of 'Arrangement' in American Protestant Homiletical Theory." Ph.D., Michigan State University, 1964.   **1648**

White, Walter H.
"Preaching Values in the Dead Sea Scrolls." S.T.M., Temple University School of theology, 1957.   **1649**

Delivery

Barton, Fred Jackson
"Modes of Delivery in American Homiletic Theory in the Eighteenth and Nineteenth Centuries." Ph.D., State University of Iowa, 1949.   **1650**

Bussis, Dale
"The Minister as Interpreter and Communicator in Worship." D.Ed., Columbia University, Teachers College, 1964.   **1651**

Caron, Gerard
"Oral Interpretation of the Sunday Gospels." M.A., Emerson College, 1955.   **1652**

Case, E. Lewis
"Application of the Critical Incident Technique for the Assessment of Effective and Ineffective Behaviors Performed by Clergy-

men While Delivering Their Sermons." M.A., University of
Pittsburgh, 1963.   **1653**

Crews, Leerie Denton, Jr.
"Modes of Delivery in American Homiletics, 1900-1961." M.A.,
University of Maryland, 1963.   **1654**

Dent, Mary Grace
"The Relationship of Speech Skills to Pulpit Communication."
M.A., Southern Methodist University, 1952.   **1655**

Goodman, Fidelis
"The Effective Reading of the Epistle and Gospel at Sunday
Mass." M.A., Catholic University of America, 1962.   **1656**

Grauer, George Albert
"The Pronunciation of Proper Names in the Bible." M.A.,
Baylor University, 1947.   **1657**

Koenig, Norma E.
"The Relation of Interpretative Reading to Preaching." A.M.,
University of Chicago, The Divinity School, 1947.   **1658**

Price, Navalyne
"The Delsarte Philosophy of Expression as Seen Through
Certain Manuscripts of the Rev. William R. Alger." M.A.,
Louisiana State University, 1941.   **1659**

Sims, Coy D.
"Oral Techniques in American Evangelism." M.A., Wayne
University, 1956.   **1660**

Williams, Howard Bruce
"The Emphasis on the Use of Voice in Sermon Delivery in the
United States, 1827-1953." Th.M., Southern Baptist Theological
Seminary, 1954.   **1661**

History—Individual Preachers

Aarvold, Ole
"Clovis G. Chappell: The Man and His Message." Th.M.,
Asbury Theological Seminary, 1953.   **1662**

Abernathy, Elton
"An Evaluation of Alexander Campbell's Debating Techniques." M.A., University of Iowa, 1937.   **1663**

Adams, Elizabeth A.
"An Analysis of Style in Representative Sermons of Dr. Peter Marshall." M.A., University of Michigan, 1953.   **1664**

Adams, Jay Edward
"Sense Appeal in the Sermons of Charles Haddon Spurgeon." S.T.M., Temple University School of Theology, 1958.   **1665**

Alder, George
"Alexander Campbell's Invention in the Debate with Robert Owen." M.A., San Jose State College, 1959.   **1666**

Alexander, Wilber
"A Rhetorical Analysis of the Speaking of H.M.S. Richards in Connection with the 'Voice of Prophecy' Radio Broadcast of the Seventh-Day Adventist Church." Ph.D., Michigan State University, 1962.   **1667**

Allbritten, Robert Gary
"John Morgan Walden: Circuit Rider." M.A., Indiana University, 1963.   **1668**

Andrews, Wayne
"A Critical Study of Jonathan Edwards' Use of the Motive of Fear in a Selected Group of Sermons." M.A., Seventh-Day Adventist Theological Seminary, 1954.   **1669**

Annich, Russel W.
"Barth, the Preacher." S.T.D., Temple University School of Theology, 1943.   **1670**

Ashbaugh, Kraid I.
"An Analysis of the Sermons of James White, Early Advent Preacher, with Emphasis on Persuasion." M.A., Seventh-Day Adventist Theological Seminary, Washington, 1951.   **1671**

Austin, Mary Teresita, R.S.M.
"The Political, Economic, and Social Aspects of Edward VI's Reign as Viewed Through the Sermons and Letters of Hugh Latimer." Ph.D., Michigan State University, 1961.   **1672**

Backstrom, David A.
"An Analysis of the Elements of Persuasion Used by Billy Sunday in the Monmouth, Illinois, Evangelistic Campaign." M.S., University of Wisconsin, 1958.   **1673**

Baggett, Hudson Doyle
"A Study of Spurgeon's Preaching Method." Th.M., Southern
Baptist Theological Seminary, 1951.   **1674**

"The Principles and Art of G. Campbell Morgan as a Bible
Expositor." Th.D., Southern Baptist Theological Seminary, 1956.   **1675**

Bailey, Richard Eugene
"A Rhetorical Study of Selected Sermons of Washington
Gladden." M.A., Ohio State University, 1964.   **1676**

Baird, John Edward
"The Preaching of William Franklin Graham." Ph.D., Colum-
bia University, Teachers College, 1959.   **1677**

Banowsky, William
"The Preaching of H. Leo Boles." M.A., University of New
Mexico, 1959.   **1678**

Barnhart, Elbert
"A Rhetorical Analysis of the Preaching of N. B. Hardeman."
M.A., University of New Mexico, 1953.   **1679**

Barrett, Daniel A.
"A Homiletical Analysis of Doctor William Franklin (Billy)
Graham's Sermon 'Our Teen-Age Problem.' " M.A., University of
Hawaii, 1961.   **1680**

Bass, George M.
"The Use of the Bible in the Preaching of Martin Luther."
S.T.D. Temple University School of Theology, 1957.   **1681**

Beers, V. Gilbert
"The Preaching Theory and Practice of John Henry Jowett."
Ph.D., Northwestern University, 1963.   **1682**

Behnke, Ralph Richard
"A Rhetorical Criticism of the Radio Preaching of Reverend
Evan A. Fry in the 'Hear Ye Him' Radio Broadcasts." M.S.,
University of Wisconsin, 1963.   **1683**

Bell, Earl Stanton
"The Preaching of John Richard Sampey." Th.M., Southern
Baptist Theological Seminary, 1954.   **1684**

Berghuis, Melvin E.
"A Rhetorical Study of the Preaching of the Rev. Peter Elders-
veld on the 'Back-to-God-Hour' Radio Broadcast." Ph.D.,
Michigan State University, 1964.   **1685**

Bernhardt, Roger B.
"Henry Ward Beecher's Application of His Own Theories of
Persuasion." M.S., University of Wisconsin, 1947.   **1686**

Bethgate, John
"Paul Tillich as a Preacher of Grace." S.T.M., Union Theological Seminary, 1959.   **1687**

Betts, Mary Lou
"Billie James Hargis: Orator in the Anti-Communist Move-
ment." M.A., California State College, Long Beach, 1964.   **1688**

Boase, Paul H.
"Peter Cartwright: Preacher and Politician." M.S., University
of Wisconsin, 1947.   **1689**

Boder, William Dunbar
"A Rhetorical Analysis of Theophilus Mills Taylor." M.A.,
Ohio State University, 1964.   **1690**

Bos, William Herman
"Henry Van Dyke's Ideas on Rhetorical Invention: The Yale
Lectures and Selected Sermons." M.A., Washington University,
1951.   **1691**

"A Study of the Preaching of Henry Van Dyke." Ph.D., University of Michigan, 1955.   **1692**

Bouwsman, Franklin G.
"A Rhetorical Analysis of Selected Sermons of Jonathan
Edwards." M.A., University of Michigan, 1950.   **1693**

Bowers, George Palmer
"An Evaluation of the Billy Graham Greater Louisville Evangelistic Crusade." Th.M., Southern Baptist Theological Seminary,
1958.   **1694**

Boyatt, Bernard Cooper
"George W. Truett, Preacher and Public Speaker." M.A., University of Tennessee, 1952.   **1695**

Boyce, Rudolph
"Four Sermons of Billy Graham Delivered in Detroit, 1953."
M.A., Wayne University, 1955.   **1696**

Brack, Harold A.
"Ernest Fremont Tittle's Theory and Practice of Preaching."
Ph.D., Northwestern University, 1953.   **1697**

Brannon, Richard Scott
"George W. Truett: Evangelist." Th.M., Southern Baptist
Theological Seminary, 1954.   **1698**

"George Washington Truett and His Preaching." Th.D., Southwestern Baptist Theological Seminary, 1956.   **1699**

Brinegar, Haywood C.
"Alexander Campbell as a Debater." M.A., University of Tennessee, 1950.   **1700**

Broadhurst, Allan R.
"A Thematic Analysis and Rhetorical Study of the Sermons of
Norman Vincent Peale." Ph.D., Michigan State University, 1961.   **1701**

Bulgarelli, Mary LaVerne
"Saint Francis of Assisi, the Medieval Orator." M.A., University
of Wisconsin, 1936.   **1702**

Bunton, Norman Desha
"A Rhetorical Analysis of Representative Sermons of John
Donne." Ph.D., State University of Iowa, 1954.   **1703**

Burks, William Hugh
"John Donne's Wit: An Analysis of the Figures of Contrariety
and Contradiction in the Lincoln's Inn Sermons." M.A., University of Tennessee, 1956.   **1704**

Burtner, Elmer Edwin
"The Use of Biblical Materials in the Sermons of Harry
Emerson Fosdick." Th.D., Boston University School of Theology,
1959.   **1705**

Cabbage, Monyne L.
"Charles R. Brown's Theories of the Art of Preaching." M.A.,
University of Michigan, 1953.   **1706**

Camp, Leon R.
  "A Rhetorical Analysis of the Speaking of Roger Williams in the Quaker Debates of 1672." M.A., Indiana University, 1961. **1707**

Carley, Glen Milton
  "A Rhetorical Study of Selected Sermons of Ellen G. White on Righteousness by Faith." M.A., Seventh-Day Adventist Theological Seminary, 1954. **1708**

Cartwright, George Washington
  "The Rhetorical Practice and Theory of Edgar DeWitt Jones." Ph.D., University of Illinois, 1951. **1709**

Cash, William
  "A Study of the Radio Addresses of Father Charles Edward Coughlin, 1938-1940." M.A., Kent State University, 1964. **1710**

Cerino, Dorothy V.
  "The Rhetoric and Dialectic of Isidorus of Seville: Translation and Commentary." M.A., Brooklyn College, 1938. **1711**

Chamberlain, Charles Abiel
  "The Preaching of the Apostle Paul, Based on a Study of Acts of the Apostles and Paul's Letters, with Special Reference to the First and Second Corinthians." S.T.D., Temple University School of Theology, 1959. **1712**

Cheesbro, Roy Alan
  "The Preaching of Charles G. Finney." Ph.D., Yale University Divinity School, 1948. **1713**

Cheney, Lois A.
  "A Rhetorical Study of Selected Speeches of Dr. Albert Schweitzer." Ph.D., Michigan State University, 1961. **1714**

Cherry, Russell Thomas, Jr.
  "The Ministry of Frederick W. Robertson." Th.D., Southern Baptist Theological Seminary, 1953. **1715**

Christensen, John A.
  "Legacy of John Chrysostom to Christian Preaching." S.T.M., Biblical Seminary in New York, 1934. **1716**

Clark, Robert D.
  "The Pulpit and Platform Career and the Rhetorical Theory of Bishop Mathew Simpson." Ph.D., University of Southern California, 1946. **1717**

Cloonan, Benignus
"The Preaching Style of St. Francis of Assisi." M.A., Catholic
University, 1953.   1718

Connolly, William Kenneth
"The Preaching of J. Frank Norris." M.A., University of
Nebraska, 1961.   1719

Conrad, F. Leslie, Jr.
"The Preaching of George Whitefield, with Special Reference
to the American Colonies." S.T.D., Temple University School of
Theology, 1959.   1720

Cook, Harold W.
"A Critical Analysis of the Use of Emotion as a Technique of
Persuasion in Selected Anti-Communist Speeches of Dr. Billy
James Hargis." M.A., Bowling Green State University, 1963.   1721

Covington, Virginia Carroll
"Rhetorical Analysis of Three Representative Sermons by
Jonathan Mayhew." M.A., University of Iowa, 1957.   1722

Cox, Robert J.
"A Study of Some Elements of the Homiletical Theory of
Charles Grandison Finney." M.A., University of Washington,
1951.   1723

Cox, Vincent Astor
"The Expository Preaching of Frederick William Robertson."
Th.D., Southwestern Baptist Theological Seminary, 1955.   1724

Cragen, Damian Bernard
"A Rhetorical Analysis of Five Sermons of Cardinal Newman
with Special Reference to Aristotle's Rhetoric." M.A., University
of Washington, 1943.   1725

Crawford, Paul K.
"The Rise of the Reverend Charles Edward Coughlin, Radio
Speaker." Ph.M., University of Wisconsin, 1936.   1726

Crim, L. Alvah
"A Rhetorical Analysis of the Preaching of Billy Graham in
the Indianapolis, Indiana, Crusade, October 6–November 1,
1959." M.A., Indiana University, 1961.   1727

Crocker, Lionel
"The Rhetorical Theory of Henry Ward Beecher." Ph.D., University of Michigan, 1933.
1728

Crook, William Herbert
"The Contributive Factors in the Life and Preaching of Charles Haddon Spurgeon." Th.D., Southwestern Baptist Theological Seminary, 1956.
1729

Currie, Andrew C.
"Modern Pulpit Persuasion: An Analysis of Selected Evangelistic Services Presented by Rex E. Humbard." M.S., Purdue University, 1963.
1730

Curtis, Richard K.
"The Pulpit Speaking of Dwight L. Moody." Ph.D., Purdue University, 1954.
1731

Curtis, Wilson A.
"A Rhetorical Study of the Sermons of Robert G. Lee." M.A., University of Houston, 1961.
1732

Derby, Matthew I.
"A Study of Rabbi Levi Yitzhok of Berdychev: Based on the Hasidic Legends and His Sermons and Comments Contained in His Kedushat Levi Ha-shalem." M.H.L., Hebrew Union College —Jewish Institute of Religion, 1960.
1733

Despland, Michel Samuel
"Kierkegaard and Communication." Th.M., Harvard Divinity School, 1960.
1734

Dodson, Margaret Cecilia
"The Use of Literary Allusions in the Sermons of Frank W. Gunsaulus." M.S., Northwestern University, 1931.
1735

Doebler, Bettie Anne
"Death in the Sermons of John Donne." Ph.D., University of Wisconsin, 1961.
1736

Drafahl, Elnora M.
"An Analysis of the Figures of Speech as Aids to Clearness in the War Sermons of Dr. Harry Emerson Fosdick." M.A., University of South Dakota, 1946.
1737

Dreher, John James
"A Rhetorical Criticism of the Epistle to the Hebrews." A.M.,
University of Michigan, 1947.   **1738**

Duncan, William Walter
"A Study of the Clergyman, Ralph W. Sockman, as a Radio
Speaker." M.A., University of Michigan, 1949.   **1739**

Dygoski, Louise Annie
"The Journals and Letters of John Wesley on Preaching."
Ph.D., University of Wisconsin, 1961.   **1740**

Eckenroth, Melvin
"A Delimited Study of Evangelistic Methodology as Contained
in the Writings of Mrs. Ellen G. White and as Applied to Contemporary Situations." M.A., Seventh-Day Adventist Theological
Seminary, 1956.   **1741**

Ellis, Beverly
"A Study of Audience Adaptation in the Speeches of the
Prophet Isaiah." M.A., University of Washington, 1963.   **1742**

Ellis, Carroll B.
"The Controversial Speaking of Alexander Campbell." M.A.,
Louisiana State University, 1949.   **1743**

Emmel, James Robert
"Speaking and Speeches of Roy T. Williams." M.A., University
of Oklahoma, 1950.   **1744**

"The Persuasive Techniques of Charles Grandison Finney as
a Revivalist and Social Reform Speaker, 1820-1860." Ph.D.,
Pennsylvania State University, 1959.   **1745**

Enfield, James R.
"The Preaching and Sermons of Peter Marshall." M.A., Baylor
University, 1960.   **1746**

Enzor, Edwin H., Jr.
"The Preaching of James M'Gready: Frontier Revivalist."
Ph.D., Louisiana State University, 1964.   **1747**

Faber, Warren Herman
"A Critical Rhetorical Study of the Effect of Horace Bushnell's
Theory of Language upon His Theory of Homiletics and His
Practice of Preaching." Ph.D., Northwestern University, 1962.   **1748**

Fahrner, William F.
"The Persuasive Techniques of Aimee Semple McPherson."
M.A., University of Redlands, 1949.   1749

Faircloth, Thomas Curtin
"The Ministry of Russell H. Conwell." Th.M., Southern Baptist
Theological Seminary, 1954.   1750

Faulconer, Joe Stanley
"Phillips Brooks." Th.M., Louisville Presbyterian Seminary,
1936.   1751

Ferri, Joseph M.
"Mary Baker Eddy: A Woman Who Founded a Church."
M.S., Emerson College, 1961.   1752

Flory, Elizabeth Bowman
"A Study of the Ethical Proof of Peter Marshall." M.A.,
Florida State University, 1955.   1753

Floyd, William Kirk
"An Examination of the Audience Adaptation of Apostle Paul
in His Speech to the Athenians." M.A., University of Oklahoma,
1958.   1754

Flynt, William T.
"Jonathan Edwards and His Preaching." Th.D., Southern
Baptist Theological Seminary, 1954.   1755

Ford, Desmond
"A Rhetorical Study of Certain Pauline Addresses." Ph.D.,
Michigan State University, 1960.   1756

Freeman, Thomas F.
"A Study in the Criteria of Effective Preaching Through an
Analysis of the Preaching of Phillips Brooks." Ph.D., University
of Chicago, The Divinity School, 1948.   1757

Fry, Donna
"A Rhetorical Analysis of P. H. Welshimer." M.A., Ohio State
University, 1964.   1758

Gable, Mariella, O.S.B.
"The Rhetoric of John Henry Newman's Parochial and Plain
Sermons with Special Reference to His Dependence on Aristotle's
Rhetoric." Ph.D., Cornell University, 1934.   1759

Garff, Royal Lovell
"A Study of Henry Ward Beecher's Methods of Controlling Hostile Audiences." M.A., Northwestern University, 1932. **1760**

Gehring, Mary Louise
"The Invention of Russell H. Conwell in His Lecture, 'Acres of Diamonds.'" M.A., Louisiana State University, 1949. **1761**

"A Rhetorical Study of the Lectures and Sermons of Russell H. Conwell." Ph.D., Louisiana State University, 1952. **1762**

Gehrki, Barbara Ann
"A Rhetorical Analysis of the Speaking of Archbishop Ireland." M.A., Saint Louis University, 1958. **1763**

Gilchrist, Bennie Jon
"A Rhetorical Analysis of Selected Discourses of Brigham Young." M.A., Texas Technological College, 1964. **1764**

Girtman, Harry Spruiell
"The Preaching of William Frank 'Billy' Graham." Th.M., Southern Baptist Theological Seminary, 1955. **1765**

Goldburg, Robert E.
"Hyman G. Enelow—Rabbi, Scholar, and Preacher." M.H.L., Hebrew Union College—Jewish Institute of Religion, 1945. **1766**

Gonce, Albert A.
"A Rhetorical Analysis of Selected Occasional Addresses of Alexander Campbell, 1835-1858." M.A., University of Alabama, 1950. **1767**

Gordon, Julius
"The Homiletics of Hasidim." D.H.L., Hebrew Union College —Jewish Institute of Religion, 1945. **1768**

Granade, Audrey Pugh
"The Devotional Preaching of Jonathan Edwards." Th.M., Southern Baptist Theological Seminary, 1950. **1769**

Grant, David McMurray
"The Homiletic Rhetoric of Hugo Blair." Ph.D., Stanford University, 1953. **1770**

Graves, Newton Abbott
"The Preaching of Robert Hall." Th.M., Southern Baptist
Theological Seminary, 1957.   **1771**

Griffith, Francis J.
"The Speeches of Daniel O'Connell on Catholic Emancipation:
The Oratory of an Agitator." Ed.D., Columbia University,
Teachers College, 1958.   **1772**

Haberman, Joshua O.
"Isak Noa Mannheimer as Preacher." M.H.L., Hebrew Union
College—Jewish Institute of Religion, 1945.   **1773**

Hagstrum, Jean Howard
"The Sermons of Samuel Johnson." Ph.D., Yale University
Divinity School, 1941.   **1774**

Hall, Joseph Calvin
"Basic Theological and Ethical Concepts of Harry Emerson
Fosdick." Th.D., Southern Baptist Theological Seminary, 1958.   **1775**

Hamel, Barbara J.
"A Structural Analysis of Selected Radio Sermons of Dr. Ralph
W. Sockman." M.A., University of Michigan, 1950.   **1777**

Hammond, Lansing van der Heyden
"The Use of Sources in the Sermons of Sterne." Ph.D., Yale
University Divinity School, 1940.   **1778**

Hance, Kenneth G.
"The Rhetorical Theory of Phillips Brooks." Ph.D., University
of Michigan, 1937.   **1779**

Hardine, Leslie
"A Study of the Pulpit Public Address of Hugh Macmillan."
Th.M., Seventh-Day Adventist Theological Seminary, 1959.   **1780**

Hardings, Leslie G.
"An Examination of the Philosophy of Persuasion in Pulpit
Oratory Advocated in the Writings of Ellen Gould White." M.A.,
Washington University, 1950.   **1781**

Harris, Robbie James
"John Chrysostom's Use of the Homily." Th.M., Southern
Baptist Theological Seminary, 1957.   **1782**

Hass, Herbert
"A Historical and Critical Analysis of Tyng's Pulpit and Public
Addresses on Issues Current from 1845 to 1865." M.A., Temple
University School of Theology, 1960.   **1783**

Hasson, Alan Guthrahan
"The Consistent Preacher: A Preliminary Investigation of
Jonathan Edwards." S.T.M., Union Theological Seminary, 1957.   **1784**

Hausman, Irving I.
"The Sermons of Isaac Nissembaum." M.H.L., Hebrew Union
College—Jewish Institute of Religion, 1940.   **1785**

Heisey, David Ray
"A Rhetorical Study of Charles Grandison Finney." M.A.,
Ohio State University, 1955.   **1786**

Hendrickson, Ernest H.
"Rhetorical Elements in Beecher's English Addresses." M.A.,
University of Iowa, 1929.   **1787**

Herman, Erwin L.
"Rabbi Johanan Bar Nappacha and His Homilies." M.H.L.,
Hebrew Union College—Jewish Institute of Religion, n.d.   **1788**

Hewgill, Murray A.
"An Analysis of the Motive and Ethical Appeals Used by Jesus
in Mark's Gospel." M.A., University of Michigan, 1953.   **1789**

Hewitt, George Street
"The Centrality of the Ethical Emphasis in the Preaching of
John Chrysostom." S.T.D., Temple University School of The-
ology, 1957.   **1790**

Hibbard, Robert Bruce
"The Life and Ministry of Ralph Washington Sockman."
Ph.D., Boston University School of Theology, 1957.   **1791**

Hietzner, Richard S.
"A Critical Analysis of William Franklin Graham as a
Speaker." M.A., University of Michigan, 1952.   **1792**

Hill, Dietrich Arno
"The *Modus Praedicandi* of John Donne: A Rhetorical Analysis of Selected Sermons of John Donne with Regard Specifically to the Theory of Preaching Which He Put into Practice." Ph.D., University of Illinois, 1962.   **1793**

Hitchcock, Orville Alvin
"A Critical Study of the Oratorical Techniques of Jonathan Edwards." Ph.D., State University of Iowa, 1936.   **1794**

Hobrecht, Hilary
"St. Francis of Assisi, the Model of Franciscan Preachers." M.A., Catholic University, 1949.   **1795**

Hochmuth, Marie
"William Ellery Channing, D.D., A Study in Public Address." Ph.D., University of Wisconsin, 1945.   **1796**

Holland, DeWitte T.
"An Analytical Study of Selected Sermons of G. W. Truett." M.A., University of Alabama, 1950.   **1797**

"A Rhetorical Analysis of the Preaching of George W. Truett." Ph.D., Northwestern University, 1956.   **1798**

Horn, George Garrison
"Elements of Power in the Preaching of John Henry Newman." Th.D., Biblical Seminary in New York, 1935.   **1799**

Hostetter, Richard
"Source of Effectiveness in the Doctrinal Preaching of Zachary Taylor Sweeney." M.A., Kent State University, 1964.   **1800**

Hotchkiss, Golda L.
"A Rhetorical Analysis of Selected Sermons of Norman Vincent Peale." M.A., University of Michigan, 1954.   **1801**

Hovee, Gene H.
"Janson Lee: A Rhetorical Criticism of His Sermon on the Oregon Mission." M.A., University of Oregon, 1963.   **1802**

Huber, Paul
"A Study of the Rhetorical Theories of John A. Broadus." Ph.D., University of Michigan, 1956.   **1803**

Huber, Robert
"Dwight L. Moody: Salesman of Salvation—A Case Study on Audience Psychology." Ph.D., University of Wisconsin, 1942.   **1804**

Hull, Lloyd Beverly
"A Rhetorical Study of the Preaching of William Bell Riley." Ph.D., Wayne State University, 1960.   **1805**

Hunter, Edward Gordon
"The Apostle Paul as a Preacher as Related to Acts and II Corinthians." S.T.M., Temple University School of Theology, 1958.   **1806**

Huntsinger, Jerald
"The Sermons of Harry Emerson Fosdick: A Study." S.T.M., Temple University School of Theology, 1959.   **1807**

Hyde, Gordon Mahlon
"A Case Study Approach to the Rhetorical Analysis of the Washington Preaching of Dr. Peter Marshall." Ph.D., Michigan State University, 1963.   **1808**

Insko, Chester Arthur
"The Biblical Preaching of Alexander Maclaren." Th.D., Southern Baptist Theological Seminary, 1950.   **1809**

Jackson, James B., Jr.
"A Study of the Sermon Illustrations Used by Ernest Fremont Tittle." Th.M., Southern Baptist Theological Seminary, 1955.   **1810**

Jacques, Brian
"An Analysis of Persuasive Techniques in the Religious Addresses of William Jennings Bryan." M.A., Seventh-Day Adventist Theological Seminary, 1954.   **1811**

Jaffa, Philip W.
"Gotthold Salomon as a Preacher." M.H.L., Hebrew Union College—Jewish Institute of Religion, 1928.   **1812**

Jones, George Alexander
"Richard Fuller and His Preaching." Th.D., Southern Baptist Theological Seminary, 1953.   **1813**

Jones, Warren S.
"G. C. Brewer: Lecturer, Debater, and Preacher," Ph.D., Wayne University, 1959.   **1814**

Katt, Arthur Frederick
"A Rhetorical Analysis of the Preaching of G. Campbell Morgan." Ph.D., Indiana University, 1963.

1815

Katzenatein, Martin
"The Homilies of Rabbi Joshua Ban Levi." M.H.L., Hebrew Union College—Jewish Institute of Religion, 1950.

1816

Kelley, Barbara Marie
"A Rhetorical Analysis of Gilbert Tennent, 1735-1745." M.A., State University of Iowa, 1951.

1817

Kennel, LeRoy Eldon
"A Rhetorical Criticism of Three Sermons by John S. Coffman, Nineteenth-Century Mennonite Educator and Evangelist." M.A., State University of Iowa, 1952.

1818

Keown, Harlice Edmond
"The Preaching of Andrew Fuller." Th.M., Southern Baptist Theological Seminary, 1957.

1819

Kline, Omer
"The Public Address of James Cardinal Gibbons as a Catholic Spokesman on Social Issues in America." D.Ed., Columbia University, Teachers College, 1963.

1820

Krensensky, Ardia Marcia
"The Style of Phillips Brooks's Sermons in 1878." M.A., State University of Iowa, 1951.

1821

Kully, Robert Delmar
"Isaac Mayer Wise: His Rhetoric Against Religious Discrimination." Ph.D., University of Illinois, 1956.

1822

Lacour, Lawrence L.
"Bishop Edwin Holt Hughes' Theory and Practice of Preaching." M.A., Northwestern University, 1950.

1823

Lantz, William C.
"An Investigation of the Field Preaching of John Wesley." M.A., Denver University, 1950.

1824

Larkin, Juanita J.
"Fulton J. Sheen's Career on Radio and Television." M.S., University of Wisconsin, 1954.

1825

Larson, Orvin Prentiss
"Phillips Brooks's Theory and Practice of Preaching." M.A., University of Iowa, 1937.

1826

"Invention in Ingersoll's Lectures on Religion." Ph.D., University of Iowa, 1969.

1827

Larson, P. Merville
"A Rhetorical Study of Bishop Nicholas Frederick Severin Grundtvig." Ph.D., Northwestern University, 1942.

1828

LaVerne, Mary
"Saint Francis of Assisi, the Medieval Orator." M.A., University of Wisconsin, 1936.

1829

Lavine, Barnard H.
"The Homilies in Leviticus Rabbah." M.H.L., Hebrew Union College—Jewish Institute of Religion, 1942.

1830

Le Vander, Theodor
"A Critical Evaluation of Dr. Fosdick's Radio Address in 'National Vespers' for the Season 1939-1940." M.A., State University of Iowa, 1940.

1831

Levin, Herschel
"The Sermons of Saul Levi Morteira." M.H.L., Hebrew Union College—Jewish Institute of Religion, 1942.

1832

Lewis, Ralph Loren
"Style and Appeals in the Book of Hosea." M.A., University of Michigan, 1952.

1833

Lien, Jerry
"Savonarola: The Speaker and His Public Address." M.A., Seventh-Day Adventist Theological Seminary, 1955.

1834

Linn, Edmund H.
"A Rhetorical Analysis of the Methods of Proof in Representative Sermons of the Reverend Dr. Harry Emerson Fosdick." M.A., State University of Iowa, 1949.

1835

"The Rhetorical Theory and Practice of Harry Emerson Fosdick." Ph.D., State University of Iowa, 1952.

1836

Livingstone, Paul Yount
"The Biblical Homiletics of Martin Luther." S.T.M., Biblical Seminary in New York, 1930.

1837

Lloyd, Mark Brooks
"An Analysis of the Pulpit Oratory of Phillips Brooks." M.A., University of Southern California, 1941.   **1838**

Lothers, William Thereon
"The Concept and Rhetorical Treatment of Sin in Selected Sermons of Timothy Dwight." M.A., University of Oklahoma, 1958.   **1839**

Loughery, James
"The Rhetorical Theory of John Cardinal Newman." Ph.D., University of Michigan, 1952.   **1840**

Love, Bill
"A Rhetorical Study of John S. Sweeny's Nashville Sermons." M.S., Abilene Christian College, 1964.   **1841**

Lucas, Richard Dark
"The Preaching of Clarence E. Macartney." Th.D., Southern Baptist Theological Seminary, 1959.   **1842**

Lunsford, Rowan
"The Evangelistic Campaigns of Dwight L. Moody." M.A., University of Redlands, 1945.   **1843**

Lymon, Herschel
"The Homilies in Numbers Rabbah." M.H.L., Hebrew Union College—Jewish Institute of Religion, 1942.   **1844**

McAlister, Virginia
"A Rhetorical Analysis of Style in Selected Recorded Sermons of Peter Marshall." M.S., Kansas State College of Pittsburg, 1964.   **1845**

McClain, Thomas
"A Rhetorical Study of Selected Sermons of Russell V. De-Long." M.A., University of Redlands, 1959.   **1846**

McClerren, Beryl F.
"An Analysis of Selected Speeches of Glenn L. Archer." M.A., Southern Illinois University, 1960.   **1847**

McClintock, James R.
"The Role of Speaking in the Career of Mary Baker Eddy." M.A., Cornell University, 1960.   **1848**

McClung, James Allen
"Dr. James Blaine Chapman's Theory of Preaching." M.A., University of Kansas, 1962.   1849

McDiarmid, A. B.
"A Critique of H. E. Fosdick's Conception of Preaching as Personal Counselling on a Group Scale." Th.D., Pacific School of Religion, 1961.   1850

McLain, Thomas
"A Rhetorical Study of Selected Sermons of Russell V. De-Long." M.A., University of Redlands, 1960.   1851

McLeod, N. Bruce
"Levels of Relevance in Preaching, a Historical Study of the Communication of the Word by a Witness, with Special Attention to the Principles of Interpretation Used in the Preaching of Phillips Brooks from 1859-1892." Th.D., Union Theological Seminary, 1960.   1852

Madden, Margaret D.
"Savonarola—the Orator." M.A., University of Wisconsin, 1936.   1853

Maheu, Antonine Marie
"A 'Dramatistic' Approach to a Rhetorical Study of the Sermon on the Mount." M.A., University of Hawaii, 1953.   1854

Malone, Henry
"The Radio Preaching Art of the Right Reverend Monsignor Fulton John Sheen." M.A., Catholic University, 1949.   1855

Mankin, Jay W.
"A Study of the Logical, Ethical, and Emotional Proofs in Three Selected Sermons by Henry Drummond." M.A., Florida State University, 1954.   1856

March, T. H.
"Bishop W. A. Quayle's Theory and Practice of Preaching." Ph.D., Northwestern University, 1947.   1857

Marlin, Charles Lowell
"The Preaching of Jemima Wilkinson: Public Universal Friend." M.A., Indiana University, 1961.   1858

Marlin, Francis Earl
"A Rhetorical Criticism of St. John Chrysostom's Homily III in the Statues." M.A., State University of Iowa, 1951.   **1859**

Martin, Albert
"Pulpit and Platform Speaking of Thomas N. Burke." Ph.D., University of Wisconsin, 1956.   **1860**

Martin, Bernard
"The Message of Emil G. Hirsch's Sermons." M.H.L., Hebrew Union College—Jewish Institute of Religion, 1951.   **1861**

Martin, Henry Lawrence
"A Study of the Sermons of Frederick William Robertson." Th.M., Southern Baptist Theological Seminary, 1954.   **1862**

Marty, Martin E.
"The Holy Spirit in Martin Luther's Preaching on the Gospel Pericopes." S.T.M., Chicago Lutheran Theological Seminary, 1954.   **1863**

Mashburn, Robert
"*Dispositio* in the Sunday Sermons of Jeremy Taylor." M.A., University of Tennessee, 1957.   **1864**

Mattis, Norman Wayne
"The Structure of a Group of Sermons of Doctor Robert Smith." M.A., Cornell University, 1929.   **1865**

Mehrling, Benjamin P.
"A Rhetorical Study of the Preaching of Dr. Henry Hitt Crane." Ph.D., Wayne State University, 1964.   **1866**

Miles, Kenneth LeRoy
"Persuasive Techniques in Selected Sermons by Dr. T. T. Shields." M.A., University of Washington, 1951.   **1867**

Miller, Arthur B.
"A Rhetorical Analysis of the Homiletic Theory and Practice of Austin Phelps." Ph.D., University of Oregon, 1964.   **1868**

Miller, Donald
"Righteousness by Faith as a Motivating Factor in the Public Address of Charles Fitch." M.A., Seventh-Day Adventist Theological Seminary, 1950.   **1869**

Miller, Donald C.
"An Analysis of Colonial Pulpit Speaking in the Salem
Witchcraft Delusion, as Evidenced by Cotton Mather's Dis-
course." M.A., University of South Dakota, 1960.   1870

Miller, George William
"A Study of Motivation in the Preaching of Harry Emerson
Fosdick." Th.M., Southern Baptist Theological Seminary, 1955. 1871

Miller, Joseph Morgan
"Anthony of Padua, Doctor Evangelicus: A Biographical Sketch
and Translations from the *Sermones.*" M.A., Indiana University,
1964.   1872

Miller, Wayne Lowell
"A Critical Analysis of the Speaking Career of Bishop G.
Bromley Oxnam." Ph.D., University of Southern California, 1961. 1873

Miller, Wray
"The Controlling Ideas in the Preaching of Phillips Brooks."
Th.M., Pittsburgh Theological Seminary, 1957.   1874

Moore, George C.
"An Analytical Study of Invention and Style in Selected Sermons of James Blaine Chapman." M.A., University of Oklahoma,
1948.   1875

Morgan, Jimmie Norton
"A Rhetorical Analysis of the Senatorial Prayers of Peter
Marshall." M.A., University of Alabama, 1956.   1876

Myers, Chester J.
"A Critical Analysis and Appraisal of the Work of Brigham
Young as a Public Speaker." Ph.D., University of Southern Cali-
fornia, 1940.   1877

Myres, William Venting
"Psychological Elements in the Sermon on the Mount." D.R.E.,
Southwestern Baptist Theological Seminary, 1949.   1878

Nelson, Theodore F.
"Charles Haddon Spurgeon's Theory and Practice of Preaching." Ph.D., State University of Iowa, 1944.   1879

Newman, Lawrence Donald
"Sermons by James Cardinal Gibbons: A Rhetorical Analysis."
M.A., Saint Louis University, 1964.   1880

Nickerson, Melvin R.
"An Analytical Study of Selected Sermons of Billy Graham
from the San Francisco Crusade of 1958, with References to Techniques and Persuasion." M.A., University of the Pacific, 1961. 1881

Nodel, Julius J.
"Study of the Homilies in Bereshith Rabbah." M.H.L., Hebrew
Union College—Jewish Institute of Religion, 1944.   1882

North, Ira L.
"The Rhetorical Method of Alexander Campbell." M.A., University of Illinois, 1945.   1883

North, Ross Stafford
"The Evangelism of Walter Scott." M.A., Louisiana State University, 1952.   1884

Olbricht, Thomas Henry
"A Rhetorical Analysis of Representative Homilies of Basil the
Great." M.A., State University of Iowa, 1959.   1885

O'Neal, Glenn Franklin
"An Analytical Study of Certain Rhetorical Factors Used by
Billy Graham in the 1949 Los Angeles Meetings." Ph.D., Uni-
versity of Southern California, 1956.   1886

Osborne, Calvin
"A Rhetorical Study of Selected Sermons of Jasper Newton
Field." M.A., University of Redlands, 1961.   1887

Page, Gladys M.
"The Comparison of the Oral and Written Style of Harry
Emerson Fosdick." M.A., University of Wisconsin, 1938.   1888

Pappas, Thomas N.
"A Study of the Rhetorical Theories and Selected Speeches
of Aeneas Sylvius Piccolomini." Ph.D., Michigan State University,
1963.   1889

Parker, Charles A.
"The Theory of Oratory of Russell H. Conwell." M.A., Temple
University, 1953.   1890

Parker, Robert Albert
"A Study of the Principles and Use of Illustrations by Henry Ward Beecher." Th.M., Southern Baptist Theological Seminary, 1951.   **1891**

Patterson, Elsie Marie
"A Rhetorical Analysis of Russell H. Conwell's Lecture 'Acres of Diamonds.'" M.A., Bowling Green State University, 1962.   **1892**

Paul, Wilson Benton
"John Witherspoon's Theory and Practice of Public Speaking." Ph.D., State University of Iowa, 1940.   **1893**

Pease, Norval F.
"Charles E. Weniger's Theory of the Relationship of Speech and Homiletics as Revealed in His Teaching Procedures, His Writings, and His Public Addresses." Ph.D., Michigan State University, 1964.   **1894**

Penner, Jonathan Gunther
"The Radio Preaching of H.M.S. Richards." M.A., Purdue University, 1958.   **1895**

Pexton, Thomas C.
"The Effect on Religious Thinking of Harry Emerson Fosdick's Speaking." M.A., Kent State University, 1960.   **1896**

Polisky, Jerome B.
"Abba Hillel Silver: Persuader for Zionism." M.S., University of Wisconsin, 1959.   **1897**

Pollock, Wallace Stanley
"The Rhetorical Theory of William G. T. Shedd." Ph.D., Northwestern University, 1962.   **1898**

Poovey, Arthur
"An Analysis of the Structure of Dwight L. Moody's Sermons." M.A., Northwestern University, 1939.   **1899**

Post, Avery D.
"The Preaching of Charles Reynolds Brown." S.T.M., Yale University Divinity School, 1952.   **1900**

Pratt, Glen R.
"Jonathan Edwards as a Preacher of Doctrine." S.T.M., Temple University School of Theology, 1958.   **1901**

Prichard, Samuel
"The Homiletic Technique of Augustus Bedlow Prichard."
M.A., University of Redlands, 1949.   1902

Pullon, Suzanne L.
"A Study of the Speaking of Reverend Merrill R. Abbey."
M.A., University of Michigan, 1954.   1903

Quimby, Rollin W.
"Dwight L. Moody: An Examination of the Historical Conditions and Rhetorical Factors Which Contributed to His Effectiveness as a Speaker." Ph.D., University of Michigan, 1951. 1904

Rabin, Henry
"Homilies of Exodus Rabbah." M.H.L., Hebrew Union College—Jewish Institute of Religion, 1941.   1905

Ransom, Eugene Arthur
"An Analysis of Selected Sermons on Social Justice by G.
Bromley Oxnam." M.A., University of Michigan, 1957.   1906

Reiber, Milton T.
"The Evangelistic Methods and Techniques of the Apostle
Paul." A.M., Seventh-Day Adventist Theological Seminary,
1957.   1907

Rezek, Clarence
"Theodore Parker, A Study in Persuasion." M.A., University
of Wisconsin, 1936.   1908

Richards, Clara
"Elements of Persuasion Used by St. Paul Based on the King
James Translation of the Bible." M.A., University of Utah, 1940. 1909

Ridge, Jessie
"Rhetorical Analysis of Two Sermons of John Peter Marshall."
M.A., Bowling Green State University, 1963.   1910

Rives, Richard R.
"The Public Address of Reverend George Duffield, D.D.,
While Pastor of the First Presbyterian Church of Detroit,
Michigan, 1838-1868." M.A., Wayne University, 1956.   1911

Robinson, Robert Jackson
"The Homiletical Method of Banajah Harvey Carroll." Th.D.,
Southwestern Baptist Theological Seminary, 1956.   1912

Romeis, David
"The Prayers of Peter Marshall in the U.S. Senate, 1947-49."
M.A., Stanford University, 1957.   **1913**

Romero, Charles I.
"An Analysis of Organization in Selected Television Addresses
of Bishop Fulton J. Sheen." M.A., University of Arizona, 1962. **1914**

Rowley, Edward A.
"A Study of the Major Methods of Persuasion Used by George
Whitefield in Ten Selected Sermons Preached in England."
M.A., University of Kansas, 1960.   **1915**

Rozak, John Joseph
"Monsignor Fulton J. Sheen, the Radio Speaker." M.A.,
University of Michigan, 1948.   **1916**

Sawyer, Syatt
"A Rhetorical Study of the Radio Sermons of W. I. Oliphant."
M.A., University of Houston, 1959.   **1917**

Schaefer, Mary Louise
"The Rhetoric of Monsignor Fulton John Sheen." M.A.,
Syracuse University, 1948.   **1918**

Schieferstein, Elizabeth M.
"A Study of the Public Speaking of the Oregon Pioneer
Reverend George Henry Atkinson, D.D." M.S., University of
Oregon, 1949.   **1919**

Schindler, Alexander M.
"The Sermons of Solomon Plessner." M.H.L., Hebrew Union
College—Jewish Institute of Religion, 1953.   **1920**

Shanks, Kenneth Howard
"A Historical and Critical Study of the Preaching Career
of Aimee Semple McPherson." M.A., University of Southern
California, 1960.   **1921**

Shaw, Horace J.
"A Rhetorical Analysis of the Speaking of Mrs. Ellen G.
White, a Pioneer Leader and Spokeswoman of the Seventh-Day
Adventist Church." Ph.D., Michigan State University, 1959.   **1922**

Shelton, L. Austin
"An Analysis of Charles Haddon Spurgeon's Lecture on the
Art of Preaching." M.A., University of South Dakota, 1963.   **1923**

Shepherd, John Paul
"A Modern Introduction to Phillips Brooks." Th.M., Louisville Presbyterian Seminary, 1950.   **1924**

Shirley, Raymond A.
"The Rhetoric of Alexander Campbell in Theory and Practice." M.A., University of Tennessee, 1962.   **1925**

Shoemaker, William
"Expository Preaching of G. C. Morgan." M.Th., Northern
Baptist Theological Seminary, 1961.   **1926**

Shor, David D.
"The Sermons of Samuel Judah Katzenellenbogen." M.H.L.,
Hebrew Union College—Jewish Institute of Religion, 1937.   **1927**

Silverman, William B.
"Homilies in the Pesikta Rabbati." M.H.L., Hebrew Union
College—Jewish Institute of Religion, 1941.   **1928**

Sleeth, Ronald E.
"The Preaching Theories of Charles E. Jefferson." Ph.D.,
Northwestern University, 1952.   **1929**

Smith, Alvin Duane
"A Study and Appraisal of the Evangelistic Preaching of J.
Wilbur Chapman, D.D., 1859-1918; Being an Investigation of
the Preaching, Ideals, Messages, and Methods of Early Twen-
tieth-Century Urban Evangelism." S.T.M., Temple University
School of Theology, 1954.   **1930**

Smith, Kirk Lamb, Jr.
"The Evangelistic Preaching of Henry Ward Beecher." Th.M.,
Southern Baptist Theological Seminary, 1951.   **1931**

Smith, Valerie Louapre
"A Rhetorical Study of the Preaching of Gilbert Tennent
During the Great Awakening 1735-1745." M.A., Louisiana State
University, 1957.   **1932**

Soukup, Cuthbert J.
"The Public Speaking of Archbishop John Ireland." M.A.,
University of Minnesota, 1948.

1933

Speckeen, Frederick J.
"A Rhetorical Study of the Preaching of Charles Edward
Jefferson." Ph.D., Michigan State University, 1961.

1934

Stager, Robert C.
"A Critical Analysis of Bishop Fulton J. Sheen's Use of Invention in Selected Radio and Television Regarding Communism
from 1936 to 1953." M.A., Bowling Green University, 1955.

1935

Stallings, Juadina Brock
"A Biographical and Rhetorical Study of the Public Address of
Dr. Louis Handley Evans." Ph.D., University of Southern
California, 1957.

1936

Stein, David Timothy
"Jonathan Edwards: A Study of Persuasive Techniques."
M.A., Saint Louis University, 1962.

1937

Stockman, Otto William
"An Evaluation of the Rhetorical Theory of the Sermon
on the Mount." M.A., Ohio State University, 1946.

1938

Sulston, Kenneth Hartley
"A Rhetorical Criticism of the Radio Preaching of Walter A.
Maier." Ph.D., Northwestern University, 1958.

1939

Svanoe, Harold Cecil
"The Preaching and Speaking of Burris Jenkins." Ph.D.,
Northwestern University, 1953.

1940

Swabb, Luke Joel
"A Rhetorical Study Based on Aristotelian Principles of Se-
lected Temperance Sermons Delivered by William Ashley
Sunday, 1911-1932." M.A., Ohio State University, 1964.

1941

Tade, George T.
"A Rhetorical Analysis of the Spiritual Exercises of Ignatius
Loyola." Ph.D., University of Illinois, 1955.

1942

Taylor, Preston Alford
"Horace Bushnell, the Preacher." Th.M., Southwestern Baptist Theological Seminary, 1956.

1943

Taylor, Richard Dowling, Jr.
"An Analysis of Method of Proof in Selected Radio Addresses of Bishop Duane G. Hunt." M.S., University of Utah, 1959.   1944

Thomas, Charles Kenneth
"The Rhetorical Practice of John Donne in His Sermons." M.A., Cornell University, 1924.   1945

Thompson, Ernest C.
"A Rhetorical Analysis of the Lectures of the Reverend Harmon Spalding." M.A., State College of Washington, 1955.   1946

Tilbury, Leon
"A Historical Analysis of Selected Sermons of Jeremy Taylor." M.A., Kansas State University, 1961.   1947

Todd, Hollis Bailey
"John A. Broadus' Theory and Practice of Speech Arrangement." M.A., Louisiana State University, 1949.   1948

Tromsness, Clair Eugene
"Isaac Backus: Colonial Apologist for Religious Freedom." M.A., Stanford University, 1964.   1949

Ulrey, Evan
"A Rhetorical Study of the Speech Training and Early Preaching of Barton Warren Stone." M.A., Louisiana State University, 1948.   1950

"The Preaching of Barton Warren Stone." Ph.D., Louisiana State University, 1955.   1951

Ungurait, Donald F.
"A Preliminary Survey of an Oral Roberts Crusade." M.S., University of Wisconsin, 1960.   1952

Valleau, M. Matthew
"The Speeches and Speaking of Bishop Thomas O'Gorman." M.A., Marquette University, 1961.   1953

Vandeman, George E.
"Spurgeon's Theory of Preaching." M.A., University of Michigan, 1946.   1954

Vinnedge, Lloyd Holden
"A Rhetorical Analysis of Ralph Waldo Emerson's Divinity
School Address." M.A., University of Illinois, 1959.   **1955**

Vondettuoli, James A., Jr.
"The English Seekers: John Jackson, the Principal Spokes-
man." Ph.D., Harvard Divinity School, 1959.   **1956**

Wagner, Maurice Earl
"Paul, the Preacher." Th.M., Northern Baptist Theological
Seminary, 1950.   **1957**

Waite, Donald Allen
"The Evangelistic Speaking of Billy Graham." Ph.D., Purdue
University, 1961.   **1958**

Walters, Edith Irene
"The Aesthetic Elements in Several Speeches by Dr. Ralph
W. Sockman." M.A., Ohio University, 1962.   **1959**

Weaver, Samuel Robert
"The Theology and Times of Harry Emerson Fosdick."
Th.D., Princeton Theological Seminary, 1961.   **1960**

Weiss, Joseph I.
"The Sermons of Nissim B. Reuben Gerondi." M.H.L.,
Hebrew Union College—Jewish Institute of Religion, 1939.   **1961**

Weniger, Charles Elliott
"A Critical Analysis and Appraisal of the Public Address
of William Miller, Early American Second Advent Lecturer."
Ph.D., University of Southern California, 1948.   **1962**

Wessell, Grant H.
"A Critical Analysis of the Methods of Persuasion Employed
by Dr. Harry Emerson Fosdick as Evidenced in Selected Ser-
mons." M.A., University of Michigan, 1953.   **1963**

White, David Lewis
"The Preaching of Phillips Brooks." Th.D., Southern Bap-
tist Theological Seminary, 1949.   **1964**

White, Eugene E.
"The Preaching of George Whitefield During the Great
Awakening of America." Ph.D., Louisiana State University, 1956.   **1965**

White, Paul A.
"Thomas Chalmers, Preacher." S.T.M., Temple University
School of Theology, 1958.   1966

Whited, Harold V.
"A Rhetorical Analysis of the Published Sermons Preached
by John Wesley at Oxford University." Ph.D., University of
Michigan, 1959.   1967

Wickman, Richard C.
"A Rhetorical Analysis of the Sermon by Billy Graham at
Yankee Stadium, New York City, July 20, 1957." M.A., Bowling
Green State University, 1958.   1968

Wilcox, Roger
"A Rhetorical Analysis of the Sermon on the Mount." M.A.,
University of Michigan, 1951.   1969

Wilson, Jack Edward
"A Rhetorical Criticism of the Preaching of Alexander Campbell." M.A., Kent State University, 1962.   1970

Winegarden, Neil A.
"A Rhetorical Analysis of Job's Speech Style." M.A., University of Michigan, 1949.   1971

Wohl, Samuel
"Jellinek, the Preacher." M.H.L., Hebrew Union College—
Jewish Institute of Religion, 1929.   1972

Worster, Donald E.
"Jonathan Edwards: The Nature of Religious Conversion
and Its Rhetorical Impetus." M.A., University of Kansas, 1964.   1973

Yarbrough, Robert Clyde
"The Homiletical Theory and Practice of Ebenezer Porter."
Ph.D., State University of Iowa, 1942.   1974

Yates, William B.
"Ethical Persuasion in the Sermons of John Donne." M.A.,
University of Tennessee, 1962.   1975

Yohe, Gladys Parsons
"A Rhetorical Analysis of the Speeches of Ralph W. Sockman
Given in the 1947-1948 National Radio Pulpit Program." M.A.,
University of Colorado, 1949.   1976

Young, James William
"John Tillotson, Preacher." S.T.M., Union Theological Seminary, 1955.

1977

Zerin, Edward
"Tanhuma Homilies of Genesis." M.H.L., Hebrew Union College—Jewish Institute of Religion, 1946.

1978

Zimmerman, Gordon G.
"A Biographical and Descriptive Study of the Speaking Career of Edgar DeWitt Jones." Ph.D., University of Michigan, 1961.

1979

History—Groups

Adams, Henry Babcock
"Selected Sermons of Fulton J. Sheen and Harry Emerson Fosdick." M.A., Stanford University, 1956.

1980

Adkerson, Sonya
"A Comparative Analysis of Selected Sermons of Jonathan Edwards and Billy Graham." M.A., Southern Illinois University, 1964.

1981

Anderson, Raezella K.
"A Comparative Analysis of the Methods of Sermon Preparation and Delivery of Twenty Contemporary Preachers." A.M., University of Chicago, The Divinity School, 1936.

1982

Atzert, Edward P.
"Subject-Matter in the New York Pulpit." M.A., University of Michigan, 1954.

1983

Averitt, James William
"A Study of Seven Contemporary Ministers." Th.M., Louisville Presbyterian Seminary, 1947.

1984

Bateman, James LaVar
"The Speaking in the Mormon Missionary System." Ph.D., University of Wisconsin, 1950.

1985

Bell, J. Milton
"Preaching Among Representative Smaller Religious Groups of the United States—A Survey of Its Effectiveness." S.T.D., Temple University School of Theology, 1954.

1986

Bennett, Fred M.
"Four Outstanding Men of the American Pulpit." S.T.M.,
Western Theological Seminary, 1948.   1987

Boecler, Paul A. O.
"The Preaching of the Law in the Sermons of Geisemann,
Fosdick, Spurgeon, and Macartney and the Application of Psychological Procedures." S.T.M., Concordia Seminary, St. Louis,
1957.   1988

Brees, Paul Rexford
"A Comparative Study of the Devices of Persuasion Used in
Ten Sermons by Harry Emerson Fosdick and Eight Sermons
by William Ashley Sunday." Ph.D., University of Southern
California, 1948.   1989

Brown, Henry Clifton, Jr.
"The Positive Elements in the Preaching of Amos and Hosea."
Th.D., Southwestern Baptist Theological Seminary, 1954.   1990

Calkins, Harold L.
"The Study and Devotional Habits of Master Preachers."
A.M., Seventh-Day Adventist Theological Seminary, 1958.   1991

Ellis, Carroll B.
"The Alexander Campbell and John B. Purcell Religious
Debate." M.A., Louisiana State University, 1945.   1992

Fogartie, James Eugene
"The Preaching of James S. Stewart, Reinhold Niebuhr, and
George W. Truett." Th.M., Union Theological Seminary in
Virginia, 1953.   1993

Gearhart, Ross Elwood
"An Analysis of the Organization of Representative Sermons
by Six Contemporary Protestant Ministers." M.A., State University of Iowa, 1957.   1994

Hauck, Arthur
"A Rhetorical Analysis of Contemporary Fundamentalist
Preachers in Boulder, Colorado." M.A., University of Colorado,
1959.   1995

Hennessy, Joseph
"A Comparison of the Use of Theological Terms in the
Speaking of D. L. Moody and Billy Graham." M.A., Pennsyl-
vania State University, 1960.   1996

Hiatt, Richard Gordon
"A Study of the Speaking in Sacrament Meetings of One Ward of the Church of Jesus Christ of The Latter-Day Saints." M.A., University of Oregon, 1956.   **1997**

Johnson, Warren Harry
"The Current Preaching of American Unitarian Ministers with Particular Reference to Use of the Bible Therein." S.T.M., Andover-Newton Theological School, 1948.   **1998**

Jones, Warren S.
"Public Speaking of Present Ministers of Churches of Christ in Detroit." M.A., Wayne University, 1954.   **1999**

Kadel, William Howard
"Contemporary Preaching in the Presbyterian Church, U.S., and the Presbyterian Church, U.S.A. in the Light of the Preaching of History." Th.D., Union Theological Seminary in Virginia, 1951.   **2000**

Lacour, Lawrence L.
"A Study of the Revival Method in America 1920-1955, with Special Reference to Billy Sunday, Aimee Semple McPherson, and Billy Graham." Ph.D., Northwestern University, 1956.   **2001**

Lewis, Ralph Loren
"The Persuasive Style and Appeals of the Minor Prophets, Amos, Hosea, and Micah." Ph.D., University of Michigan, 1959.   **2002**

McLeister, William
"The Use of the Bible in the Sermons of Selected Protestant Preachers in the United States from 1925 to 1950." Ph.D., University of Pittsburgh, 1957.   **2003**

Martin, Wilbur Lee
"A Rhetorical Analysis of American Religious Speaking During the 1954 Second Assembly of the World Council of Churches." Ph.D., State University of Iowa, 1958.   **2004**

Mitchell, Margaret Barker
"The Speech Arts as Fostered by the Mutual Improvement Associations of the Church of Jesus Christ of the Latter-Day Saints." M.A., University of Utah, 1935.   **2005**

Moseley, C. A., Jr.
"Practices of Evangelism by Negro Methodists and Baptists, Compared with Those of Negro Seventh-Day Adventists." M.A., Seventh-Day Adventist Theological Seminary (Andrews University), 1943.   2006

Pipes, William H.
"An Interpretative Study of Old-Time Negro Preaching." Ph.D., University of Michigan, 1943.   2007

Reed, John William
"The Use of the Bible in the Teaching of Eight Representative American Preachers." M.A., Bowling Green State University, 1961.   2008

Russell, R. O.
"Preaching in the South." S.T.M., Divinity School of Vanderbilt University, 1962.   2009

Schleifer, Herman William, Jr.
"The Place of Preaching in the Evangelical Lutheran Church." S.T.D., Temple University School of Theology, 1960.   2010

Shaft, Jearald J.
"Laws and Gospel in Contemporary Lutheran Preaching." S.T.M., Biblical Seminary in New York, 1959.   2011

Stewart, C. S.
"A Critical Study of the Homiletical Method of Drs. Fosdick, Jefferson, Chappell, and Morgan." Th.D., Iliff Theological Seminary, 1938.   2012

Walker, D. E., Jr.
"Invention in Selected Sermons of Ministers vs. Election of Roman Catholic Presidential Candidate." M.A., University of Florida, 1961.   2013

Wilkin, Wendell Reed
"Public Speaking in the Mutual Improvement Association of the Mormon Church." Ph.M., University of Wisconsin, 1941.   2014

Wright, O. E.
"Amos and Hosea as Preachers: Compared and Contrasted." M.A., The Graduate Seminary of Phillips University, 1937.   2015

Zeisser, Charles C.
"The Presence of Speech Techniques of Effective Preaching in the Sermons of Four Outstanding Preachers in the United States Today." M.A., Wayne University, 1946.　　2016

Zukor, Stephen Harry
"A Study of Preaching in Modern Sects." Th.D., Southern Baptist Theological Seminary, 1951.　　2017

History—Periods

Aasen, David L.
"Forty Years of New Testament Teaching and Preaching in the General Council of the Assemblies of God, 1914-1954." Th.D., Southwestern Baptist Theological Seminary, 1955.　　2018

Boase, Paul H.
"The Methodist Circuit Rider on the Ohio Frontier." Ph.D., University of Wisconsin, 1952.　　2019

Bozell, Ruth Beatrice
"English Preachers of the Seventeenth Century on the Art of Preaching." Ph.D., Cornell University, 1939.　　2020

Buffum, H. S.
"The Influence of the Puritan Minister in the Making of New England." M.A., University of Iowa, 1902.　　2021

Cain, Glen T.
"An Inquiry into the Character of Preaching as Revealed in the New Testament." Th.M., Southwestern Baptist Theological Seminary, 1951.　　2022

Church, Avery Milton
"The Reaction of the American Pulpit to the Modern Scientific Movement from 1850-1900." Th.D., Southern Baptist Theological Seminary, 1943.　　2023

Cloonan, Benignius
"The Effect of Classical Rhetoric upon Christian Preaching During the First Five Centuries A.D." Ph.D., Pennsylvania State University, 1959.　　2024

Counts, Martha Louise
"The Political Views of the Eighteenth-Century New England Clergy as Expressed in Their Election Sermons." Ph.D., Columbia University, 1956. 2025

Foote, Millard Griffin
"The Preaching of the Primitive Church." S.T.M., Andover-Newton Theological School, 1938. 2026

Frank, Victor Charles
"The Sermonic Techniques Employed over the Lutheran Hour 1931-48." M.A., Marquette University, 1953. 2027

Gaustad, Edwin Scott
"The Great Awakening in New England, 1741-1742." Ph.D., Brown University, 1951. 2028

Gray, Lloyd Jack
"A Study of Protestant Preaching in the United States, 1920-1929." Th.D., Southern Baptist Theological Seminary, 1948. 2029

Gulick, Joseph I.
"A Survey of American Preaching." M.A., George Washington University, 1933. 2030

Hare, Marion Herbert
"A Study of the Use of the Bible in Reformation Preaching." Th.M., Southern Baptist Theological Seminary, 1955. 2031

Higdon, Barbara McFarlane
"The Role of Preaching in the Early Latter Day Saint Church, 1830-1876." Ph.D., University of Missouri, 1961. 2032

Hiten, Stephen Stegmann
"The Historical Background of the Election Sermon and Rhetorical Analysis of Five Sermons Delivered in Massachusetts Between 1754 and 1755." Ph.D., University of Michigan, 1960. 2033

Howard, Martha Moffett
"A Study of Public Speaking in the First Century A.D. as Revealed in the *Acts of the Apostles*." M.A., State University of Iowa, 1950. 2034

Hudson, Roy F.
"The Theory of Communication of Colonial New England Preachers, 1620-1670." Ph.D., Cornell University, 1953. 2035

Huffines, David Allen
"Apostolic Preaching: A Study of the Sermons in Acts." Th.D.,
Union Theological Seminary in Virginia, 1952.   2036

Hunter, King B.
"The Effect of the Depression upon Disciple Preaching." A.M.,
University of Chicago, The Divinity School, 1935.   2037

Jarvis, Joseph Boyer
"Preaching in the General Conferences of the Mormon Church,
1870-1900." Ph.D., Northwestern University, 1958.   2038

Johnson, Louis Richard
"American Preaching in the Seventeenth Century." Th.D.,
Northern Baptist Theological Seminary, 1958.   2039

Jones, Paul Tudor
"The Preaching of the Apostles." S.T.M., Union Theological
Seminary, 1938.   2040

Jones, Robert D.
"America and Preaching During the Depression Years." S.T.M.,
Yale University Divinity School, 1946.   2041

Jones, Wayne Baxter
"The Christian Prophet in Acts and the Pauline Epistles."
Th.M., Southern Baptist Theological Seminary, 1957.   2042

Kahn, Robert I.
"Liberalism as Reflected in Jewish Preaching in the English
Language in the Mid-Nineteenth Century." D.H.L., Hebrew
Union College—Jewish Institute of Religion Graduate School,
1951.   2043

Kaminsky, Howard M.
"Economic Attitudes in Sermons of the Thirteenth Century."
A.M., University of Chicago, The Divinity School, 1949.   2044

Kerr, Harry P.
"The Character of Political Sermons Preached at the Time
of the American Revolution." M.A., University of Connecticut,
1962.   2045

Klein, Louis Martin
"Pulpit Oratory in Spain in the Sixteenth, Seventeenth and
Eighteenth Centuries." M.A., Cornell University, 1933.   2046

Kuster, Thomas A.
"Frontier Homily: The Preaching of Indiana Methodist Circuit Riders." M.A., Indiana University, 1962.   2047

Lacy, Edmund Emmett
"A History of Representative Southern Baptist Preaching from 1895 to the First World War." Th.D., Southwestern Baptist Theological Seminary, 1960.   2048

Lester, Lorayne
"The Christian Funeral Oration of the Fourth Century." M.A., University of Tennessee, 1960.   2049

McCain, Ray
"A Descriptive and Analytical Study of the Speaking of Atlanta Ministers on the School Desegregation Issue from February, 1961, to August 30, 1961." M.A., Louisiana State University, 1962.   2050

McCord, P. C.
"The Public Speeches of the Bible." M.A., University of Wisconsin, 1927.   2051

McGladry, L. D.
"The Changing Standards of Preaching as Revealed in the Lyman Beecher Lectures in Preaching from 1872 to 1935." M.A., University of Minnesota, 1936.   2052

McMillan, Donald Ian
"Post-Apostolic Preaching: The Approach to the Heathen as Seen in the Early Apologists, etc., (150-250 A.D.)." S.T.M., Union Theological Seminary, 1951.   2053

Masten, Charles
"Common Elements in Judaistic and Patristic Address." M.A., University of Redlands, 1949.   2054

Parker, Charles A.
"A Study of the Preaching at the Ocean Grove (New Jersey) Camp Meeting, 1870-1900." Ph.D., Louisiana State University, 1959.   2055

Parks, Kenneth Clifton
"The Progress of Preaching in England During the Elizabethan Period." Th.D., Southern Baptist Theological Seminary, 1954.   2056

Parrott, John Henry
"The Preaching of Social Christianity in the United States in the Twentieth Century." Th.D., Southern Baptist Theological Seminary, 1950.   2057

Pfander, Homer G.
"The Popular Sermons of the Medieval Friar in England." Ph.D., New York University, 1937.   2058

Preston, Robert A.
"Trends in Attitudes Toward the Bible in Disciple's Preaching of the Last Generation." A.M., University of Chicago, The Divinity School, 1935.   2059

Rose, Benjamin L.
"Learning Their Art from Great Biblical Preachers: A Study of Twelve Outstanding Examples of Biblical Preaching in the Nineteenth and Twentieth Centuries." Th.D., Union Theological Seminary in Virginia, 1953.   2060

Sager, Allen H.
"The Fundamentalist-Modernist Controversy, 1918-1930, in the History of American Public Address." Ph.D., Northwestern University, 1963.   2061

Sanford, Jack D.
"The Reformers' Concept of Preaching in Worship." Th.M., Southern Baptist Theological Seminary, 1955.   2062

Schofield, R. G.
"The Ranters in Seventeenth-Century England: Their Principles and Practices." Ph.D., Harvard Divinity School, 1949. 2063

Smith, Donald George
"Eighteenth-Century American Preaching, a Historical Survey." Th.D., Northern Baptist Theological Seminary, 1956.   2064

Stanfield, V. L.
"The Preaching of the Great Awakening and Its Contribution to Political Liberty." Th.M., Southern Baptist Theological Seminary, 1947.   2065

Steelman, Edmund H.
"The Trend in Modern Preaching." S.T.D., Temple University School of Theology, 1939.   2066

Taylor, Charles Ross
"The Old Testament Prophet as a Preacher." Th.D., Southwestern Baptist Theological Seminary, 1956. 2067

Threadgill, George G.
"Preaching of the Pietistic Movement in Germany." Th.M., Southern Baptist Theological Seminary, 1950. 2068

Trost, Harold G.
"Some Comparisons Between Fifty Sermons of the Nineteenth Century and Fifty Modern Sermons." M.A., University of Wisconsin, 1931. 2069

Umble, Roy
"Mennonite Preaching, 1864-1944." Ph.D., Northwestern University, 1949. 2070

Wakefield, Walter Leggett
"The Treatise Against Heretics of James Capelli: A Study of Medieval Writing and Preaching Against Catharan Heresy." Ph.D., Columbia University, 1951. 2071

Walker, Jessie
"An Analysis of Negro Ministry with Special Reference to the Colonial Period." M.A., Denver University, 1950. 2072

Welford, Thomas Winfred
"A Comparative Study of Two Periods of Baptist Preaching." M.A., Mississippi Southern College, 1962. 2073

Wessner, W. I.
"The *Dispositio* of Ante-Nicene Preaching." Th.M., Fuller Theological Seminary, 1961. 2074

Williams, Abraham David
"Medieval Monastic Preaching of the Twelfth Century." S.T.M., Union Theological Seminary, 1935. 2075

Witchell, Wallace
"Trends in the Rhetorcial Technique and Content of Pre-Reformation English Preaching." M.A., Wayne University, 1954. 2076

Yoder, Jess
"A Critical Study of the Debate Between the Reformed and the Anabaptists, Held at Frankenthal, Germany, in 1571." Ph.D., Northwestern University, 1962. 2077

History—Theory

Abernathy, Elton
"An Analysis of Trends in American Homiletical Theory Since 1860." Ph.D., State University of Iowa, 1941.   2078

Barton, Fred Jackson
"The Contribution of Selected Works in American Homiletics from 1860 to 1880 to the Theory of Extempore Speaking." M.A., University of Iowa, 1939.   2079

Baxter, Batsell Barrett
"An Analysis of the Basic Elements of Persuasion in the Yale Lectures on Preaching." Ph.D., University of Southern California, 1944.   2080

Cartwright, George Washington
"Modern Homiletics and the Aristotelian Tradition of Rhetoric." M.A., University of Illinois, 1948.   2081

Casteel, John L.
"Conceptions of Preaching in the Lyman Beecher Lectures, 1872-1941." Ph.D., Northwestern University, 1943.   2082

Connors, Joseph
"Catholic Homiletic Theory in Historical Perspective." Ph.D., Northwestern University, 1962.   2083

Crawford, John Woodford
"The Rhetoric of George Campbell." Ph.D., Northwestern University, 1949.   2084

Dieter, Otto A.
"Theory of Homiletical Form: A Translation of P. Kleinert's 'Homilet,' Part Three: 'Homiletische Formlehre,' 1907 Edition, with an Introduction." M.A., University of Iowa, 1931.   2085

Evans, M. F.
"Study in the Development of a Theory of Homiletics in England from 1537-1692." Ph.D., University of Iowa, 1932.   2086

Herbst, Charles
"The 'Little Method' of St. Vincent De Paul: A Reform in the Method of Preaching." M.A., Catholic University, 1951.   2087

Hughes, John Graham
"The American Contribution to Homiletic Theory." Ph.D., Southern Baptist Theological Seminary, 1907. **2088**

Lambertson, Floyd W.
"Survey and Analysis of American Homiletics Prior to 1860." Ph.D., University of Iowa, 1930. **2089**

Loughery, James
"The Rhetorical Theory of John Cardinal Newman." Ph.D., University of Michigan, 1952. **2090**

McCants, David A.
"A Study of the Criticism of Preaching Published in America Between 1865 and 1930." Ph.D., Northwestern University, 1964. **2091**

McLaughlin, Raymond W.
"Some Aspects of the Classical Rhetorical Tradition in John Albert Broadus' Textbook, *The Preparation and Delivery of Sermons.*" A.M., University of Michigan, 1947. **2092**

Martin, Julienne
"Fenelon's Theory of Pulpit Eloquence." M.S., University of Wisconsin, 1949. **2093**

Mazza, J. M.
"Joseph Glanfill's *An Essay Concerning Preaching and a Seasonable Defence of Preaching:* A Facsimile Edition with Introduction and Notes." Ph.D., University of Wisconsin, 1963. **2094**

Morrison, David MacNab
"The Criteria of Doctrinal Preaching in the Light of Its History." Th.D., Union Theological Seminary in Virginia, 1956. **2095**

Parrish, Max
"Richard Whately's Elements of Rhetoric, Parts I and II: A Critical Edition." M.A., Cornell University, 1929. **2096**

Robertz, William G.
"The Contribution of the Swedish-American Baptists to Homiletical Theory: An English Translation of J. A. Edgren's *Tankor I Homiletiken* and Eric Sandell's *Homiletik* with an Introduction." M.A., University of Illinois, 1953. **2097**

Rudin, J. J.
"Concept of *Ethos* in Late American Preaching." Ph.D., Northwestern University, 1950.   2098

Stretch, Evelyn Agnes Murphy
"Whately's Rhetorical Theory, the Relationship of Logic and Rhetoric." M.A., Stanford University, 1950.   2099

Werner, Ronald C.
"George Campbell's Homiletic Theory." M.A., University of Illinois, 1959.   2100

Teaching

Adams, Henry Babcock
"Minister's Preparation for Preaching." S.T.M., San Francisco Theological Seminary, 1951.   2101

Alexander, Wilber
"A Syllabus for an Introductory Course in Homiletics." M.A., Seventh-Day Adventist Theological Seminary, 1957.   2102

Berry, Billy Ray
"An Evaluation of the Contributions of College Speech Programs to the Education of the Minister." M.A., Baylor University, 1959.   2103

Christiansen, Charles F.
"Speech Education in the Preparation of the Protestant Minister." M.S., Syracuse University, 1959.   2104

Clark, William K.
"An Analysis of Contemporary Speech Education in American Protestant Seminaries." Ph.D., Purdue University, 1960.   2105

Donica, Donald Rex
"A Survey and Evaluation of the Traditional and Contemporary Methodologies in the Teaching of Homiletics." Th.D., Boston University School of Theology, 1962.   2106

Etheredge, Cecil D.
"An Analysis of the Speech Education of Protestant Ministers in Four Selected Denominations in Twelve Southern States." M.A., University of Alabama, 1952.   2107

Etheridge, Eugene Wesley
"A Homiletics Workbook." Th.M., Northern Baptist Theological Seminary, 1957.   **2108**

Foley, John Joseph
"A Speech Syllabus for Jesuit Theologates in the U. S." M.A., St. Louis University, 1959.   **2109**

Ford, Walter Henry
"The Role of the Speech Program in the Catholic Secular Seminaries of the Archdiocese of Detroit." M.A., Wayne State University, 1960.   **2110**

Gayle, Joe Alvin
"A Survey and Analysis of Speech Training for Ministerial Students in Southern Baptist Colleges and Universities." M.A., Baylor University, 1954.   **2111**

Hastings, Wallace W.
"An Analysis of Speech Correction Methods Used by Three Contemporary Christian Church Preachers." M.A., Christian Theological Seminary, 1959.   **2112**

Jenkins, Loren T.
"A Survey of the Speech Training of Five Hundred Seventy-Five United States Army Chaplains." M.A., State University of Iowa, 1947.   **2113**

Kirkpatrick, Caleb J.
"Pittsburgh Clergymen and a Speech Clinic." M.S., University of Pittsburgh, 1951.   **2114**

Landers, Martin Wendall
"A Survey and Analysis of Speech Training in the Study Course Program of Churches of the Southern Baptist Convention." M.A., Baylor University, 1956.   **2115**

Lundquist, Carl
"The Teaching of Preaching in Baptist Theological Seminaries of the United States." Th.D., Northern Baptist Theological Seminary, 1960.   **2116**

McCabe, George V.
"An Evaluation of the Courses in Speech in Roman Catholic Seminaries." Ph.D., Fordham University, 1949.   **2117**

McGlon, Charles A.
"Speech Education in Baptist Theological Seminaries." Ph.D., Columbia University Teachers College, 1951.　　　2118

Martin, Stanley H.
"A Twenty-Year Survey of the Functional Aspects of Methodist Theological Education." Ph.D., Boston University, 1954.　　　2119

Neeb, Martin John
"Speech Instruction Survey in Ministerial Training in Lutheran Professional Schools." M.A., St. Louis University, 1959.　　2120

Osburn, John Dixus
"An Analysis of the Speech Needs and Abilities of Representative Bachelor of Divinity Candidates." M.F.A., Texas Christian University, 1952.　　　2121

Pebley, Robert
"Oral Communication—A Curriculum Proposal for a Theological Seminary." M.A., Christian Theological Seminary, 1959.　　2122

Perry, Lloyd M.
"A Constructive Approach to the Problem of Theological Speech Education." Th.D., Northern Baptist Theological Seminary, 1948.　　　2123

"Trends and Emphases in the Philosophy, Materials and Methodology of American Protestant Homiletic Education as Established by a Study of Selected Trade and Textbooks Published Between 1834 and 1954." Ph.D., Northwestern University, 1961.　　　2124

Purcell, Robert Francis, S.J.
"A Report on an Experimental Seminar in Preaching." M.A., Saint Louis University, 1957.　　　2125

Smith, William D.
"An Analysis of Selected Homiletics Texts." M.A., Southern Illinois University, 1960.　　　2126

Soden, Minie Elmer
"Rhetorical Training Needs of the Contemporary Minister." M.A., University of Washington, 1964.　　　2127

Sullivan, Tandy Lane
"A Study of the Teaching of Preaching in Five Boston Area Theological Seminaries." M.A., Emerson College, 1963.　　　2128

Sulston, Kenneth Hartley
"A Preliminary Investigation into the Teaching of Speech on the Seminary Level." M.A. University of Kansas, 1952.   2129

Tedford, Thomas Lee
"An Investigation of Public Address as Taught by the Baptist Training Union of the Southern Baptist Convention." Ph.D., Louisiana State University, 1958.   2130

Turney, Milton Lloyd
"An Investigation of the Need for, and a Development of, A Basic Text in Speech for Sunday School Teachers and Lay Church Workers." M.A., Mississippi Southern College, 1958.   2131

Waite, Donald Allen
"A Survey of the Speech and Homiletics Program in the Protestant Theological Seminaries in the United States." M.A., Southern Methodist University, 1953.   2132

Whited, Harold V.
"A Survey of the Speech Training of Accredited Theological Seminaries in the United States." M.A., University of Michigan, 1952.   2133

Wilson, Leonard
"Speech Training for Ministers in the Area of the Northern Baptist Convention." M.A., South Dakota University, 1948.   2134

Wilson, Lon Ervin
"The Status of Speech and Homiletics in Bible Schools in the United States and Canada." Th.D., Northern Baptist Theological Seminary, 1958.   2135

Winegarden, Neil A.
"A Historical Survey of Homiletical Education in the United States." Th.D., Northern Baptist Theological Seminary, 1951.   2136

Winsor, Jerry L.
"Status of Speech and Homiletics Instruction in Accredited American Protestant Seminaries During 1964." M.S., Kansas State Teachers College (Emporia), 1964.   2137

$\mathcal{A}ppendix$

Roman Catholic Periodicals

American Ecclesiastical Review
Catholic University of America Press, Washington, D. C.

Catholic Biblical Quarterly
Catholic Biblical Association of America, Cardinal Station, Washington, D. C.

Clergy Review
Burns, Gates and Washbourne, Ltd., 28 Ashley Place, London S.W. 1, England

Downside Review
Downside Abbey, Stratton on the Fosse, Bath, England

Furrow
St. Patrick's College, Maynooth, Ireland

Homiletic and Pastoral Review
J. F. Wagner, Inc., 53 Park Place, New York, New York

Irish Ecclesiastical Record
Browne and Nolan, Ltd., 41 Nassau Street, Dublin, Ireland

Life of the Spirit
Blackfriars Publications, 34 Bloomsbury Street, London W.C. 1, England

Lumen Vitae
International Centre for Religious Education, 184 rue Washington, Brussels

Month
  Longmans, Green and Co., Ltd., 6 Clifford Street, London, W.1., England

Pastoral Life
  Society of St. Paul, Canfield, Ohio

The Priest
  Our Sunday Visitor, 30 N. Dearborn Street, Chicago, Illinois

Review for Religious
  St. Mary's College, St. Mary's, Kansas

Theological Studies
  Theological Faculties, Society of Jesus in the United States, Woodstock, Maryland

Theology Digest
  St. Mary's College, School of Divinity, St. Louis University, St. Mary's, Kansas

Worship (formerly *Orate Fratres*)
  Monks of St. John's Abbey, Liturgical Press, Collegeville, Minnesota

Protestant Periodicals

Christianity Today
  Washington Building, Washington, D. C.

Church Management
  2491 Lee Boulevard, Cleveland Heights, Ohio

College of the Bible Quarterly
  Lexington Theological Seminary, Lexington, Kentucky

Interpretation
  3401 Brook Road, Richmond, Virginia

Minister's Quarterly
  297 Park Avenue, South, New York, New York 10010

Pastoral Psychology
  400 Community Drive, Manhasset, Long Island, New York

The Preacher's Quarterly
  Epworth Press, 25 City Road, London, E.C.1., England

Princeton Seminary Bulletin
  Princeton Theological Seminary, Princeton, New Jersey

The Pulpit
407 South Dearborn Street, Chicago, Illinois 60605

Pulpit Digest
400 Community Drive, Manhasset, Long Island, New York

Religion in Life
201 Eighth Avenue, South, Nashville, Tennessee 37203

Review and Expositor
Southern Baptist Theological Seminary, 2825 Lexington Road, Louis-ville, Kentucky

Periodicals in the Field of Speech

Central States Speech Journal
c/o Robert P. Friedman, Department of Speech, University of Mis-souri, Columbia, Missouri 65202

Journal of Communication
National Society for the Study of Communication, c/o Ronald L. Smith, General Motors Institute, Flint, Michigan 48502

Quarterly Journal of Speech
Speech Association of America, Statler-Hilton Hotel, New York, New York 10001

Southern Speech Journal
c/o Owen M. Peterson, Department of Speech, Louisiana State Uni-versity, Baton Rouge, Louisiana

Speech Monographs
Speech Association of America, Statler-Hilton Hotel, New York, New York 10001

Speech Teacher
Speech Association of America, Statler-Hilton Hotel, New York, New York 10001

Today's Speech
c/o David C. Phillips, Department of Speech, University of Con-necticut, Storrs, Connecticut

Western Speech
c/o Herman Cohen, Department of Speech, University of Oregon, Eugene, Oregon 97403

Index of Authors